Foreign policy as public policy?

MANCHESTER
1824

Manchester University Press

Foreign policy as public policy?

Promises and pitfalls

**Edited by Klaus Brummer,
Sebastian Harnisch, Kai Oppermann,
and Diana Panke**

Manchester University Press

Published by Manchester University Press
Oxford Road, Manchester M13 9PL
www.manchesteruniversitypress.co.uk

British Library Cataloguing-in-Publication Data
A catalogue record for this book is available from the British Library

ISBN 978 1 5261 4069 2 hardback
ISBN 978 1 5261 6386 8 paperback

First published 2019
Paperback published 2022

Typeset by Newgen Publishing UK

Contents

Figures

Tables

Contributors

Christopher Ansell is Professor of Political Science at the University of California, Berkeley. He received his B.A. in Environmental Science from the University of Virginia and his Ph.D. in Political Science from the University of Chicago. His work focuses on how organizations and communities collaborate to improve performance, address shared problems, manage risk, build social solidarity, and deepen democracy. His current research examines collaborative governance at different scales, from local to global, and he is the co-editor (with Jacob Torfing) of *How Does Collaborative Governance Scale?* (Policy Press 2018). His policy interests focus on risk regulation, crisis management, public health, and environmental protection. He is the author of *Pragmatist Democracy: Evolutionary Learning as Public Philosophy* (Oxford University Press 2011) and the co-editor of *Public Innovation through Collaboration and Design* (Routledge 2014), the *Handbook of Theories of Governance* (Edward Elgar 2016), and *Governance in Turbulent Times* (Oxford University Press 2017).

Katja Biedenkopf is Assistant Professor of European and International Politics at the University of Leuven, Belgium. Her research centers on the external effects of European Union environmental and climate policy, carbon pricing, global environmental governance, and climate diplomacy. She has published in journals including *Global Environmental Politics* and *Environment and Planning C: Politics and Space* and co-edited the book *European Union External Environmental Policy* (Palgrave 2018). Her previous positions include Assistant Professor at the University of Amsterdam, postdoctoral research fellow at the Free University Berlin, visiting fellow at Johns Hopkins University in Washington, DC, and Fulbright Schuman fellow at the University of California at Berkeley.

Spyros Blavoukos is Associate Professor at the Department of International and European Economic Studies, at the Athens University of Economics and Business. He holds a Ph.D. from the Department of Government, University of Essex. He is the Director of a Jean Monnet Network on EU-UN Relations (EUN-NET). His research focuses on the international interactions of the EU, especially with other international and regional organizations. He is the author and (co-)editor of seven books, the most recent one being *The EU in the UN Politics* (Palgrave 2017). He has published academic articles in international journals including, among others, *Review of International Studies, West European Politics, Journal of Common Market Studies, European Journal of Political Research, Journal of Public Policy, European Union Politics, Cooperation and Conflict, European Foreign Affairs Review, Journal of European Integration, International Negotiation,* and the *British Journal of Politics and International Relations.*

Klaus Brummer holds the Chair of International Relations at the Catholic University of Eichstätt-Ingolstadt, Germany. He is Co-Editor-in-Chief of the ISA-sponsored journal *Foreign Policy Analysis.* He is a former president of ISA's Foreign Policy Analysis Section (2015–2016). He is co-principal investigator of a research project funded by the German Research Foundation (DFG) on the role of individual beliefs and leadership traits in German foreign policy (2016–2019). His research interests include comparative foreign policy analysis, political psychology, and regional integration processes. He has published in peer-reviewed journals such as *Foreign Policy Analysis, Journal of European Public Policy, British Journal of Politics and International Relations, International Politics, Acta Politica, German Politics,* and *European Political Science,* and is co-editor of, for instance, *Foreign Policy Analysis Beyond North America* (Lynne Rienner 2015, with Valerie M. Hudson), "The Boundedness of American FPA Theory" (special issue with *Global Society,* 2017, with Valerie M. Hudson), and "Coalition Politics and Foreign Policy" (symposium with *European Political Science,* 2017, with Kai Oppermann and Juliet Kaarbo).

Sebastian Harnisch holds the Chair for International Relations and Comparative Foreign and Security Policy Studies at Heidelberg University, Germany. Previously he taught at Trier University, the University of the German Federal Armed Forces, Munich as well as Beijing Foreign Studies University and Al-Farabi National Kazakh University, Almaty. He is Co-Editor of the *Oxford Encyclopedia on Foreign Policy Analysis* and Member of the Editorial Board of the ISA-sponsored journal *Foreign Policy Analysis* (2018). He is also co-principal investigator of the PhD-Research Training Group funded by the German Research Foundation (DFG) on Authority and Trust in American Politics, Economics and

Society (2017–2021). His research interests encompass comparative foreign and security policy analysis, role theory, non-proliferation and cyber security policy issues. He has published in peer-reviewed journals such as *Foreign Policy Analysis, Global Policy, Global Environmental Politics, Pacific Review, Asian Survey, European Security, German Politics,* and *Zeitschrift für International Beziehungen.* Recently, he has been Co-Editor of *China's International Roles: Challenging or Supporting International Order?* (Routledge 2016, with Jörn-Carsten Gottwald and Sebastian Bersick).

Katherine C. Hicks is a graduate of the Master of Public Administration program at Seattle University, where she collaborated with Dr. Pierce on policy process research and is a co-author on several publications. She received her B.A. in Sociology from Dartmouth College in 2011. She subsequently served as an AmeriCorps member in Seattle before earning her master's. She is currently a Research Associate with the Washington State Institute for Public Policy, a nonpartisan public research group that conducts applied policy research for the state legislature. She primarily conducts research in the area of health care.

Jeroen Joly is a Postdoctoral Research Fellow at Ghent University and Lecturer in Geopolitics at Saint-Louis University Brussels. He previously worked as a researcher at the Universities of Toronto, McGill, and Antwerp. His main research interests include political communication, party governance, and coalition politics in both the domestic and international sphere. Specifically, his research looks at domestic influences on and policy responsiveness in foreign and aid policy-making, with particular attention to the role of news media and political parties. Additionally, his work also looks at the role personality and leadership play in politics, especially among decision-makers. He has been a long-standing and active member of both the Belgian and the Comparative Agendas Project (CAP), and his work has been published in *Political Communication, Cooperation and Conflict, Foreign Policy Analysis,* and *Acta Politica.*

Juliet Kaarbo is Professor of International Relations with a Chair in Foreign Policy at the University of Edinburgh. She previously held positions at the University of Kansas and the Graduate Institute of International Studies in Geneva. She is founding co-director of Edinburgh's Centre for Security Research. Her research focuses on leadership and decision-making, group dynamics, foreign policy analysis, parliamentary political systems, and national roles and has appeared in journals such as *International Studies Quarterly, European Journal of International Relations, International Studies Review, Political Psychology, West European Politics, Cooperation and Conflict,* and

Foreign Policy Analysis. She authored *Coalition Politics and Cabinet Decision Makings* (University of Michigan Press 2012) and co-edited *Domestic Role Contestation, Foreign Policy, and International Relations* (Routledge 2016). Juliet is an Associate Editor of the journal *Foreign Policy Analysis* and the 2018 Distinguished Scholar of Foreign Policy Analysis in the International Studies Association.

Alexander Mattelaer is Associate Professor and the Academic Director of the Institute for European Studies at the Vrije Universiteit Brussel. He is also a Senior Research Fellow at Egmont—the Royal Institute for International Relations—and an assistant professor at the Vrije Universiteit Brussel. His research interests include the politics of European integration, transatlantic relations, defence policy-making, and the ongoing redefinition of state sovereignty. He is also a visiting professor at the College of Europe in Bruges and a senior editor of the online magazine *European Geostrategy*. He was a Fulbright Schuman fellow at Harvard University and at the National Defense University (Institute for National Strategic Studies) and sits on the scientific committee of the Belgian Royal Higher Institute for Defence and on the board of the United Nations Association Flanders/Belgium. His teaching portfolio includes courses on the European Union, international security, and defence policy-making. He obtained his Ph.D. in Political Science from the Vrije Universiteit Brussel and master's degrees from the University of Bath and the University of Leuven.

Kai Oppermann is Professor of International Politics at the Chemnitz University of Technology, Germany. His research centers on the domestic sources of foreign policy and international politics with a particular focus on British and German foreign policy. He won a Marie Curie Fellowship for a project on European integration referendums in 2010/2011 and is currently an associate editor of *Foreign Policy Analysis*. His work has been published in journals such as the *European Journal of International Relations, West European Politics, Foreign Policy Analysis, British Journal of Politics and International Relations*, and *Journal of International Relations and Development*. He is the co-author of a German-language book on the theories of foreign policy (2018, 2nd edition) and an associate editor of the *Oxford Encyclopedia of Foreign Policy Analysis* (2018).

Diana Panke is Professor of Political Science with a Chair in "Multi-Level Governance" at the University of Freiburg. Her research interests include international negotiations, multilateral diplomacy, comparative regionalism, small states in international affairs, European Union politics, as well as compliance and legalization. In these fields, she has published several monographs and more than forty journal articles (including in the *British Journal of Politics and International Relations, Review of International*

Organizations, International Political Science Review, European Journal of International Relations, Comparative Political Studies, Cooperation and Conflict, Millennium, Journal of Common Market Studies, Journal of European Public Policy, West European Politics, Journal of European Integration, and *International Politics*).

Jonathan J. Pierce is an Assistant Professor at the Institute of Public Service, Seattle University, where he teaches in the Master of Public Administration and Bachelor of Public Affairs programs. He received a Ph.D. in Public Affairs in 2012 from the School of Public Affairs, University of Colorado Denver. His current research examines the policy process and decision-making. He teaches courses in research methods and statistics, the policy process, policy analysis, and public and non-profit administration.

Friederike Richter holds an M.A. in Contemporary European Studies (Euromasters) from the University of Bath and a B.Sc. in Economics and Social Sciences from the Free University of Bozen-Bolzano, Italy. Friederike completed parts of her B.Sc. and her M.A. at the University of Lausanne, the University of Washington, and Sciences Po, Paris. Before starting her Ph.D. in 2015, she worked for the European Commission and a public affairs consultancy in Brussels. Her Ph.D. research, which is funded by the French Ministry of the Armed Forces, deals with agenda-setting in security and defense policy. She is particularly interested in how security and defense issues became a government priority in France and the United Kingdom between 1980 and 2015. Friederike is also a Teaching Assistant at the Paris School of International Affairs where she is in charge of M.A. classes on EU foreign policy, international organizations, and defense economics.

Siegfried Schieder, Ph.D. in Political Science from the University of Trier, is Assistant Professor in International Relations and European Politics at the University of Heidelberg and teaches International Relations at the German-Chinese Graduate School of Global Politics (GSGP), Free University of Berlin. He has been Acting Professor for International Relations and Foreign Policy at the University of Trier, Acting Professor for Global Governance at Technische Universität Darmstadt and Visiting Professor at Fudan University, Shanghai. In 2009–2010, he was a Jean Monnet Postdoctoral Fellow at the European University Institute in Florence. His books include *Theories of International Relations* (Routledge 2014, with Manuela Spindler); *Grenzen der deutschen Europapolitik* (Springer VS 2019); *Theorien der Internationalen Beziehungen* (UTB, 3rd edition, 2010 with Manuela Spindler), and *Solidarität und internationale Gemeinschaftsbildung* (Campus Verlag 2009, with Hans W. Maull and Sebastian Harnisch). Among his publications are articles appearing in the *European Journal of International Law, European Journal of International Relations, Journal of International Relations and Development, Leviathan—Berlin Journal of Social Sciences, Zeitschrift für Politikwissenschaft,* and *Zeitschrift für Internationale Beziehungen.*

Jacob Torfing, M.A., Ph.D., is Professor in Politics and Institutions at Department of Social Sciences and Business, Roskilde University, Denmark and Professor 2 at Nord University in Norway. He is Director of the Roskilde School of Governance at Roskilde University. His research interests include public sector reforms, political leadership, network governance, collaborative innovation, and co-creation. He has published several books and scores of articles on these and related topics.

Abbreviations

ACF	advocacy coalition framework
CAP	Comparative Agendas Project
CFSP	Common Foreign and Security Policy
CRS	Creditor Reporting System
DI	discursive institutionalism
EU	European Union
FPA	Foreign Policy Analysis
FRUS	Foreign Relations of the United States
HI	historical institutionalism
IR	international relations
MSA	multiple streams approach
NATO	North Atlantic Treaty Organization
NEA	Near Eastern Affairs
NGOs	non-governmental organizations
NI	new institutionalism
ODA	official development assistance
OMC	Open Method of Coordination
PA	principal-agent
PE	punctuated equilibrium
PET	punctuated equilibrium theory
PNA	Policy Network Analysis
PP	Public Policy
PPS	public policy studies
PSI	Proliferation Security Initiative
RI	rational choice institutionalism

SI	sociological institutionalism
SNA	Social Network Analysis
UN	United Nations
UNSCOP	United Nations Special Committee on Palestine
WEU	Western European Union

1

Introduction: foreign policy as public policy

Klaus Brummer, Sebastian Harnisch, Kai Oppermann, and Diana Panke

This introductory chapter outlines the rationale behind the edited volume, defines core concepts, introduces the analytical template along which the individual chapters are structured, and provides brief summaries of the individual chapters.

Foreign policy is "the sum of official external relations conducted by an independent actor (usually but not exclusively a state) in international relations" (Hill 2016: 4). Traditionally, the realm of foreign policy has been treated as a field of scientific inquiry distinct from public policy (Sprout and Sprout 1956; Snyder *et al.* 1962; Allison 1971; Hudson 2005). While public policy usually concerns policies in the domestic sphere, such as health, labor market, or infrastructure policies, foreign policy is about how a country acts in the international arena, for example vis-à-vis other state or non-state actors or within international organizations (IOs).

The two policy realms are also often seen to differ systematically with regard to the distribution of formal decision-making authority and the policy-making process more broadly. For instance, legislatures are generally considered less significant in foreign policy than in public policy. While parliaments in liberal democracies have the power to pass laws which is the foremost medium in public policy, foreign policy relies much less on formal acts of parliaments and often relegates the legislature to a more passive and reactive role, for example in ratifying international treaties. In contrast, the executive tends to be the foremost actor in foreign policy where it usually has greater authority and discretion than in public policy. This is commonly regarded as a prerequisite for the ability of a country to respond quickly and adequately to international threats and opportunities. In line with this, partisan political conflict in the domestic arena is often seen to be particularly intense in public policy which often has immediate re-distributive or regulatory consequences for a broad range of interests in society. In contrast, foreign policy has been said to have relatively little direct impact on domestic constituents so that there is less scope for domestic contestation around this policy field (Aldrich *et al.* 1989). Rather, the expectation has usually been that "politics stops at the water's edge" and that governments can rely on broad domestic support when they seek to further the "national interest" on the international stage, in particular at times of crisis or conflict.

In contrast, the starting point of this volume is that foreign policy has in many ways become more similar to (and intertwined with) "ordinary" public policies. This is true for the actors involved in the policy-making process as well as for the scope of domestic political contestation around policy-making. For once, foreign policy is no longer the more or less exclusive domain of the executive branch of government (if it ever had been). With the increasing participation and/or influence of a range of actors such as parliaments, courts, non-governmental organizations (NGOs), interest groups, etc., national governments no longer monopolize foreign policy and are even struggling to maintain their gatekeeping role. Inside governments, an ever broader range of ministries beyond the core foreign policy executive have become routinely involved in foreign affairs. Foreign policy has also become increasingly politicized in the domestic political arena (Zürn 2014) and is often contested between political parties (Rathbun 2004; Raunio and Wagner 2017), including between partners in coalition governments (Kaarbo 2017). While foreign policy remains on average less salient in the eyes of general publics than some public policies, such as tax or health policy, it still frequently emerges as a salient electoral issue (Oppermann and Viehrig 2009) and can become a significant influence on voting behavior in national elections just as domestic policies (Aldrich *et al.* 2006).

More broadly, the increasing interdependence and the greater role of transnational processes in world politics have begun to obscure the distinction between the external and the internal in policy-making (Risse 2013; Zürn 2013). Over the last decades, the integration of statehood in some world regions, in particular in Europe, and the erosion of statehood in other areas of the world have shifted the gravitational pull between hierarchy as the ordering principle in the domestic realm and anarchy in the international sphere. In addition to the plurality of actors that now characterizes foreign policy, allegedly "domestic" fields of public policy increasingly have external implications, particularly in a highly integrated region like Europe (Daugbjerg 2014). The transnational diffusion of ideas, norms, and practice shapes "domestic" as well as "foreign" policy making (Gilardi 2013). Similarly, a country's "external" relations have become more consequential for an ever broader range of "domestic" policies and actors, thereby changing the role of national (foreign) ministries and a diverse set of sub-national actors (Hocking 1999; Jönsson 2016). While certain policy areas still remain more or less insulated from their international environment, such as social security, other fields are particularly internationalized, for example finance. In any case, binary distinctions between the "external" and the "internal" or between the "domestic" and the "international" have become ever less useful categories in analyzing policy-making processes and their outcomes.

Despite the blurring of real-world boundaries between the international and the domestic, and hence between foreign policy and public policy, a divide still persists regarding the analysis of policy-making processes and substantive policies in foreign affairs on the one hand and virtually all other public policies on the other hand (Lentner 2006). Although foreign policy analysts have started to address these shifts in various ways, for instance by examining intermestic politics in foreign trade policy (Manning 1977; Russo and Haney 2012; Langhelle 2014), the consequences of this phenomenon for foreign policy studies have not yet been considered systematically. Foreign policy is still predominantly analyzed through the lens of analytical approaches developed in the field of Foreign Policy Analysis (FPA) (Carlsnaes 1992; Neack *et al.* 1995; Kaarbo 2015), focusing on individual decision-makers, policy-making processes inside the executive, or the effects of international structural factors, in particular anarchy, norms, and institutions, as well as the interactions between these forces (Hudson 2014). In contrast, analyses of all other public policy realms employ a range of "theories of the policy process" (Sabatier and Weible 2014) which involve a broad array of heuristics and concepts (Howlett *et al.* 2009; Dunn 2016) to make sense of the main drivers and constraints of policy-making. The possible contribution of such approaches to the analysis of foreign policy, however, has yet to be fully explored (see Caporaso 1997).

This lacuna is all the more surprising since calls for theoretical dialogue between the fields of FPA and Public Policy (PP) have long been voiced by key proponents from both fields (Sabatier 2007; Hudson 2014). According to Sabatier (2007: 328), one of the challenges for policy theories "is to develop a much more explicit and coherent model (or models) of the individual." FPA, in turn, puts individuals front and center since it starts from the very "assumption that human decision makers acting singly and in groups are the ground of all that happens" (Hudson 2005: 2). Clearly, there should be something in the toolbox of public policy theory that can contribute to theory development in FPA, and vice versa. Similarly, Weible (2014: 393) points to possible benefits of applying public policy theories "outside their typical scope," in particular for the further development of those theories and the delineation of their scope.

Such calls complement nicely the core goal of this volume, in the sense of getting to better understandings of policy-making processes and outcomes in the realm of foreign policy through applications of domestic-level public policy theories. Indeed, owing partly to differences in the classification of materials for national security reasons, public policy theories might be able to draw on more nuanced understandings of the policy process and, as a result, offer more sophisticated models of the policy process than those to be found in FPA. A systematic exploration of this claim extends beyond the scope of this introduction (or the edited volume in general). However, if true, this alone would represent a good reason to explore the application of public policy theories to the realm of foreign policy.

To drive home the value added by such an exercise, the public policy theories have to compete on the "home ground" of foreign policy theories by addressing "classical" topics such as decisions on the use of force, bilateral conflict, or the imposition of sanctions. If public policy theories hold explanatory power in such traditional areas of high politics, they should be similarly useful (if not even more) in accounting for decision-making in other, more "intermestic" domains of foreign policy, like foreign trade or homeland security, as well as for decision-making in highly integrated regional environments. Taking up recent calls for strengthening the conversation between different sub-disciplines of political science, the edited volume contributes to bridging the analytical divide between FPA and PP (and thus Comparative Politics more generally). Specifically, the chapters explore primarily how "domestic realm" theories and concepts developed in PP can enrich the analysis of foreign policy as well as, albeit to a lesser extent, how these theories and concepts benefit from engaging with foreign policy. The volume thus aims at establishing a theoretical dialogue that creates possibilities for analytical integration and innovation across sub-disciplinary boundaries, thereby enhancing our understanding of policy-making across issue areas.

To that end, the volume follows the dominant pattern in FPA to focus on "inside out" explanations of foreign policy which foreground the influence of domestic politics or individual leaders on foreign policy decision-making. Similar to most FPA works, it does thus not take into account in a systematic fashion how systemic pressures are translated into domestic decision-making processes. The arguably most notable exception to this is neoclassical realism which, at least in a particular version of it, seeks to bridge the different levels of analysis in an effort of developing a theory of foreign policy (Ripsman *et al.* 2016). Still, such attempts at bridging the different "images" (Waltz 1959) of international politics remain relatively uncommon in FPA. While this lopsidedness may be deplored, it is beyond the scope of this volume to remedy this as our main goal is to build bridges between different sub-disciplines of political science in order to get a better understanding of the processes and outcomes of foreign policy decision-making by individual states.

The promise of cross-disciplinary policy research

The main contention of the book is that FPA has much to benefit from more systematically taking on board scholarship in PP. This allows it to broaden the conceptual toolbox for the analysis of state policies toward external events and topics, and to capture the real-world shifts and developments in the domestic and international environment of foreign policy. More broadly, this book seeks to contribute toward re-integrating policy research across disciplinary boundaries, as the latter has increasingly hampered our capacity to understand policy processes in a globalized world. The objective of the volume is to show that a dialogue across disciplinary boundaries is necessary and to exemplify how such a dialogue can be implemented in empirical policy research. While the book focuses on bringing together public policy research and the analysis of foreign policy, the argument is a larger one: sub-disciplinary specialization is good but it should be complemented with cross-disciplinary dialogue to reap the benefits of a comprehensive policy science perspective.

Traditionally, scholars have worked on an understanding that there is a clear line to be drawn between public policy and foreign policy. In this perspective, the agents, processes, and structures in the two fields are distinct and therefore demand separate approaches and oftentimes also methods. An extension of this is the tendency in the two fields to either disregard research and advances in the respective "other" discipline or to unsystematically "misappropriate" bits and pieces of approaches from that discipline without reflecting upon their core tenets. However, this book is based on the notion that an incomplete representation of those approaches which are available in the policy science "toolbox" broadly defined seriously hampers the scientific understanding of foreign policy. Thus, the book contends that the cross-disciplinary dialogue can and should be pursued in many different ways, including, but not limited to, the application of public policy approaches to foreign policy problems. Furthermore, the book shows that even if the respective approaches have limitations, there is much to learn by reflecting about context variables, scope conditions, and theoretical or methodological constraints.

While the question of how international politics and national politics connect has been discussed for a long time (Keohane and Nye 1977), this debate has generally not been informed by public policy approaches about how policy-making in the domestic arena can be understood. This is the case, for example, for scholarship on two-level games (Putnam 1988; Moravcsik 1993) which argues that foreign policy is simultaneously shaped by international and domestic incentives and constraints, but which has little to say about how the domestic dynamics and processes of policy-making should be conceptualized. The same goes for liberal "bottom up" approaches in FPA that understand foreign policy as the aggregation of powerful interests in domestic society (Moravcsik 1997). Apart from a broadly pluralist conception of the domestic political arena, however, the workings of domestic politics remain undertheorized. While a small number of prominent works which highlight the importance of domestic structures in analyzing foreign policy have taken on board key literatures and concepts in Comparative Politics (e.g., Ikenberry *et al.* 1988; Risse-Kappen 1991), such efforts remain few and far between and have not been systematically embedded in FPA. It is thus in particular domestic politics, or "second image" explanations of foreign policy, which would have much to gain from a more solid theoretical and conceptual foundation of the domestic sphere and which a dialogue with PP promises to provide.

Moreover, the literature that focuses specifically on the public policy/ foreign policy nexus is very limited. For example, in 2006 Howard Lentner explored the cross-fertilization between foreign and domestic policy approaches, dissecting studies that called for unity, parallelism, or overlap between the two. Finding a strong dichotomy between the different approaches, Lentner (2006) pleads for "new and fruitful exchanges" between the respective literatures. More recently, Frédéric Charillon (2018) has argued that while foreign policy fully belongs to the field of public policy studies, it remains singular for several reasons. First, foreign policy tends to be more reactive than most domestic policies because of constant interdependencies with extraterritorial and unpredictable actors and events. Second, foreign policy remains more vulnerable to transnational linkages, resulting in changes of the role of public opinion, elite–mass interaction, and the feasibility of policy evaluations. Third, as the stakes are frequently high, challenges to national identity, international status, war and peace, emotions and passionate responses are more likely to shape the policy of foreign relations. Finally, the emergence of various non-state actors (NGOs, international corporations, etc.), sub-national and supra-national actors do impact upon foreign policies in a way they rarely do in other public policies.

Those accounts, helpful as they may be, are too limited in scope and number to inform the necessary dialogue between the two fields. Scholars in both policy areas should be drawing on a much broader range of approaches when focusing on the overlaps and possible synergies between their research areas than most currently do. Indeed, different trends in world politics should make both disciplines more open to talking to each other and appear to necessitate a cross-disciplinary dialogue between PP and FPA. These trends encompass first, changes in the material world that necessitate integrated solutions. For instance, there is a growing number of global problems, such as climate change, migration, public health, or internet governance, that cut across policy domains and are still predominantly but not exclusively addressed by state foreign policy. Moreover, a growing number of traditional foreign policy concerns (and the quality thereof) have unintended consequences in adjacent policy areas (interdependence effects), requiring cross-realm solutions. For example, in the realm of internet governance the emergence of high-powered transnational search engine providers, such as Google, have raised a host of privacy concerns, most notably in Europe, so that the European Court of Justice ruled in 2013 that these corporations have to find ways to implement a "right to be digitally forgotten."[1] This and other similar rulings concerning privacy rights in the digital age have not only raised eyebrows—as to the costs and effectiveness of their implementation—but also touch upon a host of national security, economic, cultural, and social sensitivities and respective policies (Kuner 2013; Allen 2015).

The second trend relates to changes in the immaterial world which equally call for cross-realm solutions. This includes changes in the character of the constitutive agents of world politics (states, IOs, NGOs) which have resulted in growing expectations and demands as to what the foreign policy of a country should address (e.g., cultural security). Most importantly, such expectations and demands have become more salient in electoral politics and require responses in multiple policy areas and arenas. One pertinent strategy of governments to cope with this challenge, moreover, has been to shift decision-making beyond the nation state and to delegate authority and responsibilities to IOs, which has, however, increased the contestation and politicization of Global Governance and created new policy conflicts between the international and national orders. These conflicts also cut across policy fields, for example trade and environment or health issues, so that public and foreign policy become mingled (e.g., Fidler 2005).

The third trend concerns changes in technology that have created new policy spheres and connected existing ones. This includes recent changes in information and communication technology that have not only created a new public policy field that transcends traditional territorial boundaries, but these technologies have also "shrunk the world" and expanded the "perceptional remit" of voters and policy-makers (Hocking and Melissen 2015). Events and developments in distant regions of the world may thus "hit home" earlier, easier, and more erratically, as Brommesson and Ekengren (2017) have recently shown in a comparative case study on the effects of mediatization in three countries (Sweden, Finland, and the United Kingdom) and on their respective humanitarian intervention behavior in two crisis situations (Libya and Côte d'Ivoire).

---

[1] This case is known as C-131/12 *Google Spain SL and Google Inc v. AEPD and Mario Costeja Gonzalez.*

The challenges of a cross-disciplinary dialogue

Thus far, we have discussed various reasons for bringing FPA and PP into conversation. At the same time, there are also a number of challenges and obstacles that could possibly hamper such a dialogue. Those challenges can be grouped into three categories: theoretical, empirical, and sociological challenges. While the following paragraphs acknowledge those challenges, they also offer arguments as to why they should not be considered as insurmountable obstacles for cross-disciplinary dialogue.

Regarding theoretical challenges, we have argued that public policy and foreign policy approaches more often than not pursue strikingly similar lines of inquiry, which at first glance bodes well for dialogue. A second glance, however, reveals that public policy and foreign policy approaches may sometimes mean different things when talking about similar concepts and variables. The advocacy coalition framework (ACF) from public policy research (see the contribution by Pierce and Hicks in this volume) serves as a case in point.

Among the main concepts of the ACF are coalitions, beliefs, and policy change (Weible *et al.* 2011). As it turns out, several strands of FPA research have dealt with the very same concepts, such as Kaarbo (2012) regarding coalitions, Schafer and Walker (2006) with respect to beliefs, and Hermann (1990) and Welch (2005) concerning policy change. While those similarities at first sight underline the scope for a dialogue, the devil is in the detail, in the sense of the specific understandings of the respective concepts. For instance, while the ACF examines coalitions that comprise a broad range of actors (legislators, interest group leaders, researchers, etc.), FPA research focuses predominantly on governing coalitions. Moreover, while the ACF stresses the importance of shared beliefs among a group of policy participants, FPA constructs assign greater importance to idiosyncratic beliefs of individual decision-makers. Finally, while the ACF examines long-term policy change, FPA constructs are typically more interested in short-term change. However, those differences should not be overdone. Indeed, it is exactly those differences in focus when examining similar independent, intervening and dependent variables that highlight the vast, albeit untapped, potential of cross-fertilization among the two fields.

Turning to empirical challenges, we have made the observation that foreign policy-making has become increasingly similar to public policy-making as a result of, among other things, the incorporation of an increasing number of actors in the formulation as well as implementation of policies. Still, it might be one step too far to argue that foreign policy-making is just like any other area of policy, even in highly integrated political contexts like Europe. Tellingly, the Common Foreign and Security Policy (CFSP) of the European Union is among the final "bastions" of intergovernmentalist decision-making in the context of European integration, which suggests that states are particularly reluctant of sharing competencies in this area of "high politics" (Hoffmann 1966). Also, in domestic contexts, the degree to which societal actors like the media or lobby groups mobilize around and seek to influence foreign policy-making might on average be lower than in areas such as tax policy, education policy, or health policy.

However, foreign policy does not need to be identical to any other area of public policy-making for the application of public policy approaches to make sense. Indeed, while the making of foreign policy might still contain features that cannot be found to the same extent in the realm of public policy-making, the differences seem to be (have become) ones in degree and not (no longer) in kind. Besides, one should not overstate the homogeneity of public policy-making in the first place, since there exist at times considerable differences concerning the formation of actors, the institutional set-up, etc. across policy areas as well. The same is true for the field of foreign policy which also includes a diverse range of issue areas, from environmental or trade policy to defense and security policy. The different areas of foreign policy might therefore be conceived as yet another domain of policy-making with their own special features and idiosyncrasies (Charillon 2018).

Finally, regarding sociological challenges, the increasing specialization within the discipline of political science impedes cross-disciplinary dialogue. The individual subfields have become so diversified, complex, and nuanced that keeping up with the recent literature has become increasingly challenging even in one's own primary area of expertise. By extension, building bridges between two subfields is increasingly daunting a task in intellectual terms (as well as with respect to time management) since it requires familiarity with two vast bodies of literature. What is more, the job market tends also to discourage rather than encourage cross-disciplinary research since job ads typically call for experts in just one field (IR or comparative politics or ...). Similar things can be said with respect to publication outlets (journals), many of which have also become increasingly specialized and thus narrow in scope, thereby disincentivizing cross-disciplinary research.

However, while for both intellectual and career reasons building bridges between two subfields of political science appears challenging, this should not prohibit exploring the theoretical, conceptual, and/or empirical added value that might possibly emerge from such an exercise. The extent to which this volume has made good on its promise of reaping the benefits as well as overcoming the challenges and pitfalls of cross-disciplinary dialogue between FPA and PP, thus contributing to a better understanding of foreign policy decision-making processes and outcomes, is up for the concluding chapter (see chapter 10) and, of course, for the reader to evaluate.

Structure of the book

The book pursues its ambition to initiate a more thorough dialogue between PP and FPA through covering arguably the most important and best-established state-of-the-art approaches in public policy research. For each of the approaches, their transferability and added value to the study of foreign policy will be discussed. We have clustered the public policy approaches along two dimensions, namely actor-centered and structural ones. This mirrors the different focal points offered by the respective approaches, highlighting the role of individual actors and agency on the one hand (e.g., advocacy coalitions or veto players) and the both enabling and constraining effects of formal or informal structural factors on the other hand (e.g., institutional settings or policy networks). What is more, this distinction can also be found in the FPA literature, where some concepts focus primarily on agency and the idiosyncrasies of individual agents (e.g., leadership traits, beliefs, or risk propensities) while others place more emphasis on structural factors (e.g., coalition arrangements, parliamentary war powers, or public opinion) (Hudson 2014; Alden and Aran 2017). The fact that similar broad distinctions of analytical perspectives can be found in both areas of research makes them a useful ordering principle for the purposes of this volume.

It is important to note that the public policy approaches discussed in the individual chapters put their emphasis on different phases of the policy cycle, thus offering more insights into some phases than others. Generally speaking, the actor-centered approaches in Part I of this volume zoom in primarily on the agenda-setting and decision-making phases of the policy cycle. Conversely, the structural approaches that are grouped together in Part II focus more on the evaluation and feedback phases. Having said that, the underlying aspiration of all public policy approaches covered in this volume is to speak to public policy-making "in toto." For that reason, the following chapters do not focus exclusively on one particular phase of the policy cycle but rather seek to explain (foreign) policy-making more generally. In so doing, the edited volume establishes how bridging the intra-disciplinary divide between studies of public and foreign policy can enrich FPA and will show it can benefit from broadening its instruments for analysis. The chapters also discuss under what conditions such a transfer is less promising due to the "sui generis" character of foreign policy.

This volume is organized in two parts. Part I consists of four chapters and looks at actor-centered approaches in PP. They are the multiple streams approach, punctuated equilibrium theory, advocacy coalitions, and veto player approaches. Part II also includes four chapters and deals with structural approaches in PP. This part has chapters on new institutionalism, network approaches, policy diffusion, and policy learning.[2]

Each chapter consists of five sections. The introductions flag up the nuts and bolts of the selected public policy approach and briefly contextualize it within the field of public policy analysis more broadly. They also indicate why and how the approach might be suitable for the analysis of foreign policy.

Second, the chapters reconstruct the original formulation of the public policy approach and illustrate how it has evolved over time. How important is the public policy approach in the realm of public policy analysis? Which core insights has it provided so far? What are the main current discussions and developments regarding substance and method within the selected public policy approach?

The third section of each chapter constitutes their analytical core. It discusses whether, how, and to what extent or under what conditions the public policy approach under study can be applied to foreign policy issues. The chapters will address questions such as how an approach speaks to FPA approaches, what and where are possible links between the domestic and the foreign realms of policy-making and analysis? Has the selected public policy approach already been applied to foreign policy before and if so in which context? Which conceptual or theoretical adjustments are required to transfer the public policy approach to foreign policy? Where are the limits of transferability?

Fourth, the chapters provide an empirical illustration of how the selected approach can be applied to study foreign policy puzzles. Although we have argued that foreign policy-making and public policy-making have become more similar over time, the case studies included in this volume address typical issues of high politics, such as bilateral interstate conflict, the foreign deployment of armed forces, or the use of coercive instruments of economic statecraft. The fact that the chapters in this volume suggest that public policy approaches have explanatory power even in those "traditional" areas of foreign and security policy further increases our confidence that they can offer viable contributions to our understanding of foreign and security policy more generally.

Finally, all chapters conclude with discussing the merits and shortfalls of the selected public policy approach for the foreign policy domain.

---

[2] While representing different strands of literature, policy diffusion and learning are clearly interconnected in the sense that learning is a specific diffusion and transfer mechanism that depicts particular forms of policy change in interaction with identifiable others. Having said that, we think that the two approaches are nonetheless sufficiently distinct to warrant a separate discussion in this volume.

What is the most promising value added and where are potential boundaries and limitations to transferability?

Summary of the chapters

This volume contains ten chapters. Following this introduction, chapters 2–5 discuss some of the most prominent actor-centered approaches in PP. Chapters 6–9 then move on to more structural approaches. Chapter 10 draws out the main lessons of this collective endeavor and discusses avenues and challenges for further efforts at bringing concepts and approaches from the fields of PP and FPA together.

Chapter 2, by Spyros Blavoukos, covers the multiple streams approach (MSA). The core objective of this contribution is to examine how MSA fares in the foreign policy realm and whether it is relevant and appropriate for the study of foreign policy. Kingdon's seminal work on public policy-making conceptualizes public policy as the intersection of three different streams (problem, policy, politics). Against this background, the theoretical component of this chapter provides an overview of the approach and discusses its transferability. The empirical thrust of the contribution derives from the analysis of two major foreign policy shifts, namely the first ever substantial Israeli–Palestinian agreement in the early 1990s that led to the Oslo Accords and the Greek–Turkish rapprochement in the late 1990s, which resulted in the substantial upgrading of the EU–Turkish relationship.

Chapter 3, by Jeroen Joly and Friederike Richter, discusses punctuated equilibrium theory (PET). This theory, which was first proposed by Baumgartner and Jones, explains how the same institutional set-up, usually preventing new policy issues from gaining political attention, is also responsible for the occasional outbursts of attention that cause disproportionately large policy shifts. PET has been successfully applied to a wide range of public policies and has increasingly generated cross-sectional and cross-national analyses, which aim at understanding and comparing the causes of stability and change in different political systems. However, the focus of these studies has mostly been on domestic policies, with only very little attention for PET in FPA. The aim of this chapter is to show that PET is not only relevant in the realm of domestic politics, but also useful for studying and understanding foreign policy-making. To illustrate this claim, this chapter looks at yearly changes in attention to foreign policy issues and examines the relationship between changes in foreign aid allocations and the size of aid administrations.

Chapter 4, by Jonathan J. Pierce and Katherine C. Hicks, covers the ACF. The ACF was developed by Paul Sabatier and Hank Jenkins-Smith in the 1980s to help explain the policy process during contentious policy-making. The main insight the theory has provided is how actors collaborating together in coalitions seek to transform their beliefs into policy by using their resources and various strategies. More specifically, this chapter discusses how the components of the ACF such as policy subsystem, policy core beliefs, coalitions, and policy change are identified and operationalized in order to demonstrate the strengths and the weaknesses of applying the ACF to foreign policy. In its empirical section, the chapter analyzes coalition stability among competing international coalitions over time by applying the ACF to the US government's decision to support the partition of Palestine under United Nations (UN) Resolution 181 in 1947.

Chapter 5, by Kai Oppermann and Klaus Brummer, addresses veto player approaches. The main contribution of veto player approaches to the study of public policy has been to provide a toolkit for the comparative analysis of the dynamics and obstacles of policy change across regime types and policy areas. Specifically, veto player approaches suggest that the possibility and conditions for policy change in a given polity depend on the veto player constellation, that is, the number of veto players and veto points, the distribution of preferences between veto players and their ability and incentives to employ veto power. While veto player arguments have already found their way into FPA, the chapter makes the case that the theoretical and empirical potential of such arguments for the study of foreign policy has not yet been systematically exploited. Against this background, the chapter first outlines the core tenets of veto player approaches and shows how they have been applied in public policy. Then, the discussion focuses on the transferability of such approaches to the field of foreign policy. This is followed by an empirical illustration of a veto player analysis of Germany's policy regarding the foreign deployment of its armed forces.

Chapter 6, by Siegfried Schieder, covers new institutionalism (NI). The purpose of this chapter is to bridge the gap between FPA and NI, providing new insights into how the former can benefit from the various strands of the latter. To do so, this chapter examines NI as one of the most prominent research programs in the field of public policy analysis and presents an overview of how NI in its rational, sociological, historical, and discursive variants has been applied to research on foreign policy and what its contribution is to the field of FPA. While FPA can be enriched by all four forms of NI, much of the relevant literature employs either rational institutionalism or a more sociological approach. To bring out the promise of NI in FPA, the chapter then looks at how historical institutionalism may be able to explain the United States' decision to impose sanctions on Russia in response to the Ukraine crisis in 2014.

Chapter 7, by Christopher Ansell and Jacob Torfing, introduces the network approach. This chapter first defines the network concept, sets out the core features of the network approach and explains how and why it has emerged as an alternative lens for understanding policy-making in dispersed and interactive settings that defy description in terms of the traditional hierarchy–market dichotomy. It then compares different theories and methods for understanding policy and governance networks and discusses how these networks can be instrumental for enhancing knowledge sharing, improving inter-organizational and cross-sector coordination, and solving wicked and unruly problems in ways that both increase effectiveness and democratic legitimacy. Subsequently, the chapter describes how and why the network approach is applicable to foreign policy-making and assesses the scope conditions as well as merits and limits of applying the approach. It argues that the network approach is useful for analyzing how states formulate, implement, and diffuse foreign policy in response to domestic interests and global problems and events. Finally, after a brief mapping of network types, the chapter provides a more extended example of how the network approach is applicable to core concerns of foreign policy. The example illustrates the role of networks in facilitating political co-operation to prevent nuclear proliferation.

Chapter 8, by Katja Biedenkopf and Alexander Mattelaer, covers policy diffusion. It argues that the analytical lens of interdependent policy decisions and mutual influence among foreign policy-makers can add a useful angle to FPA. More specifically, the focus of this chapter is on policy diffusion and transfer as independent variables in the analysis of foreign policy choices. The chapter starts with outlining policy diffusion and transfer as public policy approaches and then has a section that proposes how these two concepts could enrich FPA. The fourth section illustrates the application of a policy diffusion lens to foreign policy decisions, namely the case of planning doctrine for military crisis response operations. It explores the historical origins of North Atlantic Treaty Organization (NATO) operational planning doctrine and how it has diffused to other IOs such as the European Union (EU) and the UN. The concluding section provides some reflections on the contribution and limitations of integrating policy diffusion and transfer into FPA.

Chapter 9, by Sebastian Harnisch, discusses the policy learning approach. Learning is a change of beliefs or a development of new beliefs, skills, or procedures as a result of the observation and interpretation of experience. Policy learning has been long recognized as a central mechanism of change in public policy and it has been employed in various research approaches, such as advocacy coalition, theories of institutional change, policy diffusion and transfer, or epistemic communities. Thus far, however, its broad application has not resulted in any (substantial) additional analytical purchase because respective sub-disciplines have not communicated with and build upon each other. The chapter offers a systematic review of the extant public policy literature and discusses the competitive application of several learning approaches to the case of Soviet Union foreign policy learning under Gorbachev. In lieu of a result, it identifies three areas of common interest to PP and FPA, i.e., the historicity and cross-fertilization of domestic and foreign policy experience, the temporal pattern of specific learning episodes, and the variant patterns of sociality, including international institutions as teachers/facilitators of learning, for a future dialogue.

Chapter 10, by Juliet Kaarbo, summarizes the main findings of the eight preceding chapters on the selected public policy approaches and draws out key insights from public policy research that can be transferred to FPA. The chapter argues that bringing public policy approaches into FPA holds the promise of theoretical and methodological innovation in the field, widens the scope of FPA, helps exploring novel connections between the internal and the external in policy-making, and invites reflections on the nature of foreign policy. At the same time, the conclusion discusses possible pitfalls of linking the fields of PP and FPA, for example the dangers of adding to the theoretical incoherence in FPA and of further distancing the subfield from International Relations. Finally, the chapter provides suggestions for future research at the interface between public and foreign policies.

Taken together, this book points out how bridging the intra-disciplinary divide between PP and FPA can enrich the study of foreign policy and shows how FPA can benefit from broadening its instruments for analysis.

References

Alden, Chris and Amnon Aran (2017) *Foreign Policy Analysis: New Approaches*, 2nd edition, Abingdon and New York: Routledge.

Aldrich, John H., John L. Sullivan, and Eugene Borgida (1989) Foreign Affairs and Issue Voting: Do Presidential Candidates "Waltz before a Blind Audience?" *American Political Science Review* 83(1), 123–141.

Aldrich, John H., Christopher Gelpi, Peter Feaver, Jason Reifler, and Kristin Thompson Sharp (2006) Foreign Policy and the Electoral Connection, *Annual Review of Political Science* 9, 477–502.

Allen, Stephen (2015) Remembering and Forgetting: Protecting Privacy Rights in the Digital Age, *European Data Protection Law Review* 3, 164–177.

Allison, Graham T. (1971) *Essence of Decision: Explaining the Cuban Missile Crisis*, Boston: Little, Brown and Company.

Brommesson, Douglas and Ann-Marie Ekengren (2017) *The Mediatization of Foreign Policy, Political Decision-Making and Humanitarian Intervention*, New York: Palgrave Macmillan.

Caporaso, James A. (1997) Across the Great Divide: Integrating Comparative and International Politics, *International Studies Quarterly* 41(4), 563–592.

Carlsnaes, Walter (1992) The Agency-Structure Problem in Foreign Policy Analysis, *International Studies Quarterly* 36(3), 245–270.

Charillon, Frédéric (2018) Public Policy and Foreign Policy Analysis, in Cameron G. Thies (ed.) *Oxford Encyclopedia of Foreign Policy Analysis*, Volume 2, Oxford: Oxford University Press, 483–496.

Daugbjerg, Carsten (2014) The European Union: Balancing Trade Liberalization and Protectionism, in Oluf Langhelle (ed.) *International Trade Negotiations and Domestic Politics: The Intermestic Politics of Trade Liberalization*, London: Routledge, 76–101.

Dunn, William N. (2016) *Public Policy Analysis*, 5th edition, London: Routledge.

Fidler, David P. (2005) Health as Foreign Policy: Between Principle and Power, *The Whitehead Journal of Diplomacy and International Relations* (Summer/Fall), 179–194.

Gilardi, Fabrizio (2013) Transnational Diffusion: Norms, Ideas, and Policies, in Walter Carlsnaes, Thomas Risse, and Beth A. Simmons (eds.) *Handbook of International Relations*, 2nd edition, London: Sage, 453–477.

Hermann, Charles F. (1990) Changing Course: When Governments Choose to Redirect Foreign Policy, *International Studies Quarterly* 34(1), 3–21.

Hill, Christopher (2016) *Foreign Policy in the Twenty-First Century*, Basingstoke: Palgrave.

Hocking, Brian (1999) *Foreign Ministries. Change and Adaptation*, Basingstoke: Palgrave Macmillan.

Hocking, Brian and Jan Melissen (2015) *Diplomacy in the Digital Age*, Clingendael: Netherlands Institute of International Relations.

Hoffmann, Stanley (1966) Obstinate or Obsolete? The Fate of the Nation-State and the Case of Western Europe, *Daedalus* 95(3), 862–915.

Howlett, Michael, M. Ramesh, and Anthony Perl (2009) *Studying Public Policy. Policy Cycles and Policy Subsystems*, 3rd edition, Oxford: Oxford University Press.

Hudson, Valerie (2005) Foreign Policy Analysis: Actor-Specific Theory and the Ground of International Relations, *Foreign Policy Analysis* 1(1), 1–30.

Hudson, Valerie (2014) *Foreign Policy Analysis: Classic and Contemporary Theory*, 2nd edition, Lanham: Rowman & Littlefield.

Ikenberry, G. John, David A. Lake, and Michael Mastanduno (1988) Introduction: Approaches to Explaining American Foreign Economic Policy, *International Organization* 42(1), 1–14.

Jönsson, Christer (2016) States Only? The Evolution of Diplomacy, in Gunther Hellmann, Andreas Fahrmeir, and Miloš Vec (eds.) *The Transformation of Foreign Policy*, Oxford: Oxford University Press, 242–262.

Kaarbo, Juliet (2012) *Coalition Politics and Cabinet Decision Making: A Comparative Analysis of Foreign Policy Choices*, Ann Arbor: University of Michigan Press.

Kaarbo, Juliet (2015) A Foreign Policy Analysis Perspective on the Domestic Politics Turn in IR Theory, *International Studies Review* 17(2), 189–216.

Kaarbo, Juliet (2017) Coalition Politics, International Norms, and Foreign Policy: Multiparty Decision-Making Dynamics in Comparative Perspective, *International Politics* 54(6), 669–682.

Keohane, Robert O. and Joseph S. Nye (1977) *Power and Interdependence: World Politics in Transition*, Boston: Little, Brown and Company.

Kuner, Christopher (2013) *Transborder Data Flows and Data Privacy Law*, Oxford: Oxford University Press.

Langhelle, Oluf (ed.) (2014) *International Trade Negotiations and Domestic Politics: The Intermestic Politics of Trade Liberalization*, New York: Routledge.

Lentner, Howard H. (2006) Public Policy and Foreign Policy: Divergences, Intersections, Exchange, *Review of Policy Research* 23(1), 169–181.

Manning, Bayless (1977) The Congress, the Executive and Intermestic Affairs: Three Proposals, *Foreign Affairs* 55(2), 306–324.

Moravcsik, Andrew (1993) Introduction: Integrating International and Domestic Theories of International Bargaining, in Peter B. Evans, Harold K. Jacobson, and Robert D. Putnam (eds.) *Double-Edged Diplomacy: International Bargaining and Domestic Politics*, Berkeley: University of California Press, 3–42.

Moravcsik, Andrew (1997) Taking Preferences Seriously: A Liberal Theory of International Politics, *International Organization* 51(4), 513–553.

Neack, Laura, Jeanne A. K. Hey, and Patrick J. Haney (eds.) (1995) *Foreign Policy Analysis: Continuity and Change in Its Second Generation*, Englewood Cliffs: Prentice Hall.

Oppermann, Kai and Henrike Viehrig (2009) The Public Salience of Foreign and Security Policy in Britain, Germany and France, *West European Politics* 32(5), 925–942.

Putnam, Robert D. (1988) Diplomacy and Domestic Politics: The Logic of Two-Level Games, *International Organization* 42(3), 427–460.

Rathbun, Brian C. (2004) *Partisan Interventions: European Party Politics and Peace Enforcement in the Balkans*, Ithaca, NY: Cornell University Press.

Raunio, Tapio and Wolfgang Wagner (2017) Towards Parliamentarisation of Foreign and Security Policy? *West European Politics* 40(1), 1–19.

Ripsman, Norrin M., Jeffrey W. Taliaferro, and Steven E. Lobell (2016) *Neoclassical Realist Theory of International Politics*, New York: Oxford University Press.

Risse, Thomas (2013) Transnational Actors and World Politics, in Walter Carlsnaes, Thomas Risse, and Beth A. Simmons (eds.) *Handbook of International Relations*, 2nd edition, London: Sage, 453–477.

Risse-Kappen, Thomas (1991) Public Opinion, Domestic Structure, and Foreign Policy in Liberal Democracies, *World Politics* 43(4), 479–512.

Russo, Philip A. and Patrick J. Haney (2012) Intermestic Politics and Homeland Security, in James M. McCormick (ed.) *The Domestic Sources of American Foreign Policy: Insights and Evidence*, 6th edition, Lanham: Rowman & Littlefield, 285–300.

Sabatier, Paul A. (2007) Fostering the Development of Policy Theory, in Paul A. Sabatier (ed.) *Theories of the Policy Process*, 2nd edition, Boulder: Westview Press, 321–336.

Sabatier, Paul A. and Christopher M. Weible (eds.) (2014) *Theories of the Policy Process*, 3rd edition, Boulder: Westview Press.

Schafer, Mark and Stephen G. Walker (eds.) (2006) *Beliefs and Leadership in World Politics: Methods and Applications of Operational Code Analysis*, New York and Basingstoke: Palgrave Macmillan.

Snyder, Richard C., H. W. Bruck, and Burton Sapin (1962) *Foreign Policy Decision-Making: An Approach to the Study of International Politics*, New York: The Free Press.

Sprout, Harold H. and Margaret Sprout (1956) *Man-Milieu Relationship Hypotheses in the Context of International Politics*, Princeton: Princeton University Press.

Waltz, Kenneth N. (1959) *Man, the State, and War: A Theoretical Analysis*, New York: Columbia University Press.

Weible, Christopher M. (2014) Advancing Policy Process Research, in Paul A. Sabatier and Christopher M. Weible (eds.) *Theories of the Policy Process*, 3rd edition, Boulder: Westview Press, 391–407.

Weible, Christopher M., Paul A. Sabatier, Hank C. Jenkins-Smith, Daniel Nohrstedt, Adam Douglas Henry, and Peter deLeon (2011) A Quarter Century of the Advocacy Coalition Framework: An Introduction to the Special Issue, *Policy Studies Journal* 39(3), 349–360.

Welch, David A. (2005) *Painful Choices: A Theory of Foreign Policy Change*, Princeton: Princeton University Press.

Zürn, Michael (2013) Globalization and Global Governance, in Walter Carlsnaes, Thomas Risse, and Beth A. Simmons (eds.) *Handbook of International Relations*, 2nd edition, London: Sage, 401–425.

Zürn, Michael (2014) The Politicization of World Politics and its Effects: Eight Propositions, *European Political Science Review* 6(1), 47–71.

Part I

Actor-centered perspectives

2

The multiple streams approach in foreign policy

Spyros Blavoukos

The multiple streams approach (MSA) is based on John Kingdon's influential work, first published in 1984. In it, Kingdon identifies three kinds of processes that set agendas and specify policy alternatives. These processes comprise: first, the recognition and identification of a problem as such; second, the generation of an alternative problem specification and alternative policy options; and third, political events that alter the terms of political interaction in the policy-making process. The three streams have lives of their own; their coupling opens an "opportunity window" for change associated with focusing events or policy entrepreneurs who use it in pursuit of their favorite policy alternative (Kingdon 1995). Since its original inception and application by Kingdon in the fields of public health and transportation in the United States, the MSA has been refined and further elaborated conceptually (Zahariadis 2014; Herweg *et al.* 2015; Zohlnhöfer and Rüb 2016). It is widely recognized as one of the most prolific and influential approaches in the realm of public policy analysis (Sabatier 2007).

Kingdon identifies two "universal" elements in his analysis: first, the ambiguity and competition for attention in the policy-making process; and, second, the fact that this process is neither comprehensively rational nor linear. As regards the former, ambiguity is a key feature of the MSA, in the sense that there are several alternative ways of framing and understanding an issue (Zahariadis 2003, 2008). The vagueness and shifting nature of the problem definition results in a multitude of potential solutions to a given problem but very few of these solutions gain attention and even fewer gain support. At the same time, many problems exist but few reach the top of the policy agenda. The latter entails that actors have limited resources such as time and cognitive ability. This forces them to make choices before they have considered all possibilities and develop clear policy preferences on any given issue (Herweg *et al.* 2017). The independent nature of the three streams suggests that the policy-making process does not follow a policy cycle with clearly ordered stages. They evolve in parallel and their coupling is the critical juncture that paves the way for any public policy act.

In line with the broader objective of the edited volume, this chapter examines whether and how the MSA can be applied in the foreign policy realm. It is based on the fundamental assumption that public policy tools can be used for the analysis of foreign policy-making, appropriately adjusted to the specific and idiosyncratic features of this policy area. Following a brief overview of the MSA in the next section, we will then review scholarly works that have already made use of this approach to study foreign policy and have identified its most relevant insights. Next, our empirical illustration will examine one particular aspect of foreign policy-making, namely foreign policy change. This does not suggest that MSA can address only issues of change; however, change entails overcoming the inertia of previous policies, in which case MSA is well suited with its analytical tools to account for it. After all, the MSA allows the study of critical junctures in policy-making and foreign policy changes constitute primary examples of such policy junctures. Two cases will be studied, namely the Oslo Peace Accords and the Greek–Turkish rapprochement in the early and late 1990s respectively. We will conclude by discussing the generalizability of our findings and an overall assessment of the MSA in the field of foreign policy.

The conceptual pillars of MSA

At the core of Kingdon's analysis is the deconstruction and rejection of the rational assumptions in policy-making. Such an attempt can be traced back to the garbage can model of organizational choice (Cohen *et al.* 1972). Since then, contributions using the MSA have expanded it in three aspects: policy areas, policy stages, and different units of analysis (Zohlnhöfer *et al.* 2015: 414). The conceptual pillars of MSA as put forward by Kingdon comprise the three "Ps" in policy-making, namely problems, policies, and politics, the coupling of which by policy entrepreneurs when "opportunity windows" open paves the way for policy change (see table 2.1).

On a daily basis, numerous *problems* emerge, capture the attention of policy-makers and subsequently trigger some policy response or simply fade out. Changing policy conditions may acquire the "problem" status by different possible means: indicators that show fluctuation and call for policy revisiting and "focusing events" that may also draw attention to the existing policy conditions setting in motion the process of policy change (Kingdon 1995: 90–103). These means increase public acquiescence to the necessity of policy redirection and marginalize domestic opposition to it (Meydani 2009: 21–22).

In pluralistic political systems, *policies* emanate from policy communities that consist of specialists in a given policy area from both within and outside the government. These communities differ in their openness, fragmentation, and degree of porosity (Kingdon 1995: 117–121). They consider many ideas to address the identified problems. Most of these alternatives never take off, especially those that do not conform to the dominant normative and ideational orthodoxy, and only a few make it so far as to become concrete policy proposals vying for implementation. The size, scope, and influence of the policy communities vary according to the policy area and the degree of centralization of the domestic policy-making system. In "securitized" issue areas and/or less pluralistic, hierarchical systems, policy communities may be confined to the upper echelons of the governmental apparatus with little if any actual societal input.

The stream of *politics* encapsulates the sociopolitical environment within which policy-making is taking place, the organized political forces that cast their support or opposition to the various policy proposals, and developments at the governmental level (Kingdon 1995: 145–159). Public opinion swings vis-à-vis running policies and existing alternatives affect policy-makers, under the credible assumption that they want to ensure their political survival and are thus receptive to such changes in the "national mood." Furthermore, each policy proposal has its own constituency, the size, resources, and mobilization of which are critical in bringing an alternative proposal in the spotlight.

When these three streams that exist independently from one another are coupled, an opportunity window emerges for policy change advocates—i.e., "policy entrepreneurs"—to push forward their favorite alternative. Such windows may be predictable or unpredictable in nature, the former, for example, associated with budgetary or electoral cycles and the latter with unexpected political and socio-economic developments, such as, for example, the death of a political leader that opens the intrapartisan succession race and changes the politics dynamics (Kingdon 1995: 179–190). Policy entrepreneurs constitute a source of innovation in terms of policy content or direction, thus having a transformative effect on politics, policies, or institutions. They shape the terms of the political debate, (re)framing issues, (re)defining problems, and (re)setting policy agendas (Mintrom 1997; Sheingate 2003). They invest their own resources—special skills and expertise, vision, and/or leadership capacity—in the hope of a future return that may take the form of policy outcomes they favor, satisfaction from participation in a policy process, or even personal aggrandizement in the form of increased reputation and/or better career prospects (Kingdon 1995: 122–123). In their effort to push forward their pet proposal, they face entry barriers, the permeability of which dictates the amount of resources the entrepreneurial interloper has to invest (Schneider and Teske 1992).

A final word of caution: the emergence of a policy entrepreneur should not be conflated with the success of his/her campaign. In that vein, the challenging and even collapse of the old policy orthodoxy does not entail teleologically its replacement by a new dominant one. When an "opportunity window" opens, alternative potential "orthodoxies" are vying for domination to replace the old one (Legro 2005: 14–15). In that respect, change is more likely to occur when policy entrepreneurs espouse alternative approaches that constitute credible and feasible political options that can master the necessary political support (Walsh 2006: 491). At this stage, the role of policy entrepreneurs is also crucial, struggling for the consolidation of the "new" policy orthodoxy. New alternatives seemingly endure because they appear to generate desirable results or are expected to do so in the near future. In the absence of such results, especially in the early years of the consolidation process, setbacks and reversals are possible, undermining the political investment of the policy entrepreneur.

Kingdon's initial conceptualization of the policy-making process has been widely used. In a very meticulous literature review, Jones *et al.* (2016) trace 311 academic publications in the last fifteen years using (some of) these key MSA features. This clearly shows that the MSA has grown in popularity over the years, which is an indication of conceptual health and vigorousness. Most publications examine single domestic policy domains, mostly health, environment, governance issues, education, and welfare. Given the large number of conceptual components of the approach, it is not surprising perhaps that only one-third of the works include all major features in the analysis.

Table 2.1 The main features of MSA

Problems: changing policy conditions that may acquire the "problem" status
Policies: policy alternatives that emanate from policy communities within and outside the government; few of them manage to take off
Politics: sociopolitical environment within which policy-making is taking place; each policy proposal has its own constituency that tries to push it upwards
Opportunity windows: result of the coupling of the three "streams"; predictable (electoral cycle) or unpredictable (unexpected political development, e.g., death of a political leader) in nature
Policy entrepreneurs: advocates of policy change with a transformative effect on politics, policies, or institutions; they (re)frame issues, (re)define problems, and (re)set policy agendas; invest own resources to push forward "pet projects"

It is also interesting that about 10 percent of the identified works claim some degree of conceptual innovation, adding new sub-components to the approach. This is an indication of the MSA malleability to accommodate new research findings, although caution is required as to whether these innovations are not simply alternative specifications and/or a different operationalization of existing concepts. At the same time, as illustrated also in this volume, the MSA is in an open dialogue with other approaches to public policy analysis, most notably the punctuated equilibrium theory and the advocacy coalition framework (Jones *et al.* 2016: 18–26). Still, despite this theoretical dialogue, which should lead to some kind of osmosis, most works seem to be more focused on explaining the empirical puzzles of the individual case studies rather than contributing to the theoretical advancement of the MSA (Zohlnhöfer *et al.* 2015: 414). The reason why such a more systematic theoretical sophistication of the MSA is lacking may be found in the figurative language of the approach that renders the development of falsifiable hypotheses difficult (Sabatier 2007). Recent works try to address this criticism by developing and testing a series of hypotheses on various aspects of the approach, not least on the opening of opportunity windows, the likelihood of agenda change, the link between policy entrepreneurs and core policy-makers, and the chances of successful policy adoption (Herweg *et al.* 2015; Zohlnhöfer 2016).

Thus, two different research paths can be envisaged based on the relevant literature: the first is using the MSA as a conceptual framework of analysis to guide empirical work without deriving from it concrete hypotheses. The challenge in this option is to be as comprehensive as possible in order to fully capture the analytical dynamism of MSA. The other path entails the development of testable and falsifiable hypotheses; however, given the multi-faceted nature of the approach some selectivity is required vis-à-vis which aspects will be looked upon. Given the very few works that apply the MSA at the foreign policy domain, as will be discussed in the following section, we make a conscious choice to opt mainly for the former in order to show the overall applicability of the approach. However, in the next two sections, we will try to link the discussion with specific hypotheses to show that the MSA can offer invaluable insights regardless of the chosen research path.

The MSA in foreign policy: how does it fare?

The MSA has not been widely used in the field of foreign policy-making, some early notable exceptions notwithstanding (Durant and Diehl 1989; Travis and Zahariadis 2002; Zahariadis 2005). Comprehensive existing works apply the MSA as an analytical instrument to account for agenda-setting in the US decision to intervene in Iraq looking at the role of policy communities, focusing events, and policy windows (Mazarr 2007). They also analyze the coupling procedure by adding the emotional component of foreign policy, hypothesizing that change is less likely to occur in the foreign policy domain the more intense the fear and the longer it persists in conditions of high issue salience, complexity, and preference inconsistency (Zahariadis 2015). The approach is deemed appropriate not only for a state's foreign policy but also for the analysis of agenda-setting patterns and policy change in the formulation of EU counter-terrorism policy (Bossong 2013). Policy entrepreneurs come assertively into play to pave the way for foreign policy change (Blavoukos and Bourantonis 2012).

This lack of extensive use of the MSA in foreign policy comes despite the fact that foreign policy usefully addresses two general points of MSA criticism: first, that it is based on American politics and is thus an approach developed for a policy-making system that is highly pluralistic in nature. In that respect, the critics state, it fails to capture the hierarchical relations in many—mostly European—systems of fused legislative and executive branches of power. In such systems, the role of societal sources of alternative policy proposals should not be overemphasized and instead one should pay more attention to the intra-governmental origins of a policy. Second, that it is basically a framework for the analysis of legislative policy-making, thus it has not been appropriately applied to cast light on policies that emerge without prior public deliberation or the formal approval of legislative authorities (Page 2006: 207–208). Both points, though, can be countered by applying in a comprehensive way the MSA to the foreign policy realm.

In line with the points raised in the previous section vis-à-vis the three streams and the other features of the MSA, international developments, like for example the outbreak of an epidemic or the fall of the Berlin Wall, alter the *problem* conceptualization of a given foreign policy and the respective policy requirements. Domestic or international security crises, like a political or military imbroglio, highlight the inappropriateness of current policies and practices, triggering their re-evaluation and providing impetus for change (Welch 2005: 45–46). They break old patterns of thought and behavior, causing potentially extensive social dissatisfaction and creating a sociopolitical context more amenable to reform. Their contribution is invaluable in overcoming institutional inertia and interests vested in the previous foreign policies. In terms of *policies*, "securitized" foreign policy issue areas feature policy communities that are confined to the upper echelons of the governmental apparatus. Alternative options emanate from this small group with little if any actual societal input. Finally, *politics*-wise, change is associated with developments at the governmental level, both in terms of the administration as a whole and/or changes within an administration. The former is related with a new government in office that brings along a new foreign policy agenda, especially if the new executive enjoys an extraordinary mandate (Keeler 1993: 436–439). The latter refers to a turnover in the personnel of the administration, for example with a new minister taking over the foreign affairs portfolio. Especially in centralized, hierarchical policy-making systems where policy communities are small and compact, such developments may have cataclysmic foreign policy effects.

In this environment, the drive of policy entrepreneurs for policy differentiation originates from a different understanding, conceptualization, and prioritization of international challenges, stemming not least from their belief systems, cognitive factors, and other idiosyncratic features (Checkel 1997). Given the high salience of many foreign policy issues, their entry barriers are very high and, thus, it is reasonable to expect foreign policy change to be induced by policy entrepreneurs closely associated with the "authoritative decision unit." This may be an individual or a set of individuals with the ability and authority to make a decision and commit the resources of a society on a foreign policy issue (Hermann 2001). This resembles very much the hypothesis put forward in the MSA that the policy entrepreneur is more likely to successfully couple the streams during an open policy window the more access (s)he has to core policy-makers (Herweg *et al.* 2015: 443–444).

Several parameters condition the capacity of such a "unit" to induce change. They comprise the number of formal and/or informal veto players in foreign policy-making, the—even small—scope of societal involvement, the electoral system that leads to strong or weak, majoritarian or coalition governments, and the personal policy-making style of the regime leader. *Ceteris paribus*, less frequent changes occur in highly bureaucratic states with democratic regimes than in autocratic regimes with a minimal policy-making role for the bureaucracy and little or no regime accountability (Welch 2005: 45). In general, autonomy and insulation of the unit from political dependencies (i.e., army, veto power actors, electoral concerns, coalition partners, etc.) create a policy-making environment more conducive to change. In a democratic regime, foreign policy change is more likely to occur in cases of strong, single-party governments with a prime minister dominating decision-making in the Cabinet, few or no veto points (by a president, constitutional court, or other), and small societal involvement or interest. Again, these parameters fit well a key hypothesis of the decision-coupling process in the MSA, namely that policy adoption is more likely if the proposal meets a problem salient for the voters and is put forward by a governing party or coalition not constrained by veto actors (Herweg *et al.* 2015: 446).

Accounting for change: the Greek–Turkish rapprochement and the Oslo Accords

Foreign policy is characterized by continuity and inertia rather than change, especially in the rigid world before the collapse of bipolarity in 1989. Only in the post-1989 era did the study of foreign policy change emerge as a key research area, mainly because of the cataclysmic systemic changes and paradigm shifts that emphasize the cognitive and ideational components of foreign policy. Several contributions have addressed explicitly the issue of foreign policy change and offer useful but varying insights on its dynamics (e.g., Checkel 1997; Walsh 2006; Rynhold 2007; Blavoukos and Bourantonis 2014). Both cases we examine are primary examples of major foreign policy realignment and constitute the outcome of complex and multidimensional domestic and international processes. They constitute long-standing conflicts that have caused in the past political turbulence in the Eastern Mediterranean basin. Greece and Israel are centralized states with stable, parliamentary democratic regimes. The Greek political and electoral system nurtures strong, single-party governments usually enjoying large parliamentary majorities whereas the Israeli case is different in the sense that the formation of coalition governments is the rule rather than the exception. This variation enables us to control for the significance—among other things—of the governmental structure (single party or coalition) in foreign policy change.

The Greek–Turkish rapprochement in the 1990s

Following the 1974 Cyprus imbroglio, the relations between Greece and Turkey have often been tense, escalating occasionally very close to total military engagement. The Greek accession to the EU in 1981 introduced an additional dimension to the bilateral confrontation, with Greece vehemently and consistently opposing the enhancement of the EU–Turkish relationship. As a result, Greece was portrayed for a long time as the sole culprit for the lack of progress in EU–Turkish relations, allowing several European partners to hide their own concerns behind the cloak of Greek intransigence. Thus, the Greek consent to the Turkish EU candidacy at the Helsinki European Council, in December 1999, signaled a major shift in the Greek foreign policy. The Greek stance in Helsinki marked the culmination of a process of gradual transformation from a conflicting to a more constructive foreign policy approach.

Problems and policies

The cataclysmic 1989 events changed the systemic conditions within which the Greek foreign policy operated. The new environment raised new security challenges for Greece at the northern borders of the country.

At the same time, the end of bipolarity loosened NATO constraints over Turkish foreign policy resulting in its greater assertiveness in the Balkans and the broader region. The second focusing event was the Imia/Kardak imbroglio in January 1996 that brought Greece and Turkey on the brink of war over a couple of islets in the Aegean Sea. The escalation to an armed conflict was avoided only after a last-minute US intervention. In the eyes of the then Greek prime minister, Costas Simitis, the incident illustrated the failure of earlier approaches to Turkey's containment, urging for a new strategic approach to the bilateral relations (Simitis 2005: 72–99). The third important development was the emerging prospect of Greece's accession to the Economic and Monetary Union (EMU). Tensions with Turkey put into great jeopardy the new, EMU-related government priorities, whereas a possible détente and a subsequent restraint of the military expenditure would have a major positive spillover to the process of Greek fiscal consolidation.

In this environment, the adversarial approach lost momentum and alternative policies were sought. The most influential alternative called for a transformation of the Greek foreign policy that would entail other things the full communitarization of the Greek–Turkish relationship. This approach counted on engagement and socialization effects to bring about the normalization of bilateral relations (Heraclides 2004; Tsakonas 2010). The EU enlargement policy, based on the 1993 Copenhagen eligibility criteria, linked EU membership with domestic reforms in the candidate countries and adjustment to the EU norms and modus operandi. Thus, the argument went, Greece should actually support the Turkish membership bid instead of opposing it, in the prospect of a "Europeanized" and less aggressive Turkish foreign policy (Economides 2005). At the same time, the accession of Cyprus to the EU constituted one of the main priorities of the Greek foreign policy in the 1990s. However, several member-states were reluctant to this prospect, unwilling to import the island's political problem to the EU (Ioakimidis 1996: 75). A clear link emerged between the lifting of the Greek veto and the unobstructed accession of Cyprus in the EU, a "package deal" that was clearly reflected in the 1999 Helsinki agreement.

Greek politics and policy entrepreneurs
To avoid fragmentation and political instability after the collapse of the junta regime in 1974, the Greek political and electoral system overwhelmingly nurtured—up until recently—strong parliamentary majorities and single-party governments. The preference for a powerful, unified executive and the charismatic figures that reined political parties further contributed to the concentration of political power in the hands of the prime minister. In that respect, the prime minister evolved from *primus inter pares* to *primus solus* within the Cabinet, minimizing the role and autonomy of other ministers. Therefore, changes in the prime ministerial

post may entail substantial policy shifts even if there is no political party alteration in power. In the foreign policy domain, in particular, limited institutionalization and the personalized policy-making style and ethos suggest that a change of the person in office may spell abrupt changes in the Greek foreign policy (Ioakimidis 1999: 156).

Such change at the very center of the Greek political system occurred after the domination of the "modernization" faction in the succession race within the ruling PASOK party in the mid-1990s. The faction, led by Costas Simitis, ran on a political platform of socio-economic modernization. This platform called for the rationalization of the Greek society and economy as well as Greece's gradual reinstatement at the EU level especially through EMU membership (Tsoukalis 2000: 40–41; Lyrintzis 2005: 250). Accession to the EMU became the central point of reference for the readjustment of PASOK's ideological, programmatic, and social profile and was elevated to the country's major political priority of this period (Moschonas 2001: 14).

In such a political environment, an adversarial and conflict-prone foreign policy would have endangered Greece's chances to achieve structural reform and EMU membership. Hence, the re-prioritization of Greek foreign policy objectives after the 1996 "change of guards" in PASOK brought along a partial, albeit substantial, strategic re-conceptualization. It eventually materialized three years later and only after the intra-partisan solidification of the "modernization faction" sidelined political concerns and opposition. This re-conceptualization took off after the change of leadership at the Greek Ministry of Foreign Affairs in the beginning of 1999. The new minister, George A. Papandreou, was an ardent supporter of a more engaging and constructive relationship with Turkey already from an earlier stage of his political career. On that ground, he was selected and appointed to orchestrate the final stage of the Greek foreign policy shift regarding the European future of Turkey (Heraclides 2010: 144–151).

The making of the 1993 Oslo Accords: a major change in Israeli foreign policy

The negotiation and adoption of the Oslo Accords, in August 1993, constituted a major change in Israel's foreign policy. The Israeli prime minister and leader of the Labor Party, Yitzhak Rabin, agreed with the Palestine Liberation Organization (PLO) for a withdrawal of Israeli forces from parts of the Gaza Strip and West Bank and affirmed the Palestinian right of self-government within those areas through the creation of a Palestinian Authority. It marked a radical shift from its previous hardline foreign policy toward the Palestinians in two ways. First, Israel held direct talks with the PLO as the authentic representative of the Palestinian people, reversing its long-held rejection of the PLO as a negotiating partner (Shlaim 2001: 512). Second, in Oslo, Israel officially recognized the legitimate and political rights of the Palestinian people while in return the PLO renounced terrorism and recognized Israel's right to exist in conditions of peace and security (Rynhold 2007: 423).

Problems and policies

Like in the Greek case discussed above, international developments, in particular the end of bipolarism but more importantly the 1991 first Gulf War, brought along new preoccupations in the Israeli foreign policy. First, the United States put pressure on Israel to foster closer relations with its Arab allies in view of the Gulf War. The Israeli perception that the country's potential role as a strategic asset for the United States in the Middle East had become less significant after the end of the Cold War made Israel more vulnerable to US pressures (Barnett 1999: 18). Prime Minister Rabin was convinced that Israel should take advantage of the current situation because ultimately time was not on Israel's side (Peri 1996: 66–67). At the same time, the first Gulf War had caused serious division among the Arab states and had weakened the PLO. Arafat's stand in favor of Saddam Hussein not only caused much international concern but also resulted in the cutting off of financial assistance from Arab states, like Saudi Arabia and Kuwait (Bercovitch 1997: 224). Finally, the international systemic changes had weakened the PLO; the dissolution of the Soviet Union deprived the PLO of its most important diplomatic patron. For the Israelis, a politically and financially weaker PLO was a potentially more malleable and receptive negotiating partner. If Israel wanted a deal with the Palestinians, it could no longer avoid the PLO; the alternative would be a rejectionist and more radical section of Palestinians, like Hamas. Thus, these international developments not only generated new "problems" for Israel but also had positive spillovers, creating a conducive environment for Israel to change its policy vis-à-vis the PLO.

In terms of focusing events, the outbreak of the first Palestinian Intifada, in 1987, generated serious domestic security concerns for the Israeli public. The Palestinian uprising led to the transformation of the Arab–Israeli conflict from an interstate to an intra-state dispute, having a very negative impact on the Israeli economy and society (Makovsky 1996: 88–89; Ezrahi 1997: 71–72). As a result, the Israeli public became critical of the exclusive reliance on military force and more amenable to some form of a peaceful accommodation with the Palestinians (Arian *et al.* 1992). The shock caused by the Intifada made the domestic political setting more receptive to foreign policy change, illustrating the limits of the previous policy and highlighting the need for a new approach (Auerbach and Greenbaum 2000: 37–45; Rynhold 2007: 426). Through its impact on public opinion and Israeli statesmen, like Rabin (Peri

1996: 354–356; Shamir and Shamir 2007: 482), the Intifada accelerated the political transformation within the Labor Party that in turn paved the way for the re-orientation of Israeli foreign policy in this field.

The alternative policy approach that gained momentum and came to the political ascendance after the Intifada entailed the re-conceptualization and reprioritization of security-related national objectives (Inbar 1991). Its origins can be traced in a faction of the Labor Party, consisting mainly of a younger generation of politicians that had been less engaged in war and conflict than the old guard and, consequently, less associated with realist security approaches (Hazan 2000: 372–375). The new approach entailed a cultural shift vis-à-vis the "threat from the Arab world" (Rynhold 2007: 428–432). In contrast to the foreign and security policy of the earlier years that was based on containing conflicts through military strength, the new political culture embraced engagement in combination with a willingness to take calculated risks for building peace with the "enemy" through dialogue and compromises. Following intra-party osmosis, political heavyweights of the Labor Party, like Rabin and Peres, reached similar conclusions about the necessity for a new approach to the Palestinian question and espoused this alternative approach (Peres 1995; Peri 1996).

Israeli politics and policy entrepreneurs
Still, the Israeli U-turn had to go through the rough waters of Israeli domestic politics that revolved around intra-party frictions, coalition-building, and electoral politics (Arian 1998: 74). Because of Israel's proportional electoral system, a single Israeli party seldom enjoys an absolute majority in the Israeli Parliament (*Knesset*). That means that both major parties, Likud and the Labor Party, govern routinely in co-operation with smaller parties or, on rare occasions, in co-operation with each other in coalitions of national unity. The most important foreign and security policy issues remain in the competence of the prime minister, who usually comes from the largest party in the *Knesset*. Prime ministers have also tended to take on the defense portfolio, thus removing a potential source of intra-governmental opposition in the making of foreign and security policy. In that respect, the prime minister plays a very influential, though by no means exclusive, role in the policy-making process (Barnett 1999: 17).

The 1992 national elections were critical for the Israeli foreign policy change. In the Labor Party's primaries, the party experienced a bitter internal struggle between Rabin and Peres. Despite his win, Rabin lacked the widespread support among party activists enjoyed by his arch-rival (Arian *et al.* 2002: 122). The Labor Party ran on a political platform that acknowledged the national rights of Palestinians, hinted at a willingness to negotiate with the PLO, and promised the ending of the conflict within a short period after taking over power (Shamir and

Shamir 2007: 482–483). It successfully managed to be identified as the peace camp in the run up to the elections, capitalizing politically on the broad appeal of peace in the Israeli public at the time (Shamir and Arian 1994: 260).

In the aftermath of the party's electoral victory, Prime Minister Rabin marginalized the remaining opposition from within his own Labor Party and invested in a post-electoral co-operation with the leftist party of Meretz that shared similar foreign policy concerns (Rynhold 2007: 430–432). Peres was appointed Minister of Foreign Affairs, heading a group of advocates of the new policy approach and played a critical role in orchestrating the whole venture. Negotiations remained completely compartmentalized within the Israeli administration. The remaining Cabinet was kept in the dark and both Rabin and Peres made extensive and exclusive use of personal advisors and aides to push through the negotiations (Arian *et al.* 2002: 125).

Policy dynamics and foreign policy change

The two case studies have considerable similarities as regards the origins and the process of *problem* identification that created the impetus for change. International developments, like the collapse of the bipolar world and the first Gulf War, altered the systemic environment within which the Greek and Israeli foreign policy operated. Focusing events also contributed significantly to the reframing of existing conditions. The 1996 Imia/Kardak imbroglio between Greece and Turkey and the Palestinian Intifada illustrated the shortcomings of earlier policies followed by the two countries. In the aftermath of the crises, there emerged among the two countries' statesmen the need for a new foreign policy course (Peri 1996: 354–356; Simitis 2005: 72–99). In the Greek case, it is also possible to discern the influence of policy spillovers that derived from the emergence of EMU accession as the primary objective of the Simitis government.

The origins of alternative *policies* in the two cases also feature common elements. Both countries differ substantially from the US pluralistic model that Kingdon had in mind and tried to capture in his work. As a result, and given also the securitized nature of the issues in question, the alternative policies emanated primarily from small policy communities within the upper echelons of the government and the political system more generally with a minimal societal influence and involvement. Thus, the ascendance of the new foreign policy approach is related primarily with political developments that changed the nexus of the policy-making system, bringing into power people with a different or altered normative background. In the Greek case, the whole "modernization" faction within PASOK that came into office in 1996 had long been associated with a different political culture and policy approach, not least in the foreign policy realm. In the Israeli case, the two main political figures of the Labor Party, Rabin and Peres, despite their political grievances vis-à-vis the Party's leadership, commonly acknowledged—at different stages—and endorsed the need for change.

In terms of the stream of *politics*, public opinion, especially in Israel, had become more receptive to the idea of change, very much due to the crises mentioned above. However, although public opinion had shifted before the policy change, it did not shoot forward until after the signing of the Oslo Accords. In the Greek case, some initiatives from the civil society and the two earthquakes that hit the two countries in August and September 1999 had also contributed to a more positive disposition of the Greek public toward Turkey (Heraclides 2010: 150–151). Still, up to the closing days of the 1999 Helsinki negotiations, public opinion remained very much skeptical, not to say hostile, to the prospect of the Turkish EU candidacy.[1] Thus, it is possible to discern only a very small societal engagement in the process of change. At the governmental level, the Israeli case featured a new administration after the Labor Party's win in the 1992 elections, while the Greek one entailed changes within the PASOK administration after the death of Prime Minister Andreas Papandreou and the win of Simitis in 1996. Furthermore, the Helsinki agreement is related with the change of guards in the Greek Ministry of Foreign Affairs in early 1999 that accelerated the pace of the Greek foreign policy shift.

Further in the stream of politics and especially vis-à-vis the structure and modus operandi of the authoritative decision unit, the two cases have one difference and one common element of great significance that affect the entry barriers to policy entrepreneurship. Starting from the former, because of the Greek electoral system, Prime Minister Simitis was privileged to have a clear parliamentary majority. In contrast, the Labor Party in Israel had to join a coalition and rely on its coalition partners to push through foreign policy change. In that respect, the entry barriers for the policy entrepreneurs in each case appear different, smaller in the Greek case than in the Israeli one. However, this difference should not be overstated for two reasons. First, political domination for the Simitis administration was neither easy nor uncontested. The ascendance of the alternative political culture advocated by the "modernization faction" of PASOK was incremental both in Greek society and in the party itself. Long-held security and threat perceptions within PASOK and across the electorate more generally constituted severe political obstacles,

---

[1]   In November 1999, one month before Helsinki, only 23 percent of the Greek public was in favor of the Turkish candidacy and 69 percent against (Eurobarometer 52.0). This support was too meager to fully account for the Helsinki policy change.

holding the new strategy in abeyance up to a few months prior to the Helsinki deal and explaining to some extent the time lag in the foreign policy U-turn, from 1996 to 1999 (Tsakonas 2010: 65–72). Thus, significant entry barriers did also exist in the Greek case, mainly related to domestic intra- and cross-partisan political opposition that call into question the political viability of the prospective new foreign policy course and its agents.

Second, it is true that the entry barriers in the Israeli case revolve around the institutional political architecture that nurtures weak coalition governments with intra-coalition politics and balance emanating as significant constraints to potential policy entrepreneurs that need to appease first their coalition partners and ensure coalition viability. This is even more significant in highly salient and contested foreign policy issues, like the Oslo Accords, whereby intra-coalition dissent could easily overthrow the government and stop the realignment process. Still, despite such high entry barriers, foreign policy change did occur in Oslo, which suggests that we should not *a priori* consider coalition governments an insurmountable obstacle to foreign policy shift. The Israeli case is an example of how foreign policy reorientation may forge a coalition, with coalition politics triggering rather than hindering change. To do so, as mentioned before, Rabin had to insulate reactions from his own Labor Party and invest in a post-electoral co-operation with the party of Meretz that shared similar foreign policy objectives.

The common element in both cases is the process of foreign policy-making, which provides to a large extent an insulated environment to initiate a policy turn. Starting from the Greek case, the political and institutional features of the Greek policy-making system suggest that the authoritative decision unit takes the form of a predominant political figure, thus rendering foreign policy change seemingly feasible for a policy entrepreneur at the heart of the system. This is done so not only by means of the indisputable political role of the prime minister but also through the personalized style of foreign policy-making that renders personnel changes in the Ministry of Foreign Affairs very important. In the Israeli case, despite political dependencies from coalition politics, negotiations remained at the hands of Rabin, Peres, and their personal advisors and aides, creating a small policy community capable of pushing change ahead.

Conclusion

This chapter accounts for foreign policy change in two cases using the insights of the MSA approach. We argue that change is possible when Kingdon's three streams of problems, policies, and politics intersect and open an opportunity window, which policy entrepreneurs use to bring forward an alternative policy course. The two case studies of Greece and Israel highlight the analytical potential of the approach and its appropriateness for the study of foreign policy. It captures both systemic and conjunctural parameters of foreign policy analysis at the domestic and international level. The reframing and re-identification of problems is a process that can benefit both from realist insights about systemic changes like the collapse of the bipolar world and constructivist ones that associate the ascendance of a new policy paradigm and political culture with a generational shift, social learning processes, and socialization effects. Institutionalist-accredited factors like the policy-making power locus, electoral and coalition politics, and the political enfranchisement of socio-economic interest groups are also comfortably accommodated in the framework either in the stream of policies or politics. Conjunctural factors, like a security crisis and the death and succession of a political leader, are also captured and accounted for in all three streams. Thus, it appears that the MSA constitutes a comprehensive and holistic approach to the study of foreign policy and foreign policy change more specifically.

An issue of further study is whether the framework may be useful in addressing one additional issue that we have not touched upon, namely the consolidation of the new foreign policy. We analyze national critical junctures in the foreign policy domain without claiming that these changes are definite and cannot be reversed as the change-inducing policy entrepreneurship evolves. Neither the Greek–Turkish relations have been fully normalized, nor has the Israel–Palestine dispute been settled. Many developments have played their role in this lack of progress, but still, both changes have been compromised at some point, either because they failed to deliver the expected results or because the political entrepreneur was removed from office before the new course of action became embedded. The causal mechanisms of transforming foreign policy change to a new foreign policy path differ and equally so may differ the insights of MSA in the policy entrenchment process.

Finally, directly linked with the entrenchment prospects of a foreign policy shift, the effect of policy entrepreneurship may not only be exhibited in the content of foreign policy but also bring about structural changes in the terms and the institutional milieu of policy-making. To ensure the consolidation and longevity of the new foreign policy course, the policy entrepreneur may be inclined to further raise the political and institutional entry barriers to dissuade future competitors. This may be possible by reinforcing, for example, in the policy-making process the role of the authoritative decision unit he/she occupies or by altering the electoral system to shed off political dependencies. This point highlights and reinforces our underlying assumption of an evolving and reciprocal relationship between human agency and social structures, which lies at the heart of the agency–structure *problématique* in foreign policy and international relations.

References

Arian, Asher (1998) *Politics in Israel: The Second Republic*, New York: Chatham House Publishers.

Arian, Asher, David Nachmias, and Ruth Amir (2002) *Executive Governance in Israel*, London: Palgrave Macmillan.

Arian, Asher, Michal Shamir, and Raphael Ventura (1992) Public Opinion and Political Change: Israel and the Intifada, *Comparative Politics* 24(3), 317–334.

Auerbach, Yehudith and Charles W. Greenbaum (2000) Assessing Leader Credibility During a Peace Process: Rabin's Private Polls, *Journal of Peace Research* 37(1), 33–52.

Barnett, Michael (1999) Culture, Strategy and Foreign Policy Change: Israel's Road to Oslo, *European Journal of International Relations* 5(5), 5–36.

Bercovitch, Jacob (1997) Conflict Management and the Oslo Experience, *International Negotiation* 2(2), 217–235.

Blavoukos, Spyros and Dimitris Bourantonis (2012) Policy Entrepreneurs and Foreign Policy Change: The Greek-Turkish Rapprochement in the 1990s, *Government and Opposition* 47(4), 597–617.

Blavoukos, Spyros and Dimitris Bourantonis (2014) Identifying Parameters of Foreign Policy Change: An Eclectic Approach, *Cooperation and Conflict* 49(4), 484–500.

Bossong, Raphael (2013) *The Evolution of EU Counter-Terrorism: European Security Policy After 9/11*, London: Routledge.

Checkel, Jeffrey T. (1997) *Ideas and International Political Change: Soviet/Russian Behavior and the End of the Cold War*, New Haven: Yale University Press.

Cohen, Michael D., James G. March, and Johan P. Olsen (1972) A Garbage Can Model of Organizational Choice, *Administrative Science Quarterly* 17(1), 1–25.

Durant, Robert F. and Paul F. Diehl (1989) Agendas, Alternatives, and Public Policy: Lessons from the U.S. Foreign Policy Arena, *Journal of Public Policy* 9(2), 179–205.

Economides, Spyros (2005) The Europeanization of Greek Foreign Policy, *West European Politics* 28(2), 471–491.

Ezrahi, Yaron (1997) *Rubber Bullets: Power and Conscience in Modern Israel*, Berkeley: University of California Press.

Hazan, Y. Reuven (2000) Intraparty Politics and Peacemaking in Democratic Societies: Israel's Labor Party and the Middle East Peace Process, 1992–6, *Journal of Peace Research* 37(3), 63–78.

Heraclides, Alexis (2004) The Cyprus Problem: An Open and Shut Case? Probing the Greek-Cypriot Rejection of the Annan Plan, *Cyprus Review* 16(2), 37–54.

Heraclides, Alexis (2010) *The Greek-Turkish Conflict in the Aegean: Imagined Enemies*, London: Palgrave Macmillan.

Hermann, Margaret G. (2001) How Decision Units Shape Foreign Policy: A Theoretical Framework, *International Studies Review* 3(2), 47–82.

Herweg, Nicole, Christian Huss, and Reimut Zohlnhöfer (2015) Straightening the Three Streams: Theorising Extensions of the Multiple Streams Framework, *European Journal of Political Research* 54(3), 435–449.

Herweg, Nicole, Nikolaos Zahariadis, and Reimut Zohlnhöfer (2017) The Multiple Streams Framework: Foundations, Refinements and Empirical Applications, in Paul A. Sabatier and Christopher M. Weible (eds.) *Theories of the Policy Process*, 4th edition, Boulder: Westview Press, 17–54.

Inbar, Efraim (1991) *War and Peace in Israeli Politics: Labor Party Positions on National Security*, Boulder: Lynne Rienner.

Ioakimidis, Panayiotis (1996) *The New Enlargement of the European Union and Greece: Cyprus, Balkans, Eastern Europe: Problems, Impact, Strategy*, Athens: ELIAMEP and Sideris (in Greek).

Ioakimidis, Panayiotis (1999) The Model of Foreign Policymaking in Greece: Personalities versus Institutions, in Stelios Stavridis, Theodore Couloumbis, Thanos Veremis, and Neville Waites (eds.) *The Foreign Policies of the EU's Mediterranean and Applicant Countries in the 1990s*, London: Macmillan Press, 140–171.

Jones, Michael D., Holly L. Peterson, Jonathan J. Pierce, Nicole Herweg, Amiel Bernal, Holly Lamberta Raney, and Nikolaos Zahariadis (2016) A River Runs Through It: A Multiple Streams Meta-Review, *Policy Studies Journal* 44(1), 13–35.

Keeler, John (1993) Opening the Window of Reform: Mandates, Crises, and Extraordinary Policymaking, *Comparative Political Studies* 25(4), 433–486.

Kingdon, John W. (1995) *Agendas, Alternatives, and Public Policies*, 2nd edition, New York: Longman.

Legro, Jeffrey W. (2005) *Great Power Strategies and International Order*, Ithaca, NY and London: Cornell University Press.

Lyrintzis, Christos (2005) The Changing Party System: Stable Democracy, Contested Democratization, *West European Politics* 28(2), 242–259.

Makovsky, David (1996) *Making Peace with the PLO: The Rabin Government's Road to the Oslo Accord*, Boulder: Westview Press.

Mazarr, Michael J. (2007) The Iraq War and Agenda Setting, *Foreign Policy Analysis* 3(1), 1–27.

Meydani, Assaf (2009) *Political Transformations and Political Entrepreneurs: Israel in Comparative Perspective*, New York: Palgrave Macmillan.

Mintrom, Michael (1997) Policy Entrepreneurs and the Diffusion of Innovation, *American Journal of Political Science* 41(3), 738–770.

Moschonas, Gerasimos (2001) The Path of Modernization, PASOK and European Integration, *Journal of Southern Europe and the Balkans* 3(1), 11–24.

Page, Edward C. (2006) The Origins of Policy, in Michael Moran, Martin Rein, and Robert E. Goodin (eds.) *The Oxford Handbook of Public Policy*, Oxford: Oxford University Press, 207–227.

Peres, Simon (1995) *Battling for Peace*, New York: Random House.

Peri, Yoram (1996) Afterword, in Yitzhak Rabin, *The Rabin Memoirs – Expanded Edition*, Berkeley: University of California Press, 339–380.

Rynhold, Jonathan (2007) Cultural Shift and Foreign Policy Change: Israel and the Making of the Oslo Accords, *Cooperation and Conflict* 42(4), 419–440.

Sabatier, Paul A. (2007) Fostering the Development of Policy Theory, in Paul A. Sabatier (ed.) *Theories of the Policy Process*, 2nd edition, Boulder: Westview Press, 321–336.

Schneider, Mark and Paul Teske (1992) Toward a Theory of the Political Entrepreneur: Evidence from Local Government, *The American Political Science Review* 86(3), 737–747.

Shamir, Michal and Asher Arian (1994) Competing Values and Policy Choices: Israeli Public Opinion on Foreign and Security Affairs, *British Journal of Political Science* 24(2), 249–271.

Shamir, Michal and Jacob Shamir (2007) The Israeli-Palestinian Conflict in Israeli Elections, *International Political Science Review* 28(4), 469–491.

Sheingate, Adam D. (2003) Political Entrepreneurship, Institutional Change, and American Political Development, *Studies in American Political Development* 17(2), 185–203.

Shlaim, Avi (2001) *The Iron Wall: Israel and the Arab World*, New York: W. W. Norton.

Simitis, Constntinos (2005) *Politics for a Creative Greece, 1996–2004*, Athens: Polis (in Greek).

Travis, Rick and Nikolaos Zahariadis (2002) A Multiple Streams Model of U.S. Foreign Aid Policy, *Policy Studies Journal* 30(4), 495–514.

Tsakonas, Panayiotis J. (2010) *The Incomplete Breakthrough in Greek-Turkish Relations: Grasping Greece's Socialization Strategy*, London: Palgrave.

Tsoukalis, Loukas (2000) Greece in the EU: Domestic Reform Coalitions, External Constraints and High Politics, in Achilleas Mitsos and Elias Mossialos (eds.) *Contemporary Greece and Europe*, Aldershot: Ashgate, 37–51.

Walsh, James (2006) Policy Failure and Policy Change: British Security Policy after the Cold War, *Comparative Political Studies* 39(4), 490–518.

Welch, David A. (2005) *Painful Choices: A Theory of Foreign Policy Change*, Princeton: Princeton University Press.

Zahariadis, Nikolaos (2003) *Ambiguity and Choice in Public Policy: Political Manipulation in Democratic Societies*, Washington, DC: Georgetown University Press.

Zahariadis, Nikolaos (2005) *Essence of Political Manipulation: Emotion, Institutions, and Greek Foreign Policy*, New York: Peter Lang.

Zahariadis, Nikolaos (2008) Ambiguity and Choice in European Public Policy, *Journal of European Public Policy* 15(4), 514–530.

Zahariadis, Nikolaos (2014) Ambiguity and Multiple Streams, in Paul A. Sabatier and Christopher M. Weible (eds.) *Theories of the Policy Process*, 3rd edition, Boulder: Westview Press, 25–58.

Zahariadis, Nikolaos (2015) The Shield of Heracles: Multiple Streams and the Emotional Endowment Effect, *European Journal of Political Research* 54(3), 466–481.

Zohlnhöfer, Reimut (2016) Putting Together the Pieces of the Puzzle: Explaining German Labor Market Reforms with a Modified Multiple-Streams Approach, *Policy Studies Journal* 44(1), 83–107.

Zohlnhöfer, Reimut and Friedbert W. Rüb (eds.) (2016) *Decision-Making under Ambiguity and Time Constraints: Assessing the Multiple-Streams Framework*, Colchester: ECPR Press.

Zohlnhöfer, Reimut, Nicole Herweg, and Friedbert W. Rüb (2015) Theoretically Refining the Multiple Streams Framework: An Introduction, *European Journal of Political Research* 54(3), 412–418.

3

Punctuated equilibrium theory and foreign policy

Jeroen Joly and Friederike Richter

> *Congress does two things well:*
> *nothing and overreacting.*
>
> Michael Oxley

Governmental policies generally change only marginally over time; however, every once in a while, policies also change dramatically.[1,2] The pun-
gent quote from former Republican US Representative Michael Oxley
very well reflects this main idea behind punctuated equilibrium (PE) as
a policy-making theory. Punctuated equilibrium theory (PET), first put
forward by Frank Baumgartner and Bryan Jones (1993), explains how
the same institutional set-up, usually preventing new policy issues from
gaining political attention, is also responsible for the occasional outbursts
of attention causing disproportionately large policy shifts. While previous public policy theories had been relatively successful at explaining
either policy stability or large policy changes, the main originality and
novelty of PET was that it proposed a single theoretical model of policy-
making that explains how the same governmental processes cause both
stability and major policy shifts.

[1] We thank Frank Baumgartner and Stefaan Walgrave for their valuable comments on
earlier drafts of this chapter.
[2] The research for this chapter was financially supported by the French Ministry of the
Armed Forces, Directorate General for International Relations and Strategy (DGRIS).
Disclaimer: The opinions expressed in papers or publications by Ph.D. students, who
receive doctoral funding through the International Relations and Strategy program, are
those of the author(s) and do not reflect the official opinion of the French Ministry of the
Armed Forces. Neither the DGRIS nor the Institute for Strategic Research (IRSEM) may
be held responsible for the use which may be made of the information contained therein.

PET is based on the assumption that, due to their cognitive limitations, policy-makers cannot simultaneously attend to all the problems society is facing (Simon 1957). Hence, most policy-making is delegated to policy subsystems, that is, groups of elites consisting of elected officials, career civil servants, or interest groups. The politics of subsystems generally prevents large policy changes, leading to mostly small, incremental changes instead of policies that are proportionate to solving the problem. Yet, disproportionately large policy changes can occur when the way an issue is understood changes (*issue definition*) and/or previously uninterested people get involved (*agenda-setting*). This process can be triggered by sudden or steady attention of an influential political actor or as the result of a major focusing event (Birkland 1997, 1998). The combination of these two principles—issue definition and agenda-setting—is at the heart of PET: it explains why most policies remain stable most of the time and how they can sometimes alter drastically and radically.

Initially developed as an agenda-setting theory to examine why certain issues gain political attention, PET has evolved into a more general theory on information processing in decision-making (Green-Pedersen and Princen 2016: 69). By looking at the distribution of changes in policy, it is possible to examine and explain resistance to change—or institutional friction—throughout the policy process (Jones and Baumgartner 2005; Baumgartner *et al.* 2009). PET has been successfully applied to a wide range of public policies in numerous countries and has increasingly generated cross-sectional and cross-national analyses that aim at comparing and better understanding the causes of stability and change in different political systems. However, the focus of these studies has mostly been on domestic policies, with only very little attention for PET in a foreign policy context.

Therefore, the aim of this chapter is to demonstrate that PET is not only relevant in the realm of domestic politics, but also useful for the analysis of foreign policy. The next section reconstructs the original formulation of PET and illustrates how PET has evolved over the past two decades. Then, we outline how to study foreign policy using a PE approach, its benefits and challenges. Subsequently, we test PET in a foreign policy context by looking at yearly changes in attention to foreign policy issues, and examining the relationship between changes in foreign aid allocations and the size of the aid administrations. The chapter concludes with a reflection about the transferability of PET to the study of foreign policy more broadly.

Policy changes: doing nothing and overreacting

In the early 1990s, Baumgartner and Jones (1993) set a landmark within policy research by proposing PET, a theory which, for the first time, accounted for both incremental and dramatic policy changes. PET was a reaction to earlier public policy theories, which suggested that policy change was either highly frenetic or incremental (i.e., slow and gradual, with adjustments being based on past actions). While incrementalism seemed to be the best available alternative to explain the bulk of changes at the time, it did not account for large—and often disproportionate—policy changes in US politics. In 1984, John Kingdon's work on multiple streams (see chapter 2 in this volume) explained how an issue suddenly " 'hits', 'catches on', or 'takes off' " (Kingdon 2003: 80). Refusing to oppose radical and incremental changes, Baumgartner and Jones (1993) argued that any theory of public policy should provide an explanation for both and, therefore, advanced PET as such a comprehensive alternative.

Original formulation

PET was initially developed as an agenda-setting theory to understand policy change in the United States. The main idea behind agenda-setting is that political attention is a necessary precondition for change. Attention, however, is scarce: policy-makers are rationally bounded (Simon 1957), and can therefore only focus on a limited number of problems at the same time. This implies that policy-makers cannot constantly evaluate which problems need to be addressed first, and which policies have to be adjusted (and by how much). Instead, most policy-making is delegated to policy subsystems, allowing political institutions to process a greater number of issues at the same time (through parallel instead of serial processing). These subsystems are best understood as small communities of experts from non-governmental organizations, academics, civil servants, and the media—experts whose work is related to a specific issue.

Subsystems can grow to become policy monopolies when they are dominated by a single interest, whereby all those involved share the same goals and benefit from the existing policies (Kingdon 2003: 33). Policy monopolies are associated with a powerful and popular image or idea that relates closely to core political values (like safety, fairness, or progress). These policy images are not easily questioned, and used by the subsystem to justify its competence and actions. Through a process of negative feedback, subsystems try to prevent policy change that might reduce their importance or current benefits. This process of negative feedback strongly relates to the early work of Bachrach and Baratz (1962) and Cobb and Elder (1971), who described the mechanisms of exclusion that prevent new ideas and their proponents from gaining traction. Policy stability, consequently, does not derive from a broad societal consensus, but rather from a consensus among those holding power. When an issue and its advocates receive attention, other subsystems may mobilize to counter this effect. This mechanism of countermobilization (as one subsystem mobilizes, others react) is the basis of the negative feedback process that tends to prevent large policy changes. Hence, negative feedback is the source of the equilibrium, the stability in policy, causing the system to be self-correcting, as the changes are merely small policy adjustments (Baumgartner and Jones 1993).

This stability, however, does not mean that policy is totally gridlocked, as large policy changes also occur. Two related dynamics are central to these larger changes. The first is a change in the issue's policy image, or the way an issue is generally understood and approached. The second aspect is venue shopping, whereby policy entrepreneurs advocate their issue and an alternative policy image at different relevant policy venues, in the hope that it is picked up and catches on to spread. Policy venues are institutions or groups, such as committees and commissions, with the authority to make decisions regarding an issue (Baumgartner and Jones 1993). Much like Schattschneider's (1960) expansion of the scope of conflict, Baumgartner and Jones (1993) argue that defying the existing stability requires involving previously uninterested and uninvolved groups of people. Therefore, policy advocates on the losing side will move from one venue to another, according to their perceived efficiency in an attempt to gain "attention of potential allies not currently involved in the issue" (Baumgartner and Jones 1993: 36).

PET, thus, argues that disproportionally large policy shifts are caused by the interaction between changing policy images and policy venues—also referred to as positive feedback. While most issues gain prominence through steady advocacy over a longer period of time, struggling their way up the agenda to eventually be picked up, others are propelled and impose themselves onto the political agenda, for example through focusing events, characterized by their very dramatic and urgent nature (Birkland 1997).

Developments in PET

Over the past two decades, PET has significantly evolved, both from a theoretical and an empirical perspective. From a theoretical perspective, PET evolved from a US agenda-setting theory to a more general decision-making theory. While the concept of attention is still central to PET, the theory no longer accounts for changes in the American political agenda only, but explains policy-making and politics more generally—both in the United States and abroad. This evolution can be traced back to three main developments: (1) the emergence of the distribution approach to studying PET and the concept of institutional friction; (2) the proliferation of comparative research since the late 2000s; and (3) further theorization of existing concepts.

The distributional approach and institutional friction

The most important and noticeable development in PET has been the introduction of the distribution approach and the concept of institutional friction, which has further developed into the progressive friction hypothesis. The distribution approach consists of looking at patterns of annual changes in attention to policies over a longer period of time, whether in governmental activities like budgets, the parliament or the media. If policy changes are proportionate to changes in social inputs, we would expect frequency distributions to look like a classic bell-shaped Normal curve. However, if, as Jones and Baumgartner (2005) argue, PE characterizes the political system, the frequency distribution will have a slender central peak around the mean and very long and dominant tails (indicating disproportionate punctuations). In other words, the many small changes are concentrated around the mean (i.e., the central peak), with fewer large punctuations found in the 'fat tails', but rarely medium-sized changes in between. For an example of such a leptokurtic distribution see figure 3.1.

To explain this leptokurtic pattern of change, Baumgartner and Jones introduced the concept of institutional friction. Friction refers to the resistance to adjustment that is built into each political system; that is, the more friction there is, the more inert a political institution will respond to input and the more leptokurtic policy outputs will be (Jones and Baumgartner 2005: 170). Jones *et al.* (2009) found this leptokurtic pattern of distribution in public budgets across seven different political systems. The differences in friction they observed between those countries corresponded to differences in government structures, similar to how veto points affect policy change (see chapter 5 in this volume). Baumgartner *et al.* (2009) further developed this pattern into the progressive friction hypothesis, whereby friction increases when moving from input (information) to output (policy) due, mainly, to higher decision-making costs. This implies that attention from news media and parliament is, for example, less incremental than policy outputs, like budgets, where changes in attention involve considerably more costs. The penultimate section of this chapter details what these distributions look like and how we can use and interpret them.

The proliferation of comparative research

Focusing on the distribution of policy change has led to a better understanding of attention allocation across the policy process, and policy-making in general. Moreover, it invigorated PET and agenda-setting research studies in numerous countries, leading to an increase in comparative research. The confirmation of leptokurtic frequency distributions among countries of varying institutional design, and increasing friction throughout the policy process have strongly contributed to the evolution of PET from a specific theory of agenda-setting in the United States to a general theory of decision-making. To date, research groups in over twenty countries collect and categorize information on political agendas in different polities, including the EU and sub-national entities, using comparable coding schemes. Research on a wide variety of political activities, from news media to speeches, hearings, and budgets, not only allows for the study of policy-making across issues, over time, and between countries, but also of the influence one political agenda has on the other.

In addition to the vast expansion in countries and agendas being studied, empirical work on PET and agenda-setting now also deals with a growing number of—mostly domestic—policy issues, such as environmental policy (Repetto 2006), health care (Hardin 2002), immigration (Hunt 2002), same-sex marriage (Dziengel 2010), schools (Robinson 2004), sciences and technology (Feely 2002), and telecommunications (MacLeod 2002). This vast expanding body of research underlines the usefulness of PET and its key concepts, like subsystems, policy images, and venues, to study and understand policy-making in different institutional and topical contexts (Sheingate 2000; Pralle 2003; Daugbjerg and Studsgaard 2005). Only few scholars have, so far, used PET to study stability and change in foreign and defense policy. We review those studies in greater detail in the next section where we also discuss the general applicability of PET in foreign policy.

Further theorization of existing concepts

Finally, agenda-setting scholars have continued to improve our understanding of some mechanisms and key concepts of PET. Several agenda-setting studies, for example, examined how friction and cascading contribute to the typical pattern of policy punctuations. Cascading is best understood as a self-reinforcing process of positive feedback whereby attention from one actor generates attention from another actor, which, again, draws even more attention from the initial actor, overthrowing the existing friction mechanisms (Jones and Baumgartner 2005; Walgrave and Vliegenthart 2010). Looking at mass media and parliament, Walgrave and Vliegenthart (2010) found friction and cascading to operate independently from each other to create punctuations, and showed under which conditions these mechanisms are more likely to occur.

The notion of cascading closely relates to the wider agenda-setting literature examining how attention from one actor influences that of another. We know, for example, that political parties heavily influence each other regarding the issues they focus on in parliament (Vliegenthart et al. 2011). Several studies have also confirmed the mutual influence between news media, parliament, and government influence in the issues they focus on (for a comprehensive review of the literature on the media's influence on parliament and government, see Van Aelst and Walgrave (2016) and Walgrave *et al.* (2006)), also for foreign policy issues (Wood and Peake 1998; Edwards and Wood 1999).

Furthermore, Worsham (1998, 2006) proposed a more sophisticated understanding of policy subsystems, arguing that their degree of control actually depends on the policy issue. Other scholars have worked on venues, showing how groups and institutions are not equally created and, thus, do not follow the same dynamics, potentially inciting subsystems to opt for venue shopping to push their ideas to higher political levels (Guiraudon 2000; Sheingate 2000; Pralle 2003, 2006). John and Bevan (2012), then again, proposed a typology of policy punctuations, including low-salience punctuations, procedural changes, and high-salience punctuations, arguing that different punctuations reflect distinct types of political change. Hence, the work on specific aspects of the theory, such as policy punctuations, venues/venue shopping, and policy subsystems, has largely contributed to the development of PET and, consequently, the evolution toward a more general theory.

Overall, PET has significantly evolved in both theoretical and empirical perspectives. We have shown in this section that this evolution can be traced back to three main developments: (1) the emergence of

Table 3.1 Overview of the punctuated equilibrium theory and approach

	Stability	Change
Manifestation	- Incrementalism (small policy adjustments)	- Punctuations (disproportionately large policy changes)
Origins	- Bounded rationality (Simon 1957) - Two faces of power (Bachrach and Baratz 1962) - Incrementalism (Wildavsky 1964) - Agenda building (Cobb and Elder 1971)	- Issue-attention cycle (Downs 1957) - Scope of conflict (Schattschneider 1960) - Multiple streams (Kingdon 1984)
Sources and process	- Negative feedback	- Positive feedback
Mechanisms and key elements	- Politics of subsystems - Institutional friction	- Changing issue definition - Involvement of new or previously uninterested actors (venue shopping) - Cascading - Focusing events

the distribution approach to studying PET and the concept of institutional friction; (2) the proliferation of comparative research since the late 2000s; and (3) further theorization of existing concepts. Table 3.1 briefly summarizes the PET approach, with its origins, key concepts, and mechanisms.

Punctuated equilibrium in foreign policy

PET has, so far, rarely been applied to study stability and critical junctures in the realm of foreign policies. Hence, this literature review also includes studies that relate to and support PET, albeit not always addressing the theory directly or explicitly. Most case studies in this field focus only on American foreign and security policy. In one of the first studies analyzing what determines the presidential foreign policy agenda, Andrade and Young (1996) showed the important impact of international events, alongside approval ratings and the president's relationship with Congress. Wood and Peake (1998) partially confirmed this result, observing that US foreign policy is characterized by strong inertia, which is only disrupted in times of international crises or by increased media coverage. Looking at five domestic and foreign policy issues, Edwards and Wood (1999) studied the relationship between the US president, the media, and Congress. While the president is able to focus attention on his domestic policy initiatives, their study also shows that in foreign policy he mainly responds to events and fluctuations in media attention.

So far, we know of only three studies that examine the dynamics of foreign policy based on PET in very different contexts. Looking at international rivalries, Diehl (1998) and Diehl and Goertz (2001) used PE to explore the origins, dynamics, and termination of long-standing military conflicts, concluding that instability is usually associated with the initiation and termination of rivalries. True (2002), then again, compared traditional approaches to the study of national security with PE, demonstrating that change in US security policy only occurs erratically. Like other scholars, he concluded that policy-makers cannot fully control security policy as the context and, thus, policy objectives may change rapidly. In one of the rare studies outside the United States, Joly (2016) showed how news media influence the political agenda through dynamics similar to focusing events and steady advocacy. Specifically, media were able to influence which humanitarian situations the Belgian government paid attention to by focusing briefly and heavily on a given situation, but also determined how much emergency assistance was provided through long-term media attention to the affected countries.

The three previous studies are very complementary as they, each in their own way, show that PET is transferrable to different policy contexts and different types of external relations. Yet, perhaps the best empirical illustration of the dynamics of positive feedback and policy entrepreneurship in foreign policy—although not explicitly referring to PET—is probably Mazarr's (2007) analysis of the United States' decision to invade Iraq in 2003. In line with Kingdon's approach (see chapter 2 in this volume), Mazarr convincingly shows how certain groups, advocating a more aggressive policy course toward Iraq, were able to "use" the events of 9/11 to impose their own, alternative understanding of what needed to be done about Iraq on the president, the US Congress, the media, and the public.

Mazarr (2007) details how, during the Clinton administration, several groups had been advocating an active regime change in Iraq. A number of these activists later found themselves in senior policy positions in President Bush's administration in 2001. They quickly started focusing on Iraq but, given that they did not represent a majority voice within the Cabinet, did not manage to reach a consensus on how to best pressure Saddam Hussein, resulting in inaction vis-à-vis Iraq—until 9/11. The dramatic focusing event of 9/11 drew immediate attention from all political actors and initiated the War on Terror, initially against Al-Qaeda and the Taliban. In line with PET, this represented a unique window of opportunity for these policy entrepreneurs to redefine the Iraq issue and impose their alternative policy image. Mazarr shows how the "terrorism frame" was used to qualify Iraq as a threat to US national security due to its possession of weapons of mass destruction and support of international terrorism.

Decision-making quickly moved from the subsystem level to Congress and the executive. 9/11 also increased the general domestic support for the war in Iraq. This positive feedback, however, was only temporary, as it rapidly declined with the increasing casualties and returning body bags. Mazarr's 2007 analysis neatly shows how the dynamics of PET translate to a foreign policy context, with few to no significant policy changes until policy entrepreneurs are able to seize the right opportunity to impose an alternative understanding of the issue—a solution waiting for a problem—resulting in a major policy change. Moreover, it shows the important role focusing events can play in this process. Before we detail how PET can be used in quantitative analyses, we discuss the promises and potential pitfalls of using PET in a foreign policy context.

Promises and pitfalls of transferring PET to FPA

The example of the decision to invade Iraq has shown that PET can help us understand when and why an issue's time has come: it provides for the necessary tools to examine how societal problems turn into policy priorities and allows us to unravel the dynamics that facilitate or impede policy change. For the analysis of foreign policy, this means that we can understand why certain issues, countries or international situations receive attention while others are ignored. Based on PET, we can study actors and their interactions, analyze institutional structures, such as foreign relations committees, take into account public perceptions and beliefs, and examine how the media frames focusing events. In its more recent formulation, the distributional approach can unveil a great deal about the policy-making dynamics of foreign policy like, for example, the impact of specific actors or institutional rules and set-ups.

The previous theoretical sections, as well as the next empirical section, aim to show how useful PET can be to the study of foreign policy and how easily its key concepts translate to a foreign policy-making context. While we certainly advocate for more applications of PET in foreign policy studies, we also believe that it is useful to explore, and perhaps caution, how such applications might be different from applications in domestic policies. Hence, we try to systematically review possible differences between domestic and foreign policy issues and how this may affect their policy dynamics. We focus on four main features that might make the application of PET to foreign policy issues less straight-forward: (1) issue attributes; (2) focusing events; (3) policy venues; and (4) friction and cascading. While it is important to keep these elements in mind when using PET in a foreign policy context, we are also convinced that these challenges constitute interesting avenues for future (comparative) research regarding specific theoretical questions that need to be addressed.

Issue attributes

Most domestic issues generally do not have the same issue attributes as those in foreign policy (Peake 2001, 2016). Foreign policy issues are usually not highly salient, as the media, the public, or politicians do not pay a lot of attention to them. Moreover, foreign policy issues are rather unobtrusive, meaning that the public, as well as most policy-makers, do not experience the effects of foreign policy in a direct way. Therefore, we heavily rely on information from the media to learn about current foreign policy issues, which are often very complex and technical. That is why foreign policy is often categorized as a "governmental issue" (Soroka 2002). However, foreign and international matters can quickly turn from an abstract governmental issue into a concrete and dramatic "sensational issue" (Soroka 2002), receiving lots of attention from different actors, including the general public. This is particularly true in times of international crises and conflicts, especially with clear opposing sides (and especially if we can clearly distinguish the "good" from the "bad" guys), as opposed to more complex crises with numerous warring factions and diverging interests, like the current Syrian conflict. Foreign policy can, then, become salient to the entire political system and particularly observable to the media and the wider public.

This governmental aspect and the highly complex nature associated with many international and foreign policy issues might make it much harder to redefine specific policy issues. In people's minds—policy-makers and the general public alike—stereotypes are very hard to debunk, despite objective contradictory information. Most of the time, foreign policy issues are linked to specific groups of people. Hence, once we perceive one side of a conflict as the victims and the other as the perpetrators, it is very difficult to adjust our perception and the way we understand a given situation. This form of cognitive dissonance might be very resistant and, thus, make it harder for policy entrepreneurs to advance a different policy frame and an alternative policy related to international affairs than for domestic issues.

Focusing events

Given their general perceived importance in foreign policy, we would like to caution not to overly rely on focusing events as being the only drivers of policy change in foreign policy, or to ignore the essential dynamics associated with policy change following exogenous shocks, like focusing events. Given the prominence and importance of focusing events, like international crises or humanitarian disasters, PET provides a framework to understand why policy-makers respond to certain (types of) events while ignoring others. Moreover, PET, with its politics of subsystems, shifting policy images, and venue shopping, allows us to understand the specific dynamics that enable focusing events to have such an impact. Additionally, it also enables researchers to track and understand the dynamics that lead to policy change without a particular focusing event or a change in power. However, as the work of Mazarr (2007) shows, the events of 9/11 did not cause the war in Iraq. Instead, policy entrepreneurs used the terrorism and national security frame to impose an alternative approach, developed before 9/11, to deal with Iraq. These dynamics are an equally important part of the story and should therefore not be ignored or downplayed.

Policy venues

Foreign policy decision-making is known to be highly concentrated at the top of the executive. Unlike domestic policies that are often made in a more pluralistic atmosphere, with involvement of industry stakeholders or civil society, foreign policy tends to cut across multiple subsystems, many of which are exclusive and shrouded in secrecy (Archuleta 2016). Hence, with little media coverage, low public interest, and often scarce parliamentary scrutiny, most governments enjoy great leeway in their foreign policy-making. There might, consequently, be fewer potential policy venues where policy entrepreneurs can advocate their alternative policies. Moreover, while there are many civil society organizations advocating specific policies, they are often scattered, as they focus on their own issues, region, or country, contrary to powerful labor or industry organizations we find active in other policy domains. This combination of scarce policy venues and scattered civil society might make it harder to produce larger policy changes.

Friction and cascading

In their analyses of public budgets in several countries, Jones *et al.* (2009) did not observe any differences between domestic and defense outlays. This result, however, does neither discard the possibility of differences between domestic and defense budgets, nor does it indicate that friction is more or less prevalent in defense spending. Similarly, differences in cascading dynamics have only been examined indirectly through agenda-setting studies. Edwards and Wood (1999), for example, examined fluctuations in attention from the US president, Congress, and the media to domestic (crime, education, and health care) and foreign policy (US–Soviet relations and the Arab–Israeli conflict) issues. They found more interactions and a more influential president in domestic— as compared to foreign—policy issues. Peake (2001), however, nuanced this finding, as he observed that the president is more influential on low salient foreign policy issues where there is more leeway for determining the agenda. Given the indirect and somewhat superficial evidence, it is clear that Foreign Policy Analysis (FPA) would benefit from a more direct and systematic examination of friction and cascading processes in foreign policy, especially from a comparative perspective.

Finally, there is no consensus, or even a debate, among PET scholars about how often punctuations should be observed, as some policy areas seem to be more prone to change than others. Hence, longitudinal, cross-sectional, and cross-national analyses are recommended to understand the impact of issue attributes and institutions on the dynamics of stability and change. In other words, do different institutional set-ups witness the same policy-making dynamics and patterns of foreign policy change? These differences between domestic and foreign policies may explain scholars' hesitance to apply PET to external affairs, but certainly do not suggest that foreign policy and PET are incompatible. On the contrary, as one of the most important policy domains in many countries, often involving a large and active community of miscellaneous interest groups, it is clear that PET can provide extremely useful insights into how and why foreign policy decisions are made.

How to make sense of punctuations?

To illustrate the value and applicability of PET to the study of foreign policy, we first explain how to interpret punctuations and kurtosis measures. Then, we test the progressive friction hypothesis by comparing the distribution of attention to a variety of foreign policy issues across several countries, from information input to policy output. We assume a relatively high degree of friction in foreign policy and believe that institutional friction increases as we move down the policy stream (H_1). Finally, we explore the relationship between the size of aid administrations and institutional friction in aid programs. Here, we expect larger bureaucratic administrations to generate more leptokurtic distributions (H_2).

As we explained above, if yearly policy changes are proportionate to changes in incoming information, we would expect them to follow a normal distribution. Instead, PET scholars found percent change distributions to be highly concentrated around the mean, with more occasional large changes. Since the classic kurtosis measure is not normalized and particularly vulnerable to outliers, it is recommended to use the L-kurtosis (LK), which is based on the fourth moment of a distribution (Breunig 2006; Walgrave and Vliegenthart 2010). LK indicates the "peakedness" of a distribution and is, therefore, used to measure the degree of friction, or general resistance to change. The higher the LK, the more friction there is, and the more change is concentrated around the mean; the "fat tails" indicate a higher number of large changes than we would observe in a normal distribution.

As an illustration of how this translates to a foreign policy context, figure 3.1 shows the yearly percent changes in US official development assistance (ODA) to individual recipient countries between 1995 and 2014, as compared to a normal distribution. Although development assistance is a very specific field within foreign policy, it has been shown to be an excellent quantifiable indicator for individual donors' interests and preferences in international politics (Meernik *et al.* 1998; Schraeder *et al.* 1998; Van Belle *et al.* 2004). Data used here was obtained through the Creditor Reporting System (CRS)[3] of the OECD and pertains to the total disbursements to individual recipient countries per year for twenty-three

---

[3] The OECD publishes data on development aid flows based on individual projects (CRS). CRS is available at https://stats.oecd.org/Index.aspx?DataSetCode=CRS1 (last accessed February 2, 2017).

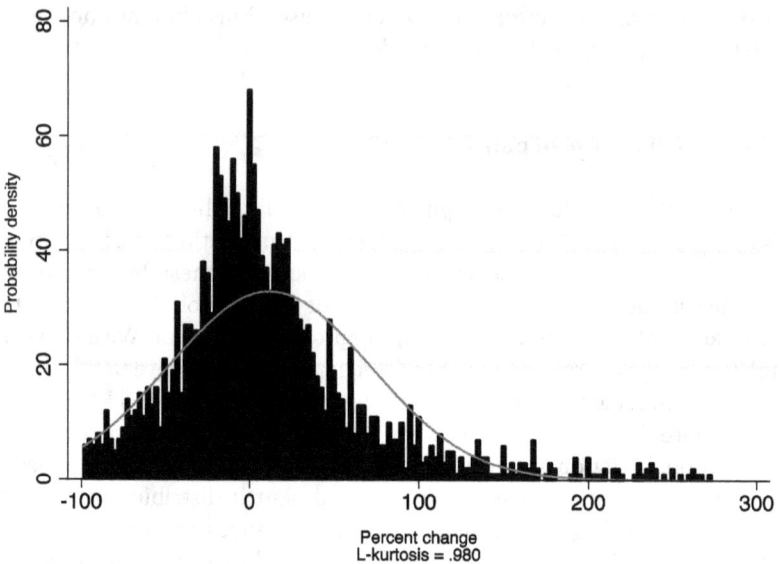

Figure 3.1 Annual change in US official development assistance (1995–2014) with overlaid normal distribution

OECD countries.[4] Disbursement data were chosen over commitments to examine data that would have been subjected to all possible forms of institutional friction. Analyses are limited to those twenty-three countries for which data on aid administration costs are also available (see Anderson 2012).

The distribution in figure 3.1 has a high central peak (concentration around the mean), "weak shoulders" (i.e., lower medium changes), and "fat tails" (i.e., more than normal large changes).[5] The LK is 0.980, compared to an LK score of about 0.123 for a normal distribution. Hence, in line with our first hypothesis, American foreign aid perfectly fits the PET distribution pattern: it is characterized by predominantly incremental changes and regular disproportionate changes. This suggests that the United States' interests and preferences toward other countries, as expressed through its aid program, is relatively stable, but also subject to larger (punctuated) changes.

[4] The 23 countries included in this study are: Australia, Austria, Belgium, Canada, Denmark, Finland, France, Germany, Greece, Ireland, Italy, Japan, Korea, Luxemburg, the Netherlands, New Zealand, Norway, Portugal, Spain, Sweden, Switzerland, the United Kingdom, and the United States.
[5] To avoid excess zeroes due to non-existing aid programs, disbursement values below zero were excluded from our analyses.

As we explained in the second section, the progressive friction hypothesis argues that institutional friction increases as we move down the policy stream, and institutional decision-making costs go up (Jones and Baumgartner 2005; Baumgartner *et al.* 2009). Hence, as we progress from policy input to policy outcome, we expect the LK of annual policy changes to increase, too. To examine this hypothesis, we look at the distribution of attention to foreign policy issues from different political and governmental activities and news media. The LK measures displayed in table 3.2 are based on the yearly percent changes in attention to each of the twenty-six individual foreign policy issues (in international defense, trade and general international affairs issues[6]) used in the Comparative Agendas Codebook.

This method involves the coding of political actors' activities on their policy content (news articles, parliamentary interventions, policy speeches, legislation, or budgets), and has become commonplace among an increasing number of agenda-setting scholars. Data were taken from the Comparative Agendas Project (CAP) website.[7] Based on CAP and ODA data, we chose to look at distributions of change in those five agendas to compare differences in friction of policy input (news media and parliamentary questions), policy process (bills and laws), as well as policy output (aid budgets). This way, we examined punctuations across the policy process. Furthermore, these five agendas are similar and comparable across countries unlike, for example, US presidential executive orders or Belgian ministerial councils, which are very country-specific. We focused on four specific countries—Belgium, Spain, Switzerland, and the United States—to examine whether there is a general pattern of stability and change across countries with different characteristics and institutional designs, for example with majority (United States and Spain) and proportional (Belgium and Switzerland) electoral systems.

Table 3.2 shows that the LK measures on the right side of the table are generally higher than those on the left side, especially compared to the LK of the policy output. This supports our first hypothesis for which we

---

[6] Foreign policy issues include: *Defense*: 1602: Alliances; 1603: Intelligence; 1605: Nuclear Arms; 1606: Military Aid; 1610: Procurement; 1619: Foreign Operations; 1699: Other – *Foreign Trade*: 1800: General; 1802: Trade Agreements; 1803: Exports; 1804: Private Investments; 1806: Competitiveness; 1807: Tariff & Imports; 1808: Exchange Rates; 1899: Other – *International Affairs*: 1900: General; 1901: Foreign Aid; 1902: Resources Exploitation; 1905: Developing Countries; 1906: International Finance; 1910: European Union; 1925: Human Rights; 1926: Organizations; 1927: Terrorism; 1929: Diplomats; 1999: Other.

[7] The Comparative Agendas Project Website brings together coded datasets from agenda-setting projects around the world. These data include activities from political and societal actors, involved in the policy process. Codebooks and datasets are available at www.comparativeagendas.net/datasets_codebooks (last accessed February 2, 2017).

Table 3.2 Levels of kurtosis for eighteen government activities in Belgium, Spain, Switzerland, and the United States

	Input		Process		Output
	Media	Parliamentary questions	Bills	Laws	Budgets
US	**0.29**[a] (*New York Times* 1996–2006)	**0.24** (Congressional hearings 1995–2014)	**0.41** (Congressional bills 1995–2015)	**0.22** (Public laws 1995–2014)	**0.98** (ODA 1995–2014)
BE	**0.27** (*De Standaard* newspaper 1999–2008)	**0.27** (Oral questions 1995–2010)	**0.14** (Bills 1995–2010)	**0.23** (Laws 1995–2010)	**0.80** (ODA 1995–2014)
CH	**0.22** (*Züricher Zeitung* 1995–2003)	–	–	**0.72** (Laws 1995–2008)	**0.79** (ODA 1995–2014)
ES	**0.32** (*El País* 1996–2011)	**0.23** (Oral questions 1995–2014)	**0.19** (Bills 1995–2010)	**0.41** (Laws 1995–2015)	**0.91** (ODA 1995–2014)

Lowest friction ————→ Highest friction

Source: The Comparative Agendas Project (CAP), available at: www.comparativeagendas.net/datasets_codebooks (last accessed February 2, 2017).

[a] LK for *New York Times* is based on data excluding the almost "institutional" coverage on the War on Terror. When taking those media stories into account, LK=0.37.

expected institutional friction to increase as we move down the policy stream and decision-making costs go up. The agendas on the left side of the table are more volatile and have more medium and large changes from one year to another. Using the same categorization as Baumgartner *et al.* (2009), news media and parliamentary questions are considered to be part of the input or information side of the political system; bills and laws belong to the policy process, and budgets represent the policy output. Hence, we find yearly distributional changes that follow the same pattern as those found by Baumgartner *et al.* (2009) on a variety of policy agendas in Belgium, Denmark, and the United States. Figure 3.2 presents the average LK scores of each policy stage for all four countries and confirms that foreign policy outputs are generally more punctuated than the input and process stages of policy-making. Table 3.2 and figure 3.2, thus, confirm that foreign policy follows the same dynamics generally found in domestic policies: policy changes are highly incremental with occasional disproportional "corrections." We also find institutional friction—or resistance to change—to increase, as political decision-making costs get higher. Only Belgium displays a slightly different pattern, with relatively low friction for bills and laws, even though outcomes are still very highly punctuated.

Table 3.2 and figure 3.2 also display one of the major advantages of PET, which is to compare governmental processes and dynamics across

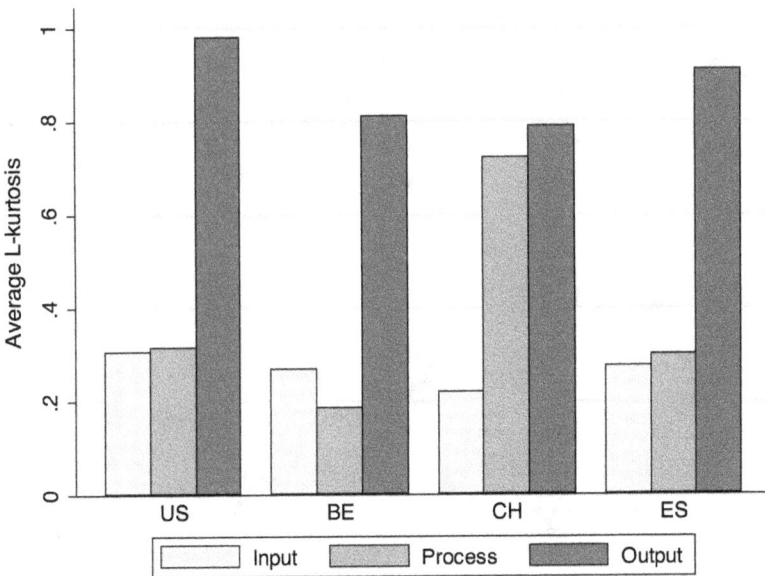

Figure 3.2 Average punctuatedness, from policy input to outcome, in four countries

countries and different political systems. Hence, we observe that there are differences in friction between countries, as Belgian bills and laws are less punctuated than those in Spain, Switzerland and the United States, or even than its own input series. Moreover, looking at foreign aid allocations for each country, which is perhaps the most comparable policy measure, it is clear that the Belgian and Swiss aid programs are less punctuated than the American and Spanish ones. This brings us to one of the challenges and possibilities generated by the distributional approach, which is to explain differences in distributional patterns and institutional friction. Hence, if the leptokurtic pattern of policy distributions is due to the processes of negative and positive feedback, as described above, we expect larger bureaucratic administrations to generate more leptokurtic distributions. Therefore, if we examine the relationship between the actual size of the aid administration, in million US$, and the amount of institutional friction, as measured by the LK scores, we should find a positive correlation according to PET.

To examine the relationship between administrative size and institutional friction, we looked at LK measures for twenty-three OECD donor countries (for which data was available), based on annual percent changes in aid distributions to developing countries. Figure 3.3, then, shows the relationship between LK scores and the absolute administrative cost in

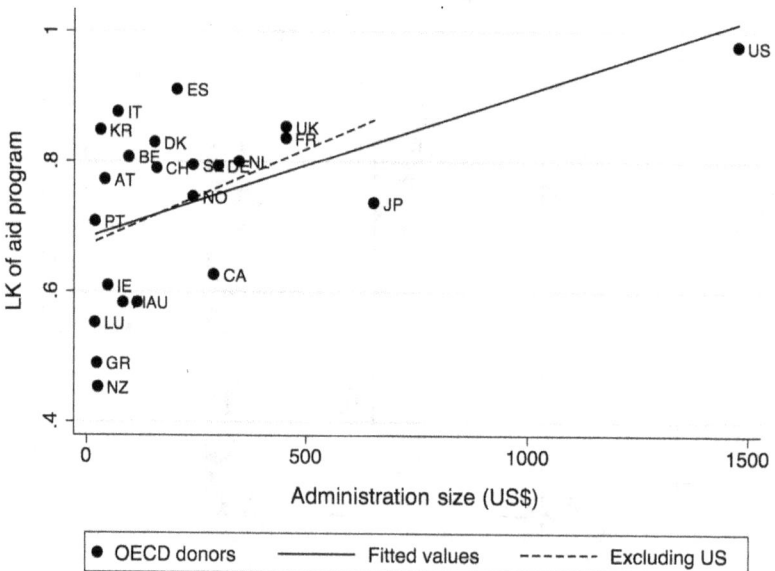

Figure 3.3 The relationship between friction (LK scores) and the size of the administration (in millions of US$)

millions of US$, as a measure for the size of the aid administration. The fitted values on the solid line clearly show that there is a relatively strong positive correlation (r=0.51), thus validating our second hypothesis. This correlation is still moderately positive when we exclude the United States as an outlier (r=0.39), as evidenced by the dashed fitted regression line. While this does not represent any direct or causal evidence, it supports our argument that aid distributions and, thus in a way, relations between and preferences toward other countries also behave according to a pattern of PE, whereby incremental policy changes are followed by occasional disproportional policy corrections.

Conclusion

The aim of this chapter was to show that PET is not only relevant in the realm of domestic politics, but also a useful approach to studying and understanding foreign policy-making. After explaining the key theoretical concepts and how they apply to FPA, we analyzed the yearly changes in attention to foreign policy issues and examined the relationship between changes in foreign aid allocations and the size of aid administrations. Based on these results, we came to the following three conclusions. First, American foreign aid perfectly fits the PET distribution pattern: it is characterized by many incremental and few disproportionate changes. This suggests that the United States' interests and preferences toward other countries are relatively stable, but also subject to larger changes. Second, we tested and applied the progressive friction hypothesis to a foreign policy context. We examined punctuations across the policy process, and found that institutional friction increases as we move down the policy stream and decision-making costs go up. Last but not least, we analyzed the relationship between administrative size and institutional friction in twenty-three OECD donor countries. Results support our argument that aid distributions and, thus in a way, relations between and preferences toward other countries behave according to PET, whereby incremental policy changes are followed by occasional disproportional policy corrections. These three conclusions, therefore, demonstrate that PET constitutes a unique tool for examining why and how certain foreign policy issues move up and down the political agenda.

Despite the recent surge in research on the influence of domestic politics on foreign policy, many prevalent theories in international relations still look for explanations of countries' behavior at the systemic level. While PET might not be the most suited theory to account for policy changes related to shifts in power at the systemic level, it provides a uniquely comprehensive approach to examine how policy issues evolve over time. It is particularly useful in explaining how steady advocacy from powerful political actors or groups can provide alternative policy solutions, or how focusing events can overthrow existing policies. Moreover, PET can be applied to analyze the policy dynamics that lead to specific decisions qualitatively (e.g., through process tracing) as well as to quantitatively study patterns of behavior and decision-making processes for a wider variety of foreign policy issues over a longer period of time.

Thus far, however, PET has not received much attention from foreign policy and international relations scholars. Foreign policy decision-making is generally assumed to be more concentrated within the executive, leaving fewer venues for policy entrepreneurs to advocate their alternative policy ideas. However, past literature discussed in this chapter indicates that there is an important role for the media and parliament in directing attention to specific issues, as is the case with domestic issues. Moreover, as our example on the Iraq war shows, PET can be a powerful tool, even—or especially—in explaining foreign policy decisions and how they came about. Particularly, PET incorporates the impact of focusing events as an important drive for policy change. Given the general importance of focusing events as well as the possibility to quantify their impact—e.g., through the number of victims, the cost, or the public and media attention they generate—it is relatively easy and straightforward to include them in both quantitative and qualitative explanatory models.

Finally, we believe that the strengths of PET lie in its applicability across political systems and policy issues. Several authors have shown that similar patterns of change and decision-making dynamics apply to a wide range of issues and polities, including international rivalries (Diehl and Goertz 2001) and humanitarian aid (Joly 2016). Given the potential PET provides for comparative research, much work can and needs to be done to further unravel the core mechanisms that constitute PE. FPA would surely benefit from a more systematic investigation of the patterns of policy distributions at different stages of the policy process. While comparisons across countries will uncover the impact specific institutions and mechanisms have on policy stability and change, comparison between issue domains will inform us on the role of subsystems and policy venues associated with specific issues. Similar to our investigation of the influence of the size of an administration, comparative research can also further inform us about drivers of stability or change in specific policy domains. At a lower, disaggregated level, we can also learn a great deal from examining differences in punctuations and what causes them, including mechanisms and conditions of positive feedback, like cascading.

References

Anderson, Edward (2012) Aid Fragmentation and Donor Transaction Costs, *Economics Letters* 117(3), 799–802.

Andrade, Lydia and Garry Young (1996) Presidential Agenda Setting: Influences on the Emphasis of Foreign Policy, *Political Research Quarterly* 49(3), 591–605.

Archuleta, Brandon J. (2016) Rediscovering Defense Policy: A Public Policy Call to Arms, *Policy Studies Journal* 44(S1), S50–S69.

Bachrach, Peter and Morton Baratz (1962) Two Faces of Power, *American Political Science Review* 56(4), 947–952.

Baumgartner, Frank R. and Bryan D. Jones (1993) *Agendas and Instability in American Politics*, Chicago: University of Chicago Press.

Baumgartner, Frank R., Christian Breunig, Christoffer Green-Pedersen, Bryan D. Jones, Peter B. Mortensen, Michiel Nuytemans, and Stefaan Walgrave (2009) Punctuated Equilibrium in Comparative Perspective, *American Journal of Political Science* 53(3), 603–620.

Birkland, Thomas A. (1997) *After Disaster: Agenda Setting, Public Policy, and Focusing Events*, Washington, DC: Georgetown University Press.

Birkland, Thomas A. (1998) Focusing Events, Mobilisation and Agenda Setting, *Journal of Public Policy* 18(1), 53–74.

Breunig, Christian (2006) The More Things Change, the More Things Stay the Same: A Comparative Analysis of Budget Punctuations, *Journal of European Public Policy* 13(7), 1069–1085.

Cobb, Roger W. and Charles D. Elder (1971) The Politics of Agenda-Building: An Alternative Perspective for Modern Democratic Theory, *Journal of Politics* 33(4), 892–915.

Comparative Agendas Project (2017) Datasets/Codebooks, available at www.comparativeagendas.net/datasets_codebooks (last accessed February 2, 2017).

Daugbjerg, Carsten and Jacob Studsgaard (2005) Issue Redefinition, Venue Change and Radical Agricultural Policy Reforms in Sweden and New Zealand, *Scandinavian Political Studies* 28(2), 103–124.

Diehl, Paul Francis (ed.) (1998) *The Dynamics of Enduring Rivalries*, Urbana: University of Illinois Press.

Diehl, Paul Francis and Gary Goertz (2001) *War and Peace in International Rivalry*, Ann Arbor: University of Michigan Press.

Downs, Anthony (1957) *An Economic Theory of Democracy*, New York: Harper.

Dziengel, Lake (2010) Advocacy Coalitions and Punctuated Equilibrium in the Same-Sex Marriage Debate: Learning from Pro-LGBT Policy Changes in Minneapolis and Minnesota, *Journal of Gay & Lesbian Social Services* 22(1–2), 165–182.

Edwards, George C. and B. Dan Wood (1999) Who Influences Whom? The President, Congress, and the Media, *The American Political Science Review* 93(2), 327–344.

Feely, T. Jens (2002) The Multiple Goals of Science and Technology Policy, in Frank R. Baumgartner and Bryan D. Jones (eds.) *Policy Dynamics*, Chicago: University of Chicago Press, 125–154.

Green-Pedersen, Christoffer and Sebastiaan Princen (2016) Punctuated Equilibrium Theory, in Nikolaos Zahariadis (ed.) *Handbook of Public Policy Agenda Setting*, Northampton, MA: Edward Elgar, 69–86.

Guiraudon, Virginie (2000) European Integration and Migration Policy: Vertical Policy-Making as Venue Shopping, *Journal of Common Market Studies* 38(2), 251–271.

Hardin, John W. (2002) Multiple Topics, Multiple Targets, Multiple Goals, and Multiple Decision Makers: Congressional Consideration of Comprehensive Health Care Reform, in Frank R. Baumgartner and Bryan D. Jones (eds.) *Policy Dynamics*, Chicago: University of Chicago Press, 96–124.

Hunt, Valerie F. (2002) The Multiple and Changing Goals of Immigration Reform: A Comparison of House and Senate Activity, 1947–1993, in Frank R. Baumgartner and Bryan D. Jones (eds.) *Policy Dynamics*, Chicago: Chicago University Press, 73–95.

John, Peter and Shaun Bevan (2012) What Are Policy Punctuations? Large Changes in the Legislative Agenda of the UK Government, 1911–2008, *Policy Studies Journal* 40(1), 89–108.

Joly, Jeroen (2016) Disentangling Media Effects: The Impact of Short-Term and Long-Term News Coverage on Belgian Emergency Assistance, *Cooperation and Conflict* 51(4), 428–446.

Jones, Bryan D. and Frank R. Baumgartner (2005) *The Politics of Attention: How Government Prioritizes Problems*, Chicago: Chicago University Press.

Jones, Bryan D., Frank R. Baumgartner, Christian Breunig, Christopher Wlezien, Stuart Soroka, Martial Foucault, Abel François, Christoffer Green-Pedersen, Chris Koski, Peter John, Peter B. Mortensen, Frédéric Varone, and Stefaan Walgrave (2009) A General Empirical Law of Public Budgets: A Comparative Analysis, *American Journal of Political Science* 53(4), 855–873.

Kingdon, John W. (1984) *Agendas, Alternatives, and Public Policies*, Boston: Little, Brown and Company.

Kingdon, John W. (2003) *Agendas, Alternatives, and Public Policies*, New York: Longman.

MacLeod, Michael C. (2002) The Logic of Positive Feedback: Telecommunications Policy through the Creation, Maintenance, and Destruction of a Regulated Monopoly, in Frank R. Baumgartner and Bryan D. Jones (eds.) *Policy Dynamics*, Chicago: Chicago University Press, 51–72.

Mazarr, Michael J. (2007) The Iraq War and Agenda Setting, *Foreign Policy Analysis* 3(1), 1–23.

Meernik, James, Eric L. Krueger, and Steven C. Poe (1998) Testing Models of U.S. Foreign Policy: Foreign Aid During and After the Cold War, *Journal of Politics* 60(1), 63–85.

Organisation for Economic Co-operation and Development (2017) Creditor Reporting System, available at https://stats.oecd.org/Index.aspx?Data SetCode=CRS1 (last accessed February 2, 2017).

Peake, Jeffrey S. (2001) Presidential Agenda Setting in Foreign Policy, *Political Research Quarterly* 54(1), 69–86.

Peake, Jeffrey S. (2016) Agenda Setting Dynamics and Differences across Issues: Agenda Setting on the Economy and Foreign Policy, in Nikolaos Zahariadis (ed.) *Handbook of Public Policy Agenda Setting*, Cheltenham: Edward Elgar, 314–331.

Pralle, Sarah B. (2003) Venue Shopping, Political Strategy, and Policy Change: The Internationalization of Canadian Forest Advocacy, *Journal of Public Policy* 23(3), 233–260.

Pralle, Sarah B. (2006) Timing and Sequence in Agenda-Setting and Policy Change: A Comparative Study of Lawn Care Pesticide Politics in Canada and the US, *Journal of European Public Policy* 13(7), 987–1005.

Repetto, Robert (ed.) (2006) *Punctuated Equilibrium and the Dynamics of US Environmental Policy*, New Haven: Yale University Press.

Robinson, Scott E. (2004) Punctuated Equilibrium, Bureaucratization, and Budgetary Changes in Schools, *Policy Studies Journal* 32(1), 25–39.

Schattschneider, Elmer E. (1960) *The Semisovereign People: A Realist's View of Democracy in America*, New York: Holt, Rinehart & Winston.

Schraeder, Peter J., Steven W. Hook, and Bruce Taylor (1998) Clarifying the Foreign Aid Puzzle: A Comparison of American, Japanese, French, and Swedish Aid Flows, *World Politics* 50(2), 294–323.

Sheingate, Adam D. (2000) Agricultural Retrenchment Revisited: Issue Definition and Venue Change in the United States and European Union, *Governance* 13(3), 335–363.

Simon, Herbert A. (1957) *Models of Man: Social and Rational: Mathematical Essays on Rational Human Behavior in a Social Setting*, New York: Wiley.

Soroka, Stuart N. (2002) *Agenda-Setting Dynamics in Canada*, Vancouver: UBC Press.

True, James L. (2002) The Changing Focus of National Security Policy, in Frank R. Baumgartner and Bryan D. Jones (eds.) *Policy Dynamics*, Chicago: University of Chicago Press, 155–183.

Van Aelst, Peter and Stefaan Walgrave (2016) Political Agenda Setting by the Mass Media: Ten Years of Research, 2005–2015, in Nikolaos Zahariadis (ed.) *Handbook of Public Policy Agenda Setting*, Cheltenham: Edward Elgar, 157–179.

Van Belle, Douglas A., Jean Sébastien Rioux, and David M. Potter (2004) *Media, Bureaucracies, and Foreign Aid: A Comparative Analysis of the United States, the United Kingdom, Canada, France, and Japan*, New York: Palgrave Macmillan.

Vliegenthart, Rens, Stefaan Walgrave, and Corine Meppelink (2011) Inter-Party Agenda-Setting in the Belgian Parliament: The Role of Party Characteristics and Competition, *Political Studies* 59(2), 368–388.

Walgrave, Stefaan and Rens Vliegenthart (2010) Why are Policy Agendas Punctuated? Friction and Cascading in Parliament and Mass Media in Belgium, *Journal of European Public Policy* 17(8), 1147–1170.

Walgrave, Stefaan, Frédéric Varone, and Patrick Dumont (2006) Policy with or without Parties? A Comparative Analysis of Policy Priorities and Policy Change in Belgium, 1991 to 2000, *Journal of European Public Policy* 13(7), 1021–1038.

Wildavsky, Aaron (1964) *The Politics of the Budgetary Process*, Boston: Little, Brown and Company.

Wood, B. Dan and Jeffrey S. Peake (1998) The Dynamics of Foreign Policy in Agenda Setting, *American Political Science Review* 92(1), 173–184.

Worsham, Jeffrey (1998) Wavering Equilibriums, *American Politics Quarterly* 26(4), 485–512.

Worsham, Jeffrey (2006) Up in Smoke: Mapping Subsystem Dynamics in Tobacco Policy, *Policy Studies Journal* 34(3), 437–452.

4

Foreign policy applications of the advocacy coalition framework

Jonathan J. Pierce and Katherine C. Hicks

The advocacy coalition framework (ACF) is an actor-specific theory of the policy process. The unit of analysis is the policy subsystem, within which advocacy coalitions compete to translate their beliefs into public policy. The framework is based on a series of assumptions at the systemic, meso-, and individual levels of analysis (Sabatier and Weible 2007), and identifies three theories: advocacy coalitions, policy learning, and policy change (Sabatier and Jenkins-Smith 1999; Jenkins-Smith *et al.* 2014).

The framework has been applied hundreds of times to understand the policy process with almost all applications examining domestic policy processes (Weible *et al.* 2009; Pierce *et al.* 2017). Developed in the United States (Sabatier 1988; Sabatier and Jenkins-Smith 1993), the ACF is now more widely applied by European scholars (Pierce *et al.* 2017). Over the decades, the ACF has evolved as a framework as identified in Sabatier and Jenkins-Smith (1999), Sabatier and Weible (2007), and Jenkins-Smith *et al.* (2014), each time in response to past criticisms and empirical applications. A flow diagram of the main components is in figure 4.1.

Although domestic ACF applications outnumber those examining foreign and defense policy issues (Pierce *et al.* 2017), the ACF can readily be applied to understand foreign policy. The ACF (Jenkins-Smith *et al.* 2014) and Foreign Policy Analysis (FPA) (Snyder *et al.* 1954; Holsti 1977; Hudson 2005) share an analytical focus on actor beliefs. A core ACF assumption that considers actor beliefs to be hierarchical originates from Converse's (1964) work examining public opinion about foreign policy. Past applications have demonstrated that with some minor adjustments, the assumptions, components, and theories of the ACF hold up when applied to FPA (Pierce and Hicks 2017). For example, the ACF has been applied to understand coalition stability in relation the creation of Israel

(Pierce 2011), policy learning by German during the war in Afghanistan (Schroer 2014), and the change and stasis of Swiss foreign policy toward South Africa and Iraq (Hirschi and Widmer 2010). These and other applications demonstrate that the ACF can be applied to understand advocacy coalitions, policy learning, and policy change in relation to FPA.

Advocacy coalition framework overview

The ACF provides a simplifying lens for understanding the policy process. First developed in the 1980s by Paul Sabatier and Hank Jenkins-Smith to understand contentious policy processes, the ACF was a response to perceived weaknesses in extant policy process theoretical frameworks (Sabatier and Jenkins-Smith 1999). Early iterations of the ACF attempted to expand the analytical complexity to better reflect the policy process (Sabatier 1988). This was accomplished by introducing bottom-up policy change to complement top-down paths; encouraging a long-term per- spective; expanding the definition of policy actors to include researchers, scientists, media among others; and replacing the perception of the indi- vidual as a rational actor with a model grounded in psychology and belief systems (Weible *et al.* 2011).

As a framework, the ACF establishes broad parameters such as scope, theoretical assumptions, and key concepts, while supporting multiple theoretical emphases (Weible *et al.* 2011). Major framework components include the policy subsystem, advocacy coalitions, policy learning, and policy change (Jenkins-Smith *et al.* 2014). Key founding research questions ask how people mobilize through advocacy coalitions, how people learn from their political allies and opponents, how science and technical information influence the policy process, and the causes of policy change (Weible *et al.* 2011).

Several key assumptions comprise the framework. The first three describe structural elements of the ACF. (1) The primary unit of analysis is the policy subsystem, delineated by a policy issue, territorial scope, and the actors attempting to influence an issue (Jenkins-Smith *et al.* 2014). A subsystem incubates policy outputs and outcomes. Semi-independent social structures, subsystems are dynamic units that may overlap and/or be nested within each other. Subsystems may be characterized by periods of stability, minor change, or major change, and they tend to contain a policy-making authority. (2) Any person consistently attempting to influ- ence the subsystem's policy issue is considered a relevant policy actor. This definition broadens the scope of policy participation from strictly traditional iron triangle actors such as legislators, government agencies, and interest groups to also include unofficial or third-party actors, such as members of the business or non-profit sector, as well as journalists, academics, members of the judiciary, among others (Heclo 1978). (3) These actors are grouped into advocacy coalitions united by shared beliefs. The logic in grouping by belief rather than alternative member attributes, such as organizational affiliation, is that it simplifies membership orientation and allows for stability over time (Sabatier and Jenkins-Smith 1999).

A fourth assumption outlines the ACF's fundamental philosophical understanding of human behavior. (4) The ACF posits that individuals are boundedly rational, or limited in their capability to process cognitive stimuli. They therefore employ a hierarchical belief system to simplify, sort, and make use of the unremitting stream of information that is cognition (Converse 1964). The ACF suggests a three-tiered belief system with broader beliefs often constraining more specific beliefs (Peffley and Hurwitz 1985). These broader, or deep core beliefs, are normative, axiomatic values resistant to change. Because they are not issue-specific, deep core beliefs can span subsystems. Intermediary policy core beliefs deal with views of a policy problem, including empirical assessments of the seriousness of a problem, its causes, as well as solutions. They are specific to the subsystem, with topical and/or territorial dimensions, and represent the glue that binds the advocacy coalition. Superficial secondary beliefs are the instrumental means of achieving a desired policy outcome. They may be specific to a subset of policy actors or coalition within the subsystem (Sabatier and Jenkins-Smith 1999). Additionally, based on prospect theory, the ACF assumes that people remember losses more than gains (Quattrone and Tversky 1988). Such negative bias means policy actors are susceptible to a "devil shift," whereby they overestimate both the power and the malice of opponents. This may lead to demonization of opponents and prolonged conflict.

Additional ACF assumptions characterize policy itself. (5) Mirroring the heuristic role of beliefs in actors, policies themselves are projections of the goals, values, and practices of constituent coalitions and their members (Lasswell and Kaplan 1950). Public policies therefore contain basic conceptions of causality in their very design. This may help to explain both dogged determination among coalitions as well as polarization between coalitions with varying belief systems. (6) Scientific, technical, and other empirical information filters through belief systems to help shape the perceived causes, magnitude, and probable impacts of various problems and solutions (Sabatier and Jenkins-Smith 1999). (7) Finally, because the policy process is never static but in a constant state of evolution (Lindblom 1968), researchers and political scientists should adopt a long-term lens for analysis. A period of a decade or more may be necessary to capture whether a policy was a success or a failure and to appreciate the various strategies actors engage in (Mazmanian and Sabatier 1980). This perspective will give the most robust insight into causality and patterns among and within subsystems.

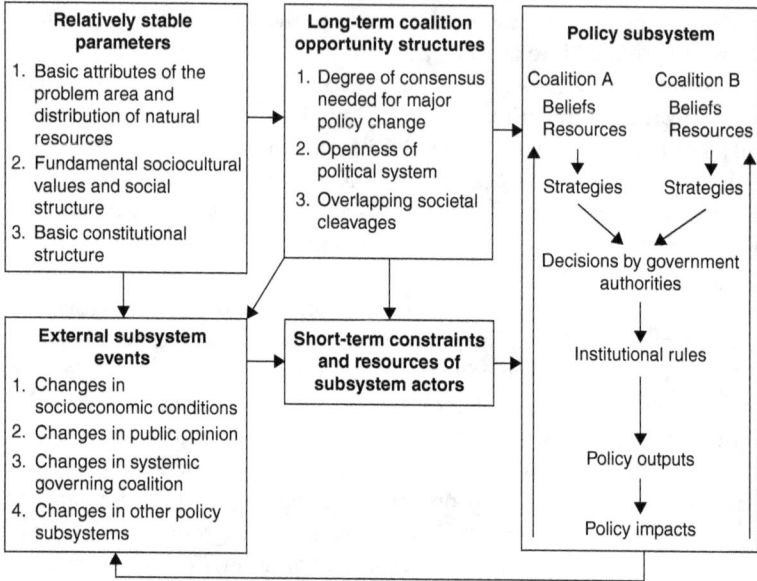

Note: Source is Jenkins-Smith *et al.* 2014.

Figure 4.1 Flow diagram of the advocacy coalition framework

Comprised of coalitions jockeying for political influence, the policy subsystem is the arena where policy inputs are transformed into outputs. These outputs, via governmental decisions, can in turn become inputs into other subsystems. Subsystems exist within an ecosystem of both (1) stable parameters and (2) external events, which influence the policy subsystem through different pathways (Jenkins-Smith *et al.* 2014).

Stable parameters include institutional/constitutional structures as well as cultural, social, and economic conditions, among others (Jenkins-Smith *et al.* 2014). A country's constitutional framework, for example, might be considered a stable parameter. By contrast, external events may act as focusing events or shocks (e.g., Birkland 2006) to subsystems. Examples are shifts in public opinion or socio-economic conditions, developments in other subsystems, crises and disasters, and/or elections. These dynamic changes are in turn influenced by the short-term constraints and resources of a subsystem like a window of opportunity.

The framework contains three key theories concerning the formation and stability of advocacy coalitions, policy oriented-learning, and policy change (Sabatier and Jenkins-Smith 1999; Jenkins-Smith *et al.* 2014). Advocacy coalitions are made up of actors united by policy core beliefs who seek to translate those beliefs into policy. These actors, whether principal or auxiliary, strategically coordinate their actions to influence the policy subsystem. In forming belief-based alliances, actors and coalitions may become combative in their attempts to enact their own versions of policy (Pierce and Weible 2016). A coalition's resources, which may include formal legal authority, public opinion, information, mobilizable troops, financial resources, and leadership (Sabatier and Weible 2007) moderates its influence on the policy subsystem. Nohrstedt (2011) has found that formal legal authority may be the most influential resource. Policy actors are most likely to achieve collective action when they have similar beliefs, engage in both weak and strong coordination, and/or experience the devil shift as a catalyst for action (Sabatier and Weible 2007). Five hypotheses concerning advocacy coalitions that can be found in Jenkins-Smith *et al.* (2014). One of these hypotheses that is tested in this chapter is that when policy core beliefs are in dispute, the lineup of allies and opponents tends to be stable over periods of a decade or so (Jenkins-Smith *et al.* 2014: 195).

Policy-oriented learning is defined as "enduring alternations of thought or behavioral intentions that result from experience and which are concerned with the attainment or revision of the precepts of the belief system of individuals or collectives" (Sabatier and Jenkins-Smith 1993: 42–56). In other words, learning is lasting changes in beliefs because of experienced stimuli. Altered beliefs may concern problem perception and causality, viable alternatives, or strategies for influence (Jenkins-Smith *et al.* 2014). In scenarios involving policy-oriented learning, researchers are particularly concerned with how and to what extent the makeup of belief systems change (i.e., secondary, policy core, or deep core beliefs); the spread of learning across the subsystem to opposing coalitions; and the role of policy brokers as well as professional forums in facilitating learning among coalition opponents (Jenkins-Smith *et al.* 2014). Five hypotheses available in Jenkins-Smith *et al.* (2014) about the conditions that facilitate policy-oriented learning between coalitions assume that coalitions will tend not to change their policy core beliefs and therefore only empirical evidence is likely to lead to such changes.

The ACF strives to explain the causes and nature of policy change, the third key ACF theory. Policy change may be either major or minor in nature, depending on the level of belief in question. Like the three-tiered belief system of actors and coalitions, the ACF also understands policies to be reflections of underlying hierarchical beliefs (Jenkins-Smith *et al.* 2014). Thus, major policy changes occur when core beliefs are altered (a change in the normative or empirical components of the policy). Likewise, minor changes are the result of altered secondary beliefs (a change in the instrumental decisions or informational processes).

Policy change in the ACF may be a top-down or bottom-up process. Subsystems in federal governments that do not operate at the national level may have policy change imposed vertically by a hierarchical superior jurisdiction. Subsystems may also be forced to change policy based on actions of horizontal subsystems, such as the courts. Furthermore, policy implementation is dependent upon the power and legitimacy of enacting bodies within their legal and temporal terms. Thus, except in cases of superior jurisdiction, policy core attributes of a given government program will remain stable so long as the affiliated advocacy coalition remains in power (Sabatier and Jenkins-Smith 1993).

The remaining four pathways to policy change are bottom-up and deal with coalitions as agentic actors in a dynamic environment. The hypothesis states that, *Significant perturbations external to the subsystem, a significant perturbation internal to the subsystem, policy-oriented learning, negotiated agreement, or some combination thereof are necessary, but not sufficient, sources of change in the policy core attributes of a governmental program* (Jenkins-Smith *et al.* 2014).

Transfer to foreign policy

Traditional FPA has remained outside the scope of theories of the policy process, instead falling into the domain of international relations (IR) (Litfin 2000). However, IR approaches have been found limited to explain foreign policy, in part because they favor societal and institutional forces over the role of beliefs (Goldstein 1988). Therefore, a policy process theory that focuses on the role of beliefs in uniting policy actors may be relevant to the foreign policy process (Friman 1993).

Past studies examining how policy actors translate beliefs into foreign policy tend to identify epistemic communities (Haas 1992), ethnicity (Smith 2000; Ambrosio 2002; Rubenzer 2008), business and labor organizations (Lipset 1986), or religious affiliation (Mearsheimer and Walt 2007) as the rationale behind coalition formation and stability. The ACF uses actor beliefs about the problem and proposed solution as the focus for studying coalitions. The ACF includes government officials, interest groups, media, and academics/scientists who are all active and share beliefs (Sabatier and Jenkins-Smith 1999). This approach of including all policy actors in a subsystem instead of focusing on a coalition government (Oppermann and Brummer 2014), or an individual (Walker *et al.* 1999) differs from traditional FPA.

The ACF should be used to conduct FPA because it focuses on the beliefs of actors which are consistent with FPA (Snyder *et al.* 1954; George 1969; Axelrod 1976; Holsti 1977; Hudson 2005). The ACF is generally associated with domestic policy processes and most frequently applied to environmental and energy issues (Weible *et al.* 2009; Pierce *et al.* 2017), but there have been past applications of the ACF to FPA (e.g.,

Pierce 2011). These past applications demonstrate the utility of the ACF to understand FPA (Pierce and Hicks 2017).

Four recent exemplary applications of the ACF to FPA are Haar (2010), Hirschi and Widmer (2010), Pierce (2011), and Schroer (2014). While these applications differ in terms of their topic of inquiry, theoretical foci and methodology, each applies the ACF to foreign policy. Haar (2010) examines US policy change under the George W. Bush administration in its decision to go to war with Iraq after the terrorist attacks of September 11, 2001 (9/11). Similarly, Schroer (2014) examines changes in German policy oriented learning around its involvement in the war in Afghanistan following 9/11. Hirschi and Widmer (2010) examine Swiss foreign policy change toward Iraq during the Gulf War in 1990 and 1991 in comparison to Swiss foreign policy toward South Africa. Pierce (2011) studies coalition stability and changes in beliefs about the "Question of Palestine" following World War I and during World War II. This demonstrates the range of theoretical questions and hypotheses that the ACF can be utilized to study FPA. Pierce (2011) studies advocacy coalitions and their stability over time, Haar (2010) and Hirschi and Widmer (2010) study policy change, and Schroer (2014) analyzes policy oriented learning. These studies represent the range of theories within the ACF.

In terms of methodology, all four applications employ qualitative methods with varying degrees of data collection and analysis. Haar (2010) and Schroer (2014) examine a single case study using qualitative methods to interpret documents. Hirschi and Widmer (2010) collect data from documents and interviews using qualitative comparative case study design. Pierce (2011) also uses documents as a source of data, applying content analysis to create quantitative data that is statistically analyzed. This demonstrates that the ACF applied to FPA can support a range of methods, including qualitative interpretation, comparative case study, and quantitative analysis.

There are some potential obstacles to applying the ACF for FPA (Pierce and Hicks 2017). One potential issue stems from the characteristics of the policy subsystem, the ACF's primary unit of analysis. Territorial scope is one of the relatively stable parameters of the policy subsystem. The purpose of this component is to delineate the scope of inquiry (Jenkins-Smith *et al.* 2014), but it raises obstacles to FPA where a clear territorial scope is not always identifiable (e.g., Richardson 1996; Farquharson 2003). However, it should be noted that territorial scope is a legacy of the ACF's origins in the environmental and energy sectors. Litfin (2000) argues that a single territorial dimension is not necessary for ACF applications. An alternative method for delineating the scope of inquiry is to focus on a government body that has authority to make and implement foreign policy. The ACF prescribes that subsystems will include some authority or potential authority (Jenkins-Smith et al. 2014), making this method a viable alternative for studying FPA (Pierce and Hicks 2017).

The ACF was designed to study sub-national processes. National-level application raises concern with key ACF concepts such as limiting the policy actors and institutions involved, differentiating between internal and external events and many other concepts as the ACF was originally designed to explain policy processes at the sub-national level (Sabatier and Jenkins-Smith 1993). However, a plurality of applications of the ACF over the past decade have been at the national level (as opposed to constituent political bodies such as states or provinces) (Pierce et al. 2017). Therefore, these limitations to the framework are not unique to FPA.

Scientific and technical information is important to understand policy subsystems (Jenkins-Smith et al. 2014). However, the purpose of this ACF assumption is to indicate that the transparent, unbiased nature of scientific and technical information creates potential for learning between and among coalitions (Sabatier and Jenkins-Smith 1999). Thus, the ACF sees scientific and technical information as a useful, but not requisite tool for policy-oriented learning and negotiation. In terms of FPA, Schroer (2014) explores policy-oriented learning among coalition members without the need to focus on scientific and technical information.

The ACF proposes to understand and evaluate policy change inclusive of implementation, a period of a decade or more should be taken (Jenkins-Smith et al. 2014), this is often not the case in practice. For example, Haar (2010), studying US foreign policy after 9/11, analyzes a period of approximately one year, and while Hirschi and Widmer (2010) use multiple decades to study Swiss foreign policy toward South Africa, they use a period of only a year to study Iraq. Therefore, in practice often around focusing events such as wars and terrorist attacks the ACF can be utilized to understand policy change over periods of time much shorter than a decade.

Empirical application

The development and evolution of coalitions that compete to shape public policies is an enduring field of political science (e.g., Heclo 1978; Sabatier and Jenkins-Smith 1993). The relative stability of coalition membership and beliefs, and the effects on policy-making, has been a topic of analysis among ACF scholars (Ingold 2011; Nohrstedt 2011). This study analyzes coalition stability among competing international coalitions over time by applying the ACF to the US government's decision to support the partition of Palestine under UN Resolution 181 in 1947. As the study analyzes coalition stability and its relationship to policy processes, the case selected is considered typical (Gerring 2007).

Mearsheimer and Walt (2007) argue that modern US policy toward the Middle East, specifically the Israeli–Palestinian conflict, is dominated by a loose coalition of pro-Israel interest groups. The influence of this "Israel Lobby" on the US government is in part responsible for the minimal support for a Palestinian state (Mearsheimer and Walt 2007). As the US government continues to be involved with issues of sovereignty in Palestine, the study of historical policy processes is essential because past policies have been found to help shape modern US foreign policy in the Middle East (May 1973; Hemmer 2000). This study tests a hypothesis about the stability of advocacy coalitions over time.

> **Hypothesis:** On major controversies within a policy subsystem, when policy core beliefs are in dispute, the lineup of coalition members as allies and opponents tends to be rather stable over periods of a decade or so. (Sabatier and Jenkins-Smith 1999)

This research analyzes the development of US government foreign policy in relation to the question of sovereignty over Palestine. Palestine was a mandate territory under the British Empire from 1922 to 1948, during which the British government attempted to balance Jewish and Arab demands for sovereignty (Smith 2001). This research focuses on the period between January 1, 1945 and November 29, 1947 when the UN voted to partition Palestine. The data for this study was collected from the US Department of State, *Foreign Relations of the United States* (FRUS) like past studies of this policy issue (Cohen 1990; Benson 1997; Radosh and Radosh 2009). The FRUS is the official archive of documents pertaining to US government foreign policy. The archives used for this study are identified as "Palestine 1945," "Palestine 1946," and "Palestine 1947" in the FRUS. Almost all the documents are official memorandum among or between the US Department of State and other US government agencies, foreign governments, or interest groups. The study is divided into three time periods that reflect new policy proposals and changes in venues within the subsystem.

Time Period 1: January 1 to August 31, 1945

Under US President Franklin D. Roosevelt, the US government generally did not seek to interfere with how the British government administered Palestine (US Department of State 1968: 699–700). President Roosevelt made statements supporting both Jewish and Arab claims for sovereignty, and established a policy of dual consultation that no major changes to US policy would be made without first consulting both parties (US

Department of State 1968: 698). When President Roosevelt unexpectedly died in April 1945, he was succeeded by Vice-President Harry S. Truman, who maintained Roosevelt's policies of dual consultation and allowed the US Department of State, Bureau of Near Eastern Affairs (NEA) to administer policy on Palestine (US Department of State 1968: 707).

During the summer of 1945, the war in Europe came to an end and the magnitude of the Holocaust emerged for the American public (Clifford 1978). The Holocaust left hundreds of thousands of displaced persons (DPs), many of them Jews, living in former concentration and refugee camps across Europe (Segev 1993). President Truman began meeting with Jewish interest group leaders who lobbied him to connect the issues of the Jewish DPs in Europe to British restrictions on Jewish immigration into Palestine (Benson 1997). Subsequently, the president ordered a report to determine how to address the Jewish DPs issue, and in August 1945 it concluded that 100,000 Jews should immediately immigrate to Palestine (Clifford 1978).

Time Period 2: August 31, 1945 to April 2, 1947

Based on this report, President Truman wrote to newly elected British Prime Minister Clement Attlee asking him to allow the prescribed 100,000 Jewish DPs to enter Palestine (US Department of State 1968: 737–739). This act marked a major change in US policy as now the United States was directly interfering in the British Mandate for Palestine, was advocating for immigration of Jews without consulting the Arabs, and President Truman did not consult the Department of State (US Department of State 1968: 746). The British government responded by inviting the US government to form a joint Anglo-American Inquiry to investigate the future of sovereignty over Palestine, and Jewish DPs in Europe (US Department of State 1968: 771–775). This began a period in which the United States collaborated with the United Kingdom on the future of sovereignty over Palestine, and directly connected Jewish DPs in Europe to immigration in Palestine.

The resultant Anglo-American Inquiry report recommended that 100,000 Jewish DPs be allowed to immigrate into Palestine, but argued against partitioning Palestine in favor of a single federal state (US Department of State 1969: 585–586). The proposal was rejected by both the Arab governments and the Jewish Agency (Jewish authority in Palestine), and the American and British governments soon followed in their rejection (US Department of State 1969: 682). After this failure, the British government convened a conference in London and invited the Arabs and Jewish Agency to negotiate a resolution with the United States acting as an observer (Smith 2001). The London Conference failed by early 1947 because the two sides refused to meet with each other (Smith 2001).

At the global level, World War II ended and there was rising tension between the USSR and the US and UK governments. The USSR had utilized a "wait and see" approach on the Question of Palestine, but now became increasingly engaged and sought to balance the influence of the United States in the region while opposing the British (Gorodetsky 2003). This meant making statements aligning it with Arab governments. In April 1947, British Foreign Minister Ernest Bevin announced that the issue of Palestine was no longer Great Britain's responsibility and it would instead be formally delegated to the newly formed UN (US Department of State 1971: 1047–1048).

Time Period 3: April 3 to November 29, 1947

In May 1947, the UN formed the United Nations Special Committee on Palestine (UNSCOP) to investigate the future of Palestine. UNSCOP conducted interviews and hearings in multiple locations, including in Palestine where Jewish leaders provided testimony and evidence to support their claims, but the Arabs refused to take part because they perceived UNSCOP as illegitimate. In September 1947, UNSCOP submitted its majority report to the UN prescribing the partitioning of Palestine into Jewish and Arab states along with the internationalization of Jerusalem (US Department of State 1971: 1143). The Arabs rejected the partition plan and lobbied the United States, Great Britain, and the Soviet Union along with its allies to vote against the proposal in the General Assembly. However, King Abdullah of Trans-Jordan collaborated with the British government as well as the Jewish Agency in Palestine, seeking to expand his kingdom into Palestine including capturing Jerusalem (Sela 1992). This meant that the Arab states were not a hegemonic coalition opposing the British and Jewish Agency. With some reservations, the Jewish Agency and American Jewish interest groups lobbied in favor of UNSCOP's proposal.

On November 29, the partition plan was passed by the General Assembly with the support of the US and Soviet governments among many others. The British government abstained. The Arab states walked out in protest, while the Jewish Agency and their supporters celebrated a victory. By the next day civil war broke out in Palestine. A Jewish or Arab state was not declared, but it was clear that the US policy was now in support for the creation of an independent Jewish state in Palestine. This represented a major change in US foreign policy since 1945 when it sought dual consultation and minimal involvement, to 1947 when it became one of the primary actors, favored the creation of an independent Jewish state in Palestine, as well as Jewish immigration into Palestine.

From the FRUS archives, the unit of analysis is the statement iden-tified at the organizational level (e.g., "British Government" or "Jewish Agency"), which is consistent with ACF studies examining advocacy coalitions (Jenkins-Smith and St. Clair 1993; Zafonte and Sabatier 2004; Nohrstedt 2011). Therefore, the level of analysis is the national government or interest group in the case of Jewish and Palestinian organizations, except for the US government as there was significant disagreement on the issue within the Department of State and the White House (Cohen 1990; Wilson and Quandt 2009).

Content analysis was conducted operationalizing policy core beliefs identified by Sabatier and Jenkins-Smith (1999). This was based on a review of the secondary literature and primary sources leading to the identification of fifteen policy core beliefs identified in table 4.1. All 505

Table 4.1 Operationalization policy core beliefs

Policy core beliefs (Sabatier and Jenkins-Smith 1999)	Operationalization policy core beliefs
Orientation on basic value priorities	1. The Jews are a nation
	2. The Arabs of Palestine are a nation
	3. The United States should seek to maintain security in the Middle East
	4. The United States should seek to maintain security in Palestine
	5. The United States should seek to maintain security for the Jewish people
Identification of groups whose welfare is of greatest concern	6. The welfare of the Jews is important
	7. The welfare of the Arabs of Palestine is important
Basic causes of the problem	8. Jewish immigration into Palestine should be prevented
	9. Jewish immigration into Palestine should be limited
	10. Jewish immigration into Palestine should be unlimited
	11. The Jews should be blamed for the problems in Palestine
	12. The Arabs should be blamed for the problems in Palestine
	13. The British should be blamed for the problems in Palestine
Proper distribution of authority	14. Sovereignty over Palestine should come from the Jews
	15. Sovereignty over Palestine should come from the Arabs

statements from January 1, 1945 to November 29, 1947 (UN Vote) were coded for all fifteen beliefs on a scale from -1 disagreement to 1 agreement. Statements that included two or fewer beliefs were excluded to prevent against Type II errors resulting in 398 statements being analyzed. Intercoder reliability was conducted on all codes using Cohen's Kappa (1960) and were at an acceptable level of fair (Fleiss 1971).

The resulting data was put into matrices for each time period representing beliefs per organization during the time period. The number of organizations per time period varied, and the number of statements per time period is as follows: n=55 (Time 1), n=227 (Time 2), and n=116 (Time 3). The Manhattan distance or absolute distance was calculated for each belief for every organization ranging from 0 or complete agreement to 30 or complete disagreement on all fifteen beliefs. Tabu search cluster analysis (Borgatti *et al.* 2002; Hanneman and Riddle 2005) was used to identify an organization's coalition membership (see Henry *et al.* 2010), a method similar to identifying discursive coalitions based on public statements (see Leifeld 2013). Tabu search cluster analysis identifies clusters of actors based on their relative difference on the fifteen beliefs and is used because it provides a relative goodness of fit (R^2) that can be utilized to discern the optimal number of clusters (Borgatti *et al.* 2002; Hanneman and Riddle 2005).

To analyze the variation in coalition beliefs and shifting membership, the mean Manhattan distances among coalition members and between coalitions are used. The lower the Manhattan distance the greater the level of agreements among and between coalitions on the fifteen beliefs. The number of observations reported for each coalition corresponds to the number of organizations in the coalition and not the number of statements in the time period. The findings are shown in table 4.2.

Table 4.2 Mean Manhattan distances among and between coalitions

Time Period	Coalition	Coalition		
		Arab	Zionist	Anglo-American
Time 1	Arab (n=5)	3.8	18.4	12
	Zionist (n=2)		4	13.3
	Anglo-American (n=4)			6.7
Time 2	Arab (n=9)	4.4	14	10.3
	Zionist (n=2)		3	11.5
	Anglo-American (n=4)			2.7
Time 3	Arab (n=6)	6.8		11.7
	Anglo-American (n=8)			7

Source: US Department of State (1968, 1969, 1971).

For Time Period 1, the analysis identifies five organizations as part of the Arab Coalition (Arab Higher Committee (AHC), Egyptian Government (EG), Iraqi Government (IZ), Saudi Arabian Government (SA) and the Syrian Government (SY)), two organizations as part of the Zionist Coalition (Jewish Agency (JA) and Zionist Organization of America (ZOA)), and four organizations belonging to the Anglo-American Coalition (Department of State (DOS), Department of State Near Eastern Affairs (DOS NEA), British Government (UK), and White House (WH)). The level of disagreement among coalition members is relatively lower among the Arab and Zionist Coalitions compared to the Anglo-American Coalition.

In terms of distance between the coalitions, the Anglo-American Coalition is about equidistant between the Arab (12) and Zionist (13.3) Coalitions. This represents an absolute value of disagreement on about six beliefs by the Anglo-American Coalition with either coalition. The distance between the Arab and Zionist Coalition is 18.4, representing disagreement on a majority of beliefs. The distances among and between the coalitions as well as the beliefs that they have in common and disagree on are graphically represented in figure 4.2.

This figure is a two-mode network map of the beliefs (grey squares with numbers correlating to table 4.1) and organizations (black circles with initials) using a stress minimization (Multidimensional Scaling (MDS)) of graph-theoretic distances (Brandes and Pich 2009) as implemented in UCINET (Borgatti *et al.* 2002). All figures in this chapter use MDS. The figure displays the beliefs of these organizations and connections among these organizations based on their common beliefs.

Coalitions overlap on several beliefs. The Zionist and Anglo-American Coalitions share several beliefs, including agreement that the Jews are a nation (1) whose security (5) and welfare (6) are important, and the White House supports unlimited Jewish immigration into Palestine (10). The Arab and Anglo-American Coalitions share beliefs that the Arabs are a nation (2) whose welfare is important (7) and that the United States should maintain security in Palestine (4) and the Middle East (3). Within the Anglo-American Coalition, the British Government and the Department of State (NEA) share the belief with the Arab Coalition that the Jews are to blame for the problems in Palestine (11). The Zionist and Arab Coalitions do not share any beliefs. This indicates intermediate levels of conflict between the Anglo-American Coalition and the other coalitions, but high levels of conflict and relative polarization between the Arab and Zionist Coalitions.

Each coalition also has unique beliefs. Only the Zionist Coalition believes that the British are to blame for the problems in Palestine (13) and that the Jews should have sovereignty over Palestine (14). Only the Arab Coalition believes that immigration of Jews should be prevented

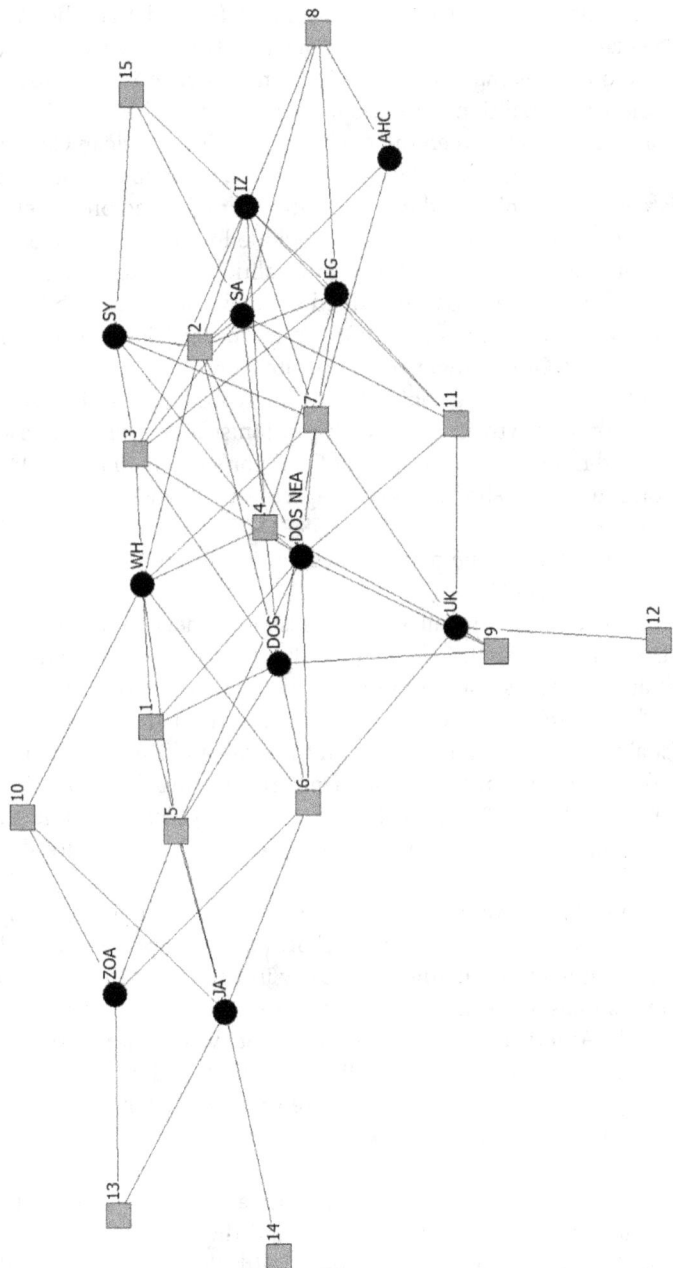

Figure 4.2 Organizations and policy core beliefs for Time Period 1

(8) and that the Arabs should have sovereignty over Palestine (15). The beliefs that only the Anglo-American Coalition possess are that Jewish immigration into Palestine should be limited (9) and that the Arabs should be blamed for the problems in Palestine (12).

This demonstrates that the major divisions between the Zionist and Anglo-American Coalitions are about sovereignty and blame. In contrast, major divisions between the Arabs and Anglo-American Coalition concern immigration and sovereignty, while beliefs about blame are inconsistent. The Zionists and Arab Coalitions are divided on all beliefs.

For Time Period 2, the Arab Coalition added four new members for a total of nine organizations. The Arab Coalition continued to include the AHC, EG, IZ, SA, and SY and added the newly formed Arab League (AL), the Soviet Government (USSR), Trans-Jordan Government (TJ), and the Lebanese Government (LB). Despite its growth in size, the level of disagreement on beliefs only slightly increased to 4.4. Unlike the Arab Coalition's growth in membership, Zionist and Anglo-American Coalitions did not change. The Zionist Coalition's two members (JA and ZOA) continued at a similar level of agreement (3), while the Anglo-American Coalition's four members (UK, DOS, DOS NEA, and WH) increased agreement as the distance decreased from 6.7 in Time Period 1 to 2.7 in Time Period 2.

The distances between all coalitions slightly decreased, reflecting an increase in agreement. This may be due to the consistent attempts at negotiations and use of committees. The Anglo-American Coalition continued to be relatively equidistant from the Arab (10.3) and Zionist (11.5) Coalitions. The distance between the Arab and Zionist Coalitions remained the greatest, but decreased from 18.4 during Time Period 1 to 14 during Time Period 2. Figure 4.3 depicts the organizations and their corresponding beliefs. The same MDS layout is used for figure 4.3 as figure 4.2.

Zionist and Anglo-American Coalitions share beliefs that the Jews are a nation (1) whose security (5) and welfare (6) are important, and that the United States should maintain security in Palestine (4). The Zionist Coalition also has some notable agreements with individual members of the Anglo-American Coalition, such as the White House supports unlimited Jewish immigration into Palestine (10), and agreement with the British government that the Arabs are to blame for the problems in Palestine (12).

The Arab and Anglo-American Coalitions share beliefs that the Arabs are a nation (2) whose welfare is important (7) and that the United States should maintain security in Palestine (4) and the Middle East (3). The Department of State now shares the belief with the Arab Coalition that the Jews are to blame for the problems in Palestine (11). By contrast, the British government now blames the Arabs (12). The Zionist coalition

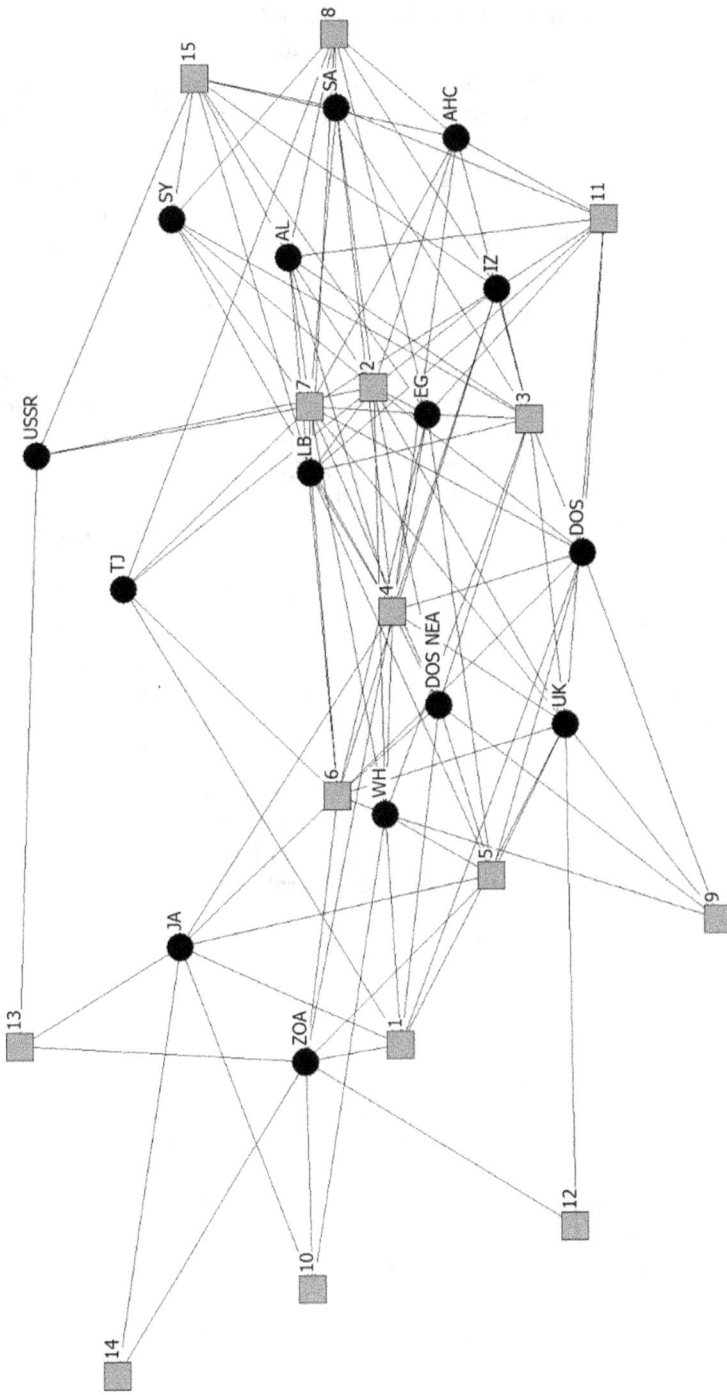

Figure 4.3 Organizations and policy core beliefs for Time Period 2

shares the belief with the Soviet government (Arab coalition) that the British are to blame for the problems in Palestine (13).

The belief only held by the Zionist Coalition is that the Jews should have sovereignty over Palestine (14). In contrast, the beliefs only held by the Arab Coalition are that immigration of Jews should be prevented (8) and that the Arabs should have sovereignty over Palestine (15). The beliefs that only the Anglo-American Coalition possess are that Jewish immigration into Palestine should be limited (9), and that the Arabs should be blamed for the problems in Palestine (12).

This demonstrates that the major divisions between the Zionist and Anglo-American Coalitions continue from Time Period 1 to be about sovereignty and blame. The Anglo-American and Zionist Coalitions agree that the Jews should immigrate to Palestine, but disagree on the limits of that immigration. The disagreements between the Arabs and Anglo-American Coalition continue from Time Period 1 and are about immigration and sovereignty, while beliefs about blame are inconsistent. The major divisions between the Zionist and the Arab Coalitions continue from Time Period 1 and are on all beliefs.

For Time Period 3, there are six members of the Arab Coalition (AHC, AL, IZ, SA, LB, and SY). The level of disagreement among the members increased since Time Period 2, despite fewer members. Two members defected membership from the Arab Coalition to the Anglo-American Coalition: the USSR and Trans-Jordan. The USSR supported the UN resolution to partition Palestine, and King Abdullah of Trans-Jordan sent a telegram to the US Department of State arguing that security in the Middle East and Palestine is imperative, and this includes security for the Jewish people and that their welfare is important. In addition, the statement blamed both the Jews and the Arabs for the problems in Palestine. While this statement was not in support of Jewish sovereignty and immigration, it departed from the rest of the Arab Coalition in terms of recognizing Jewish security and welfare as well as blame on the Arabs. Also, Egypt did not make any statements in the FRUS archives during this time period.

The Anglo-American Coalition for Time Period 3 also changed its membership growing to include eight members (DOS, DOS NEA, UK, JA, ZOA, WH, USSR, and TJ), an increase from four members during Time Period 2. New members include the former Zionist Coalition members (JA and ZOA) as well as former Arab Coalition members (USSR and TJ). This demonstrates defection from the Arab Coalition and the merging of the Zionist and Anglo-American Coalition in Time Period 3. The level of disagreement among Anglo-American coalition members is 6.96, a clear increase from the previous disagreement level of 2.67. However, the Anglo-American Coalition's level of disagreement in Time Period 3 is similar to that of Time Period 1 (6.67), as well as the Arab Coalition during Time Period 3 (6.8).

The distance between the Anglo-American Coalition and the Arab Coalition is 11.7, representing an increase in disagreement from 10.3 during Time Period 2. As there is no longer a Zionist Coalition, there is no distance. The policy actors and beliefs for Time Period 3 are graphically represented in figure 4.4.

Figure 4.4 demonstrates a clear change in the policy core beliefs among the policy actors. Policy actors no longer tend to hold beliefs in isolation. Instead multiple policy actors in a coalition agree on policy core beliefs and share many beliefs with the other coalition. Only members of the Arab Coalition believe that Jewish immigration into Palestine should be prevented (8) and only the Arabs should have sovereignty over Palestine (15). In comparison, only members of the Anglo-American Coalition believe that the Jews are a nation (1) whose welfare is important (6) and the United States should maintain their security (5), and that the Arabs should be blamed for the problems in Palestine (12). The beliefs that the two coalitions have in common are that Arabs of Palestine are a nation (2) whose welfare is important (7); the United States should maintain security in the Middle East (3) and in Palestine (4); Jewish immigration into Palestine should be limited (9); and the Jews (11) as well as the British (13) should be blamed for the problems in Palestine.

This demonstrates that the Arab Coalition continued to hold absolute positions on immigration and sovereignty that were not shared by any other policy actors. The other policy actors supported UN Resolution 181 or at least in the case of Trans-Jordan acknowledged the importance of Jewish welfare and security in Palestine. The Jewish Agency and the Zionist Organization of America no longer demanded unlimited immigration (10) and Jewish sovereignty over Palestine (14), at least as stated in the FRUS. These changes in publicly and privately stated beliefs to the US Department of State are arguably strategic as demonstrated by the subsequent war and attempt to gain sovereignty over all of Palestine and unlimited immigration by the Jewish Agency (Morris 1988). However, the Zionist Coalition supported the UN Resolution 181 aligning most of their expressed beliefs with the Anglo-American Coalition. In the final analysis, the lack of changes in beliefs by the Arab Coalition on issues of Jewish sovereignty and immigration, the refusal to collaborate with UNSCOP, the defection of the USSR and Trans-Jordan from the Arab to the Anglo-American Coalition between Time Periods 2 and 3, as well as changes in beliefs by the Zionist Coalition to align themselves with the Anglo-American Coalition help explain the success of the UN resolution and the defeat of the Arab Coalition. In the end, UN Resolution 181 was approved by the General Assembly on November 29, 1947. This led directly to the declaration of an Independent Israel and general war in the region in May 1948.

This research has many limitations. Using only the FRUS as a data source may have disproportionately represented the beliefs of US policy

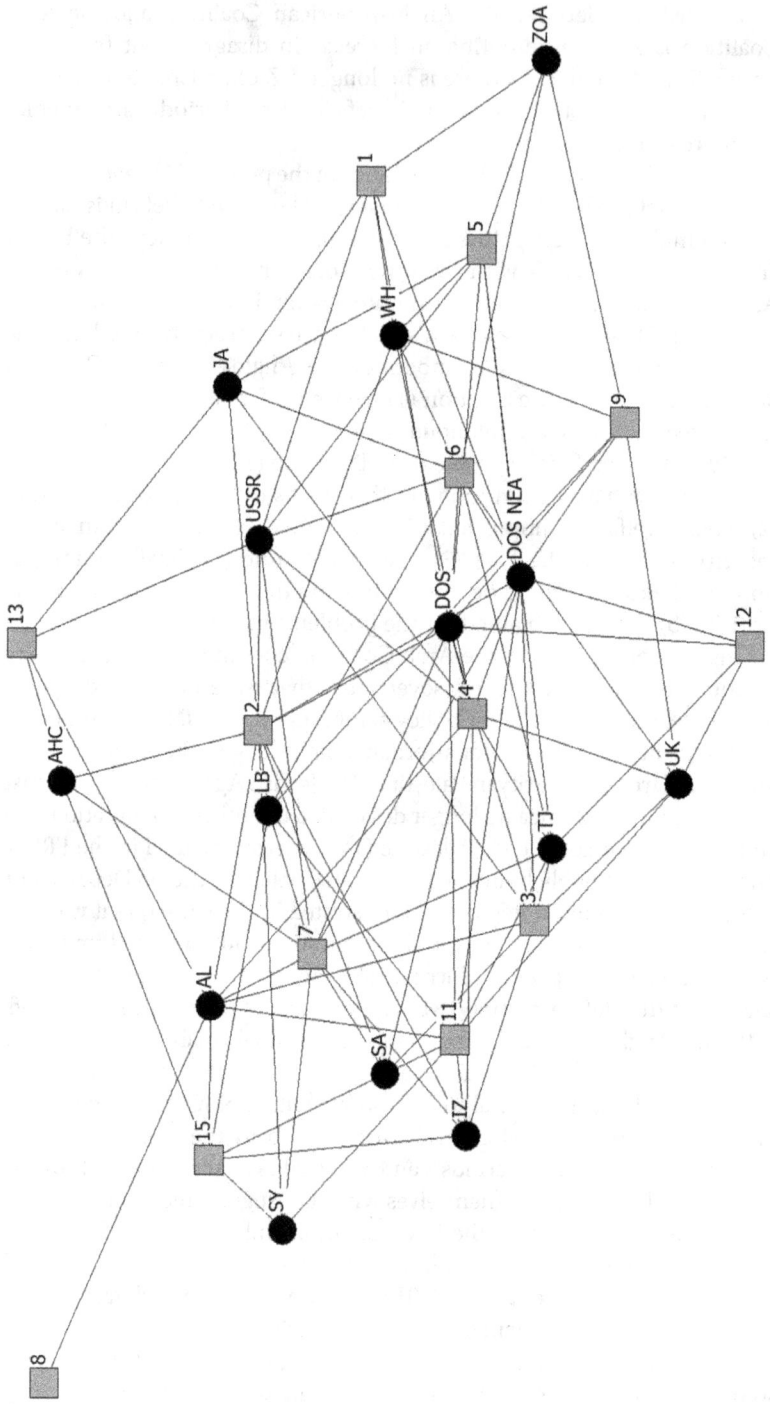

Figure 4.4 Policy actors and policy core beliefs for Time Period 3

actors, did not capture the dimensions of beliefs and actors within other governments, and probably did not capture all of the actors in the subsystem. Regardless, the purpose of this study was to analyze US foreign policy. Additionally, any study using documents to ascertain policy actor beliefs also suffers from limitations due to subjectivity of expressed beliefs (Larson 1988). However, the use of content analysis of text to analyze beliefs is a common method within both the ACF (Zafonte and Sabatier 2004) and FPA (Holsti 1977).

This research tested the hypothesis that the lineup of opponents and allies should be stable over time (Sabatier and Jenkins-Smith 1999). This study found that within a three-year time period (1945–1947) members of the Zionist Coalition as well as members of the Arab Coalition (USSR and Trans-Jordan) joined the Anglo-American Coalition. This research does not support the hypothesis that coalition membership was stable over time and is counter to the findings of Jenkins-Smith and St. Clair (1993), and Zafonte and Sabatier (2004). Advocacy coalitions may change their beliefs over time. Such belief change may indicate defection of coalition members or the change of beliefs for larger strategic goals such as winning elections. This last finding about coalitions strategically changing beliefs in pursuit of winning elections supports the finding of other ACF research (e.g., Nohrstedt 2010).

Conclusion

This empirical research found that the ACF can be used as a theoretical lens to better understand the formation and changes among policy actors within the field of foreign policy. It found that coalitions of actors with shared beliefs may face defection over time. In this case, defection led to changes in the balance of power between competing coalitions and subsequently a major policy change, in terms of the adoption of a UN resolution and the creation of Israel. Understanding coalition stability and defection over time can help shed light on how policy change occurs.

The study of policy actors competing to influence foreign policy by coordinating in coalitions is a topic of scholarly interest in FPA (e.g., Haas 1992; Smith 2000; Mearsheimer and Walt 2007). As demonstrated by this empirical case study, the ACF can be used to study such coalitions that organize around policy core beliefs seeking either to maintain or change policy. In addition, the ACF can also be used to study policy-oriented learning as well as policy change within the context of FPA. The ACF and FPA are compatible as both are actor-centric and focus on beliefs.

Potential obstacles in applying the ACF to FPA can be overcome without complication. The first obstacle, the ACF's inclusion of a geographic region in the definition of a policy subsystem, must be shifted to instead focus on a government authority responsible for foreign policy. A second obstacle is the ACF's assumption that scientific and technical information is central to the policy process. While such information may be relevant to FPA in some contexts, such as foreign aid or defense issues, it is not necessary as the ACF also supports research that is more normative in nature (Sabatier and Jenkins-Smith 1999).

Overall, this chapter demonstrates that the ACF is well suited to address FPA research questions and hypotheses. Questions about how the beliefs, strategies, and coordinated behavior of actors can lead to policy change can be better understood by utilizing the ACF. The ACF should be more readily adopted by FPA scholars, in particular those seeking to analyze the beliefs of actors and how they form coalitions whose objective is to influence politics and policy.

References

Ambrosio, Thomas (ed.) (2002) *Ethnic Identity Groups and U.S. Foreign Policy*, Westport: Praeger.

Axelrod, Robert (ed.) (1976) *Structure of Decision: The Cognitive Maps of Political Elites*, Princeton: Princeton University Press.

Benson, Michael (1997) *Harry S. Truman and the Founding of Israel*, Westport: Praeger.

Birkland, Thomas (2006) *Lessons of Disaster: Policy Change after Catastrophic Events*, Washington, DC: Georgetown University Press.

Borgatti, Stephen, Martin Everett, and Linton Freeman (2002) *UCINET 6 for Windows*, Cambridge, MA: Analytical Technologies.

Brandes, Ulrik and Christian Pich (2009) An Experimental Study on Distance-Based Graph Drawing, in *Proceedings of the 16th International Symposium on Graph Drawing*, Berlin: Springer, 218–229.

Clifford, Clark (1978) Factors Influencing President Truman's Decision to Support Partition and Recognize the State of Israel, in Clark Clifford, Eugene Rostow, and Barbara Tuchman (eds.) *The Palestine Question in American History*, New York: Arno, 24–45.

Cohen, Jacob (1960) A Coefficient of Agreement for Nominal Scale, *Education and Psychological Measurement* 20(1), 37–46.

Cohen, Michal (1990) *Truman and Israel*, Berkeley: University of California Press.

Converse, Philip (1964) The Nature of Belief Systems in Mass Publics, in David Apter (ed.) *Ideology and Discontent*, New York: Wiley, 206–261.

Farquharson, Karen (2003) Influencing Policy Transnationally: Pro- and Anti-Tobacco Global Advocacy Networks, *Australian Journal of Public Administration* 62, 80–92.

Fleiss, Joseph (1971) Measuring Nominal Scale Agreement among Many Raters, *Psychological Bulletin* 76 (November), 378–382.

Friman, Richard (1993) From Policy Beliefs to Policy Choices: The Resurgence of Tariff Retaliation in the U.S. Pursuit of Fair Trade, *Journal of Public Policy* 13(2), 163–182.

George, Alexander L. (1969) The "Operational Code": A Neglected Approach to the Study of Political Leaders and Decision-Making, *International Studies Quarterly* 13(2), 190–222.

Gerring, John (2007) *Case Study Research: Principles and Practices*, New York: Cambridge University Press.

Goldstein, Judith (1988) Ideas, Institutions, and American Trade Policy, *International Organization* 42(1), 179–219.

Gorodetsky, Gabriel (2003) The Soviet Union's Role in the Creation of the State of Israel, *Journal of Israeli History: Politics, Society, Culture* 22(1), 4–20.

Haar, Roberta (2010) Explaining George W. Bush's Adoption of the Neoconservative Agenda after 9/11, *Politics and Policy* 38(5), 965–990.

Haas, Peter (1992) Introduction: Epistemic Communities and International Policy Coordination, *International Organization* 46(1), 1–35.

Hanneman, Robert and Mark Riddle (2005) Introduction to Social Network Methods, available at http://faculty.ucr.edu/~hanneman/nettext/Introduction_to_Social_Network_Methods.pdf (last accessed October 13, 2016).

Heclo, Hugh (1978) Issue Networks and the Executive Establishment, in Anthony King (ed.) *The New American Political System*, Washington, DC: American Enterprise Institute, 46–57.

Hemmer, Christopher (2000) *Which Lessons Matter? American Foreign Policy Decision Making in the Middle East, 1979–1989*, Albany: SUNY.

Henry, Adam, Mark Lubell, and Michael McCoy (2010) Belief Systems and Social Capital as Drivers of Policy Network Structure: The Case of California Regional Planning, *Journal of Public Administration Research and Theory* 21(3), 419–444.

Hirschi, Christian and Thomas Widmer (2010) Policy Change and Policy Stasis: Comparing Swiss Foreign Policy toward South Africa (1968–94) and Iraq (1990–91), *Policy Studies Journal* 38(3), 537–563.

Holsti, Ole (1977) *The "Operational Code" as an Approach to the Analysis of Belief Systems*, Durham, NC: Duke University Press.

Hudson, Valerie (2005) Foreign Policy Analysis: Actor-Specific Theory and the Ground of International Relations, *Foreign Policy Analysis* 1(1), 1–30.

Ingold, Karin (2011) Network Structures within Policy Processes: Coalitions, Power, and Brokerage in Swiss Climate Policy, *Policy Studies Journal* 39(3), 435–459.

Jenkins-Smith, Hank and Gilbert St. Clair (1993) The Politics of Offshore Energy, in Paul A. Sabatier and Hank Jenkins-Smith (eds.) *Policy Change and Learning: An Advocacy Coalition Approach*, Boulder: Westview Press, 149–176.

Jenkins-Smith, Hank, Daniel Nohrstedt, Christopher M. Weible, and Paul A. Sabatier (2014) The Advocacy Coalition Framework: Foundations, Evolution, and Ongoing Research, in Paul Sabatier and Christopher M. Weible (eds.) *Theories of the Policy Process*, 3rd edition, Boulder: Westview Press, 183–223.

Larson, Deborah Welch (1988) Problems of Content Analysis in Foreign-Policy Research: Notes from the Study of the Origins of Cold War Belief Systems, *International Studies Quarterly* 32(2), 241–255.

Lasswell, Harold and Abraham Kaplan (1950) *Power and Society*, New Haven: Yale University Press.

Leifeld, Philip (2013) Reconceptualizing Major Policy Change in the Advocacy Coalition Framework: A Discourse Network Analysis of German Pension Politics, *Policy Studies Journal* 41(1), 169–198.

Lindblom, Charles (1968) *The Policy-Making Process*, Englewood Cliffs: Princeton University Press.

Lipset, Seymour (1986) *Union in Transition: Entering the Second Century*, San Francisco: Institute for Contemporary Studies.

Litfin, Karen (2000) Advocacy Coalitions along the Domestic-Foreign Frontier: Globalization and Canadian Climate Change Policy, *Policy Studies Journal* 28, 236–254.

May, Ernest (1973) *"Lessons" of the Past: The Use and Misuse of History in American Foreign Policy*, New York: Oxford University Press.

Mazmanian, Daniel and Paul Sabatier (1980) A Multivariate Model of Public Policy-Making, *American Journal of Political Science* 24, 439–468.

Mearsheimer, John and Stephen Walt (2007) *The Israel Lobby and U.S. Foreign Policy*, New York: Farrar, Straus, and Giroux.

Morris, Benny (1988) *The Birth of the Palestinian Refugee Problem, 1947–1949*, Cambridge: Cambridge University Press.

Nohrstedt, Daniel (2010) Do Advocacy Coalitions Matter? Crisis and Change in Swedish Nuclear Energy Policy, *Journal of Public Administration Research and Theory* 20(2), 309–333.

Nohrstedt, Daniel (2011) Shifting Resources and Venues Producing Policy Change in Contested Subsystems: A Case Study of Swedish Signals Intelligence Policy, *Policy Studies Journal* 39(3), 461–484.

Oppermann, Kai and Klaus Brummer (2014) Patterns of Junior Partner Influence on the Foreign Policy of Coalition Governments, *The British Journal of Politics and International Relations* 16(4), 555–571.

Peffley, Michael and Jon Hurwitz (1985) A Hierarchical Model of Attitude Constraint, *American Journal of Political Science* 29 (November), 871–890.

Pierce, Jonathan (2011) Coalition Stability and Belief Change: Advocacy Coalitions in U.S. Foreign Policy and the Creation of Israel, 1922–44, *Policy Studies Journal* 39(3), 411–434.

Pierce, Jonathan and Katherine Hicks (2017) Advocacy Coalitions in Foreign Policy, in Cameron Thies (ed.) *Oxford Research Encyclopedia of Foreign Policy Analysis*, Oxford: Oxford University Press. DOI: 10.1093/acrefore/9780190228637.013.355.

Pierce, Jonathan and Christopher Weible (2016) Advocacy Coalition Framework, in Stephen Schechter (ed.) *American Governance*, Farmington Hills: Gale, Cengage Learning, 22–23.

Pierce, Jonathan, Holly L. Peterson, Michael D. Jones, Samantha P. Garrard, and Theresa Vu (2017) There and Back Again: A Tale of the Advocacy Coalition Framework, *Policy Studies Journal* 45(S1), S13–S46.

Quattrone, George and Amos Tversky (1988) Contrasting Rational and Psychological Analysis of Political Choice, *American Political Science Review* 82, 719–736.

Radosh, Allis and Ronald Radosh (2009) *A Safe Haven: Harry S. Truman and the Founding of Israel*, New York: HarperCollins.

Richardson, Jeremy (ed.) (1996) *European Union: Power and Policy-Making*, London: Routledge.

Rubenzer, Trevor (2008) Ethnic Minority Interest Group Attributes and U.S. Foreign Policy Influence: A Qualitative Comparative Analysis, *Foreign Policy Analysis* 4(2), 169–185.

Sabatier, Paul A. (1988) An Advocacy Coalition Framework of Policy Change and the Role of Policy-Oriented Learning Therein, *Policy Sciences* 21(2/3), 129–168.

Sabatier, Paul A. and Hank Jenkins-Smith (1993) *Policy Change and Learning: An Advocacy Coalition Approach*, Boulder: Westview Press.

Sabatier, Paul A. and Hank Jenkins-Smith (1999) The Advocacy Coalition Framework: An Assessment, in Paul A. Sabatier (ed.) *Theories of the Policy Process*, Boulder: Westview Press, 117–166.

Sabatier, Paul, and Christopher Weible (2007) The Advocacy Coalition Framework: Innovations and Clarifications, in Paul A. Sabatier and Christopher M. Weible (eds.) *Theories of the Policy Process*, Boulder: Westview Press, 189–222.

Schroer, Arne (2014) Lessons Learned? German Security Policy and the War in Afghanistan, *German Politics* 23(1–2), 78–102.

Segev, Tom (1993) *The Seventh Million: The Israelis and the Holocaust*, New York: Hill & Wang.

Sela, Avraham (1992) Transjordan, Israel and the 1948 War: Myth, Historiography and Reality, *Middle Eastern Studies* 28(4), 623–688.

Smith, Charles (2001) *Palestine and the Arab-Israeli Conflict*, 4th edition, Boston: Bedford/St. Martin's.

Smith, Tony (2000) *Foreign Attachments: The Power of Ethnic Groups in the Making of American Foreign Policy*, Cambridge, MA: Harvard University Press.

Snyder, Richard C., Henry W. Bruck, and Burton Sapin (1954) *Decision-Making as an Approach to the Study of International Politics*, Princeton: Princeton University Press.

US Department of State (1968) Foreign Relations of the United States, 1945 "Palestine," volume 8, Washington, DC: Government Printing Office.

US Department of State (1969) Foreign Relations of the United States, 1946 "Palestine," volume 7, Washington, DC: Government Printing Office.

US Department of State (1971) Foreign Relations of the United States, 1947 "Palestine," volume 5, Washington, DC: Government Printing Office.

Walker, Stephen G., Mark Schafer, and Michael D. Young (1999) Presidential Operational Codes and Foreign Policy Conflicts in the Post-Cold War World, *Journal of Conflict Resolution* 43(5), 610–625.

Weible, Christopher M., Paul A. Sabatier, and Kelly McQueen (2009) Themes and Variations: Taking Stock of the Advocacy Coalition Framework, *Policy Studies Journal* 37, 121–140.

Weible, Christopher M., Paul A. Sabatier, Hank C. Jenkins-Smith, Daniel Nohrstedt, Adam Douglas Henry, and Peter deLeon (2011) A Quarter Century of the Advocacy Coalition Framework: An Introduction to the Special Issue, *Policy Studies Journal* 39(3), 349–360.

Wilson, Evan and William Quandt (2009) *A Calculated Risk: The U.S. Decision to Recognize Israel*, Cincinnati: Clerisy Press.

Zafonte, Matthew and Paul A. Sabatier (2004) Short-Term versus Long-Term Coalitions in the Policy Process: Automotive Pollution Control, 1963–1989, *Policy Studies Journal* 32, 75–107.

5

Veto player approaches in public policy and foreign policy

Kai Oppermann and Klaus Brummer

Foreign policy has long been conceived of as the (more or less) exclusive domain of the executive branch. Power and responsibility was resting first and foremost in the hands of a country's "foreign policy executive" which comprises the head of government and key departmental ministers (Hill 2016: 62). A change in a country's foreign policy could thus be traced back primarily to alterations in the composition and/or the preferences, interests, beliefs, etc. of the members of the foreign policy executive. However, the executive branch's autonomy in foreign policy-making has been eroding for a number of reasons. They include processes of regional integration, which, especially in the European context, have led to a sharing of competencies between states as well as between states and supra-national institutions. At the same time, the leeway of the executive in foreign policy-making has also been curtailed in the domestic arena. Not least for reasons of increasing the executive's accountability and responsiveness, other institutions, most notably but not limited to the legislature, have received (additional) formal decision-making powers in the realm of foreign policy, which even extend to decision-making on the use of force, and thus arguably to the most salient domain of foreign policy of all (e.g., Peters and Wagner 2011).

In short, then, an increasing number of actors and institutions is nowadays involved in the process of foreign policy-making. Those actors and institutions are not only in a position to influence the substance and thus possibly the overall direction of foreign policy but also to block changes and adaptations in a country's external behavior. This is the opening for introducing veto player approaches, which are among the most prominent approaches in comparative public policy,[1] to the analysis of foreign policy.

---

[1] We refer to "veto player approaches" as a comprehensive term which comprises a variety of scholarship that explores the impact of veto power and veto opportunities in

This chapter argues that while veto player analyses of foreign policy will likely have to overcome particular challenges, veto player approaches do indeed hold significant promise for Foreign Policy Analysis (FPA). The remainder of this chapter proceeds as follows: the next section outlines the core tenets of veto player approaches and gives an overview of how they have been applied in public policy. Then, the transferability of such approaches to foreign policy is discussed. This is followed by an empirical illustration of veto player studies in foreign policy, pertaining to changes in Germany's policy regarding the foreign deployment of its armed forces.

Veto player approaches in public policy

The main objective of veto player approaches is to explain and predict the potential for policy change across different political systems and issue areas. The key argument is that policy stability increases and the capacity of political systems to implement policy change decreases with the number of veto players, the heterogeneity of their preferences, and the ability and incentives of veto players to employ their veto power (Tsebelis 1995: 293–301). Veto players are defined as "individual or collective actors whose agreement is necessary for a change of the status quo" (Tsebelis 2002: 19). The configuration of veto players is specific to particular policy areas and a relatively stable feature of political systems. If changes in the identity or preferences of veto players do occur, however, this is expected to facilitate policy change, in particular in policy areas with only one or a few veto players (Tsebelis 1995: 313).

The rise of veto player analyses is part and parcel of new institutionalist theorizing in Comparative Politics (Hall and Taylor 1996; see chapter 6 in this volume). Veto player approaches have in common that they understand policy change or stability as the result of the interplay between institutional incentives and constraints on one hand and actor preferences and strategies on the other. At the same time, they may lean more toward either the historical or the rational choice incarnations of the new institutionalism. As for the former, veto player analyses may focus on the historical development of veto player configurations, their path-dependency and impact on actor preferences. In contrast, scholarship starting out from a rational choice institutionalist perspective treats the preferences of veto players as exogenously given and is interested primarily in their strategic interaction under existing institutional constraints. However, the difference between these two varieties of veto player analyses is

policy-making (see Ganghof 2003: 2). While the works of George Tsebelis (1995, 2002) are arguably the most influential contributions to this scholarship, veto player approaches stand in a longer and broader research tradition.

down, first and foremost, to differences in the particular research focus and interest.

A further significant distinction in veto player approaches is that between the concepts of "veto players" and "veto points." While the former denotes agents who have and (potentially) exercise veto power, the latter refers to institutional opportunities which invest agents with veto power (Immergut 1992: 395–398). It should be noted, however, that the two concepts seem complementary to each other. In fact, veto players can only exercise veto power at particular veto points in the policy process. Whether or not they do so depends, above all, on their preferences and priorities. Veto points, in turn, require agents who choose to take advantage of the institutional opportunity to exercise veto power. They do, however, define at which stage of the policy process and in which sequence veto players are able to employ veto power and thus shape their strategies and preferences.

The greatest promise of veto player approaches arguably lies in their scope for comparative analysis. They provide a unified vocabulary and analytical framework that transcend well-known typologies of political regime types, such as the distinctions between parliamentary and presidential democracies, majoritarian and consensual forms of democracy, or democratic and authoritarian regimes (Tsebelis 2002: 67–90). Not least, this has enabled veto player analyses to uncover similarities between the capacities of different regime types for policy change as well as differences within the same regime type. This potential has already been explored in numerous empirical studies (for overviews, see Ganghof 2003; Hallerberg 2011). Methodologically, such works range from small-n qualitative studies to large-n quantitative analyses, mainly at the rational choice institutionalist end of the spectrum. Indeed, quantitative studies have come to dominate the field, especially since the publication of Tsebelis' works. Also, the majority of empirical applications of veto player arguments has focused on established parliamentary democracies of the Global North while relatively little attention has been put on non-democratic regimes or on developing countries from the Global South.

On the *qualitative* side of the divide, the classic example of a comparative case study approach remains Ellen Immergut's (1992) work on health care policy in France, Switzerland, and Sweden. She finds that a larger number of veto points empowers interest groups and makes health care reforms more difficult to implement. Correspondingly, Giuliano Bonoli's (2000) study of pension reforms in Britain, Switzerland, and France suggests that fewer veto points facilitate government plans for reform. Among the few qualitative studies which go beyond the Global North is Andrew MacIntyre's (2001) work on the policy responses to the 1997 East Asian financial crisis in Thailand, the Philippines, Malaysia, and Indonesia. His main argument is that a wide distribution of veto authority increases policy rigidity whereas centralized veto authority may encourage excessive policy volatility, both of which pose policy risks for investors.

The *quantitative* scholarship, in turn, tends to cluster around four themes. First, concerning government spending and budget deficits, studies have suggested, among other things, that an increase in the number of veto players in government (i.e., multiparty cabinets) reduces the likelihood of budgetary changes from the status quo (Franzese 2002) and results in higher deficits (Volkerink and De Haan 2001). Second, regarding the politics of taxation, the number of veto players has been said to be negatively related to the responsiveness of tax policy to external incentives and pressures (Hallerberg and Basinger 1998). Also, governments judge the scope for tax reforms in competitor countries in terms of these countries' veto player constellations (Basinger and Hallerberg 2004). Third, with respect to labor market policy, Tsebelis (1999) found that legislative outputs in this field decrease and policy stability increases when the ideological distance between veto players gets bigger. Also, Boockmann (2006) has used veto player approaches to examine the determinants for the ratification of International Labor Organization conventions in seventeen OECD countries. Finally, scholarship has explored broader institutional effects of different veto player constellations. Tsebelis (2002: 222–247) argued that veto player constellations which give rise to high policy stability also lead to relatively large policy discretion of bureaucracies and courts. Along these lines, a growing range of scholarship has developed similar arguments for the independence of central banks (see Hallerberg 2011: 36–38).

While the set-up of this wide range of works in different methodological traditions is obviously quite diverse, they still, in different shapes and forms, follow a similar tripartite analytical framework. First, veto player studies identify the relevant veto players and veto points. Second, they make inferences about the preferences of veto players and how they relate to each other. Finally, veto player analyses involve a discussion about the ability and incentives of veto players to actually use their veto power. Taken together, these three aspects make up the veto player constellation which constitutes the critical independent variable in veto player approaches to explain patterns of policy stability and change (see figure 5.1).

Specifically, the hypothesis is that the win-set for policy change decreases if the veto player constellation becomes more restrictive, i.e., if the number of veto players or veto points increases, the congruence between the preferences of veto players decreases and the better able and more willing veto players are to use their veto power. The illustrative case study engages this hypothesis in two ways. First, it zooms in on a veto player constellation in which the win-set for policy change was large. Since the case initially featured only one ex-ante veto player, changes

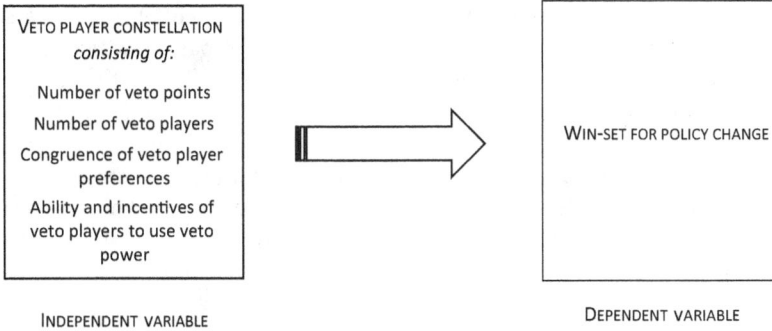

Figure 5.1 Explanatory model of veto player approaches

in the preferences of that veto player strongly predict policy change. Second, the case study involves a change in the veto player constellation. The number of veto players and veto points in the case increased which should have reduced the win-set for policy change and thus made large scale changes in foreign policy less likely.

The *first step* in operationalizing veto player constellations is to identify and count veto players and veto points. These can vary across political systems, policy areas, and time. Also, there might be political contestation about the policy process and decision-making rules and thus about the institutional opportunities to block policy proposals and the distribution of veto power. Other things equal, a larger number of veto players and points will never decrease, but usually increase policy stability.

To begin with, it is useful to distinguish between institutional and partisan veto players (Tsebelis 2002: 19–20). Institutional veto players can be read off a country's constitutional and legal framework. They are individual or collective actors, for example parliaments or presidents, who have to approve policy proposals *de jure*. In contrast, partisan veto players, for example political parties, are defined by politics, not law, and their support is required to implement policy change *de facto*. In cases in which the position of a collective institutional veto player is determined by one or more (collective) partisan veto players, the institutional veto player is substituted by the partisan veto players (Tsebelis 2000: 447). For example, if a parliament as an institutional veto player decides on a policy proposal by a simple majority and if this majority consists of a stable coalition between two parties, then the parties, not the parliament, are counted as (partisan) veto players. If the preferences of a veto player are a subset of the preferences of other veto players, that veto player is absorbed by the other veto players. Such a veto player is not being counted, because including it would not affect the degree of policy stability or change (Tsebelis 2002: 26–30).

It is important to note, moreover, that the list of potential veto players goes beyond parliaments, presidents, and political parties which were originally at the focus of Tsebelis' work. Rather, depending on the constitutional and political context the analysis might need to include a range of additional institutional or partisan veto players, for example courts, central banks, government departments, the military, or the median voter (see Tsebelis 1995: 306–308). What is critical, however, is that actors who are merely influential in policy-making, but who do not have the potential, *de jure* or *de facto*, to block policy change, are not considered as veto players.

In parallel to counting the relevant veto players, the first step in applying veto player approaches also involves identifying the veto points in policy-making. This requires an understanding of the policy process in a policy field across the three branches of government and the broader electoral arena (see Immergut 1992: 395–398). What the study of veto points contributes to the analysis, in particular, is data about how often, at which stages, and in what sequence different veto players have the opportunity to block policy change. This affects not only expectations about the potential for policy change and the degree of policy stability, but also the relative significance of different veto players and the ability of other actors to influence veto players. Closely related, the analysis needs to identify which veto player is the agenda-setter and can make policy proposals to other veto players (Tsebelis 2002: 33–37). That veto player enjoys significant first-mover advantages to shape policy outcomes according to its preferences.

Once the veto players and veto points have been spelled out, the *second step* is to specify the preferences of veto players. The larger the policy distance between veto players is and the less congruent their preferences are, the higher the level of policy stability and the smaller the win-set for policy change should be (Tsebelis 1995: 308–311). Also, the advantages of the agenda-setter are expected to become less significant, the less centrally located its preferences are relative to the preferences of other veto players (Tsebelis 2002: 34–35).

Broadly speaking, veto player analyses can be distinguished as to whether they theoretically assume or empirically measure the preferences of veto players (Ganghof 2003: 5–9). As regards the former, it is critical that the theoretical frameworks from which preferences are being derived and how these preferences are attributed are clearly spelled out. Otherwise, the risk is that preferences are "retrofitted" so that they confirm veto player arguments. As for measuring the preferences of veto players and their congruence, scholars can employ the whole array of tried and tested methodological tools and data sources in public policy, such as expert, elite, and public opinion surveys, the content analysis of speeches, party manifestos, policy documents, and media reporting, or the study of past behavior, including, for example, court rulings and legislative voting patterns. At the same time, veto player studies have to grapple with the familiar range of problems that usually befall the measurement of policy preferences (see Merkel 2003: 27–28). Chief among these problems are: the danger of circular reasoning if preferences are deduced from observed behavior; and how to distinguish between strategic adaptations of behavior and changes of underlying preferences, for example in response to external shocks or as a result of policy learning (see chapter 9 in this volume).

The *third and final step* in operationalizing the veto player constellation has to acknowledge that not all veto players, given their preferences, will be equally able and willing to block policy change all of the time. Strong veto players will be more likely to use their veto power than weak veto players (see Ganghof 2003: 19). In his original contributions, Tsebelis (1995: 311–313) had already hypothesized that policy stability will increase the more cohesive collective veto players are, i.e., the smaller the policy differences between the individual members of that veto player are. More cohesive veto players will be able to form majorities to veto a broader range of policy proposals and are thus stronger than less cohesive veto players.

However, focusing solely on the cohesion of veto players has been criticized for failing to fully grasp the variance in the likelihood that veto power will indeed be employed in a particular decision context. Most notably, veto player approaches lack a theory of action and need to be combined with assumptions about whether veto players are policy-seeking, office-seeking, or vote-seeking (Merkel 2003: 23–36). For example, it has been proposed to distinguish between co-operative and competitive veto players, depending on whether or not the analysis suggests that party political competition gives them extra strategic incentives to block policy change. While co-operative veto players do not have such incentives and are thus expected not to vote down policy proposals they prefer to the status quo, competitive veto players may have party political reasons to do so, for example in order to frustrate and undermine the government (Wagschal 1999; Zohlnhöfer 2009: 99–100). Competitive veto players should thus lead to higher policy stability than co-operative veto players. As a case in point, opposition parties can be seen as competitive veto players which might be driven to block government proposals or to demand disproportionate policy concessions because they expect to suffer political costs from supporting the government. To the contrary, coalition parties are more likely to be co-operative veto players which have a political incentive to support government proposals even if, in narrow policy terms, they prefer the status quo over the proposed change (Ganghof 2003: 19).

In addition, other things being equal, veto players should be particularly likely to veto policy proposals on issues that are highly salient to them. On low-salience issues, in contrast, they should be less prepared to spend political capital in employing their veto power and more willing to trade their support for concessions on issues they consider more salient (Oppermann 2008: 181–185). Also, veto players will likely be involved in policy-making across a range of issues and policy arenas, for example in multilevel systems, and might thus be "bought off" by strategies of issue linkage, package deals, and side payments (Merkel 2003: 28). Finally, the configuration of veto points and in particular the sequence in which veto players have to decide whether to use their veto power should also impact on their willingness to block policy change. For example, veto players which come last in that sequence, after all other veto players have already approved a policy change, might find blocking that change particularly costly.

The promise of veto player approaches in FPA

Applying veto player approaches to the analysis of foreign policy requires the same three analytical steps as in public policy. Veto players and veto points are to be identified, the foreign policy preferences of veto players have to be established, and inferences must be drawn about the ability and incentives of veto players to actually use their veto power. Still, on each of these steps certain peculiarities in studying foreign policy need to be taken into account. This section begins with discussing some such differences which might give rise to particular challenges in applying veto player approaches to foreign policy and then spells out the promise of veto player studies in FPA.

As for the first part of the veto player analytical framework, an important difference between public policy and foreign policy is that the latter relies less on formal legislative acts (bills, laws) than the former. Although legislatures often have to ratify international treaties and agreements, approve budgets for foreign policy, and vote on high-profile decisions (e.g., military interventions), a broad range of foreign policy behavior takes place without any such legislative involvement. Instead, it consists, for instance, of executive acts, diplomatic démarches, bi- and multilateral negotiations, or participation in international organizations. The implication for veto player studies, however, is not that there are no veto points or veto players in foreign policy. Rather, the challenge in FPA is that these veto points and players tend to be more ill-defined and less formal. Specifically, the balance between institutional and partisan veto players in foreign policy is likely be tilted more towards partisan veto players than in public policy, particularly in autocratic regimes.

Given the extent of executive control over foreign policy-making, moreover, veto player analyses of foreign policy should pay particular attention to veto points and players inside governments. This, in turn, links up nicely with the literature in FPA on "bureaucratic politics" (for an overview, see Jones 2010), which highlights the pursuit of organizational interests (e.g., regarding turf or budget) by governmental actors typically at the expense of other Cabinet members. Overall, the task of identifying and counting veto players and points in foreign policy will likely be less straightforward and clear-cut than it sometimes is in public policy. Literature from the field of FPA on "decision units" (Hermann 2001) could be of help for this purpose.

A similar argument can be made with respect to the second step in veto player analyses, the specification of veto player preferences. For one thing, domestic actors can be expected to have on average better defined and more clearly spelled out preferences which are easier to pin down on public policy than on foreign policy. For example, the foreign policy preferences of political parties will often be quite vague and unspecific as evidenced by comparative data on party manifestos (Volkens *et al.* 2016). Similarly, public opinion tends to form more around broad foreign policy orientations than specific foreign policy issues (Hurwitz and Peffley 1987) with the exception of issues that are highly salient in public discourse (Baum and Potter 2008). What is more, foreign policy preferences tend to sit uneasily with the traditional left–right schema for mapping the public policy positions of actors, such as political parties, in the domestic political space. Existing quantitative datasets on the left–right positioning of domestic actors, for example the Chapel Hill expert surveys, should thus be less useful for veto player studies in foreign policy than in public policy. Overall, it will likely prove more challenging to identify the precise preferences of veto players in foreign policy than in many areas of public policy.

Moving on to the third part of the analytical framework, there are arguments to suggest that veto players, other things equal, will be more reluctant to use their veto power in foreign policy than in public policy. For one thing, this is because foreign policy is for the most part less salient in the domestic arena than public policies, such as economic policy or health policy. For another, veto players have to reckon with significant political costs if they are seen to obstruct government foreign policy for narrow partisan or strategic political reasons. As the old adage that "politics stops at the water's edge" would suggest, there tends to be a premium in foreign policy on supporting governments in their pursuit of "the national interest" and a disincentive to political contestation in this field. Competitive veto players should be less common in foreign policy than in public policy. Overall, the policy discretion of the agenda-setter in foreign policy will therefore likely be larger than in public policy. It is important to note, however, that the distinction between foreign and public policy in this respect should become less relevant insofar as party political contestation around foreign policy issues increases.

Overall, the differences between applying veto player approaches in PP and in FPA must not be overdone. They point to certain shifts in emphasis and specific methodological challenges for veto player studies in foreign policy, but do not put into question the basic explanatory logic of veto player approaches or their transferability from one field to the other. To the contrary, veto player studies appear to hold great promise for FPA and fit in closely with liberal approaches in the field, in particular republican liberalism (Moravcsik 1997). The reminder of this section will flag some areas in which this promise is particularly notable.

Much for the same reasons as in public policy, veto player approaches have immense potential in reinvigorating comparative foreign policy analysis (Rosenau [1966] 2006). For example, veto player arguments have been used in quantitative large-n studies to explain levels of foreign aid provision across twenty-seven OECD countries (Wang and Jin 2013) and the propensity of 194 countries to sign up to preferential trade arrangements (Mansfield *et al.* 2007). Other notable quantitative applications include studies that have explored the relationship between veto players and the depth of regional integration agreements (Mansfield *et al.* 2008), the duration of civil wars (Cunningham 2006), the commitment of states to international human rights agreements (Lupu 2015), or the ability of developing countries to attract foreign direct investment (Choi and Samy 2008). Qualitative comparative works, in turn, have explored, for example, the quality and pace of implementing EU legislation (Haverland 2000) and domestic ratification processes of European treaties (Stoiber and Thurner 2000) across different EU member states. More specifically, Finke *et al.* (2012) have employed veto player perspectives to provide an in-depth analysis of the workings of the 2001–2003 European Convention and the negotiation and ratification of the Lisbon Treaty.

Most notably, veto player approaches provide a systematic framework that travels across different political systems and regime types and that can give guidance to theorizing the restrictiveness of domestic constraints and the weight of different domestic actors in foreign policy decision-making. This is not to deny that different regime types and political systems might set different (dis-)incentives for veto players to actually use their veto powers. Rather, it is one of the comparative promises of veto player approaches to provide a common analytical toolbox to identify and explore such differences. Along these lines, the concept of veto players has been employed, for example, to make predictions about the relative importance of domestic and international incentives in foreign policy-making (Alons 2007: 216–218). More broadly, veto player approaches can be useful in adding to the theoretical rigor of liberal second image arguments in comparative foreign policy analysis.

The same is true for research into foreign policy change. After all, the main *raison d'être* of veto player approaches in public policy precisely is to explain and predict patterns of policy stability and change. Such approaches should therefore have an obvious appeal as a ready-made theoretical framework to study drivers and obstacles to change in foreign policy as well. Specifically, a large number of veto points and "strong" veto players with a diverse range of foreign policy preferences would be expected to reduce the potential for foreign policy change and rather lead to foreign policy stability and rigidity. For example, the constellation of veto players has been shown to account for the inertia in Japan's nuclear policy, making a nuclear weapon breakout of the country highly unlikely (Hymans 2011). More generally, veto player perspectives offer themselves to complement and strengthen existing theoretical approaches to the study of foreign policy change. As a case in point, the concept of veto players might be used to formalize and operationalize one of David Welch's hypotheses according to which foreign policy change is less likely in "highly bureaucratic states with democratic regimes" (Welch 2005: 45).

Another area of research in FPA for which veto player approaches hold obvious promise are two-level game analyses of foreign policy (Putnam 1988). Specifically, incorporating veto player arguments into the two-level framework is a possible route for addressing the often-made critique that the analysis of domestic win-sets in two-level games is under-theorized. Insights from veto player approaches can also strengthen arguments in the two-level game literature about the prospects for international co-operation and the bargaining power of governments in international negotiations. Other things equal, countries should be less likely to engage in international co-operation if decision-making is more constrained by domestic veto points and veto players (see Mansfield *et al.* 2007). At the same time, such conditions should give governments greater international bargaining power. Also, veto player approaches provide a useful perspective to study domestic political contestation around the institutional ratification requirements of international agreements and to explore the strategic drivers and domestic and international effects of changes in veto player constellations in foreign policy. Specifically, this might shed new light on the rationale as well as the inherent risks of political elites using referendums and referendum promises as discretionary instruments in two-level contexts, most notably with regard to the process of European integration (Oppermann 2013).

Empirical illustration: explaining change in the foreign deployments of the German armed forces

One of the main goals of the veto player approach is to explain policy change, the scope of which is expected to depend on the veto player constellation. Some of the main expectations that follow from the theoretical discussion above are: changes in policy preferences of veto players are an important pathway to policy change; policy change occurs only if it is acceptable to all veto players (win-set for policy change); and an increase in the number of veto players should render policy change less likely. Against this background, the following empirical illustration of the veto player approach relates to a major episode of foreign policy change, pertaining to Germany's policy regarding the foreign deployment of its armed forces, the Bundeswehr. The case exhibits changes in the preferences of a key veto player in conjunction with the inexistence of other ex-ante veto players. Those values in the independent variable render the case a "most likely" case (George and Bennett 2005: 121), in the sense of strongly predicting policy change (dependent variable). The reasoning behind our case selection is that the objective of this chapter is not to confirm or disconfirm veto player approaches (whose core assumptions have been corroborated in a multitude of empirical studies) but rather to use an "easy" case to illustrate the theory's explanatory scope beyond its usual area of application. In other words, contrary to the goal that is typically associated with "most likely cases," in the sense of casting doubt on theories if they do not fit where they should be strong, our case study serves to illustrate the actual applicability of veto player approaches in the realm of foreign policy by selecting a case in which veto player arguments not only should, but in fact do hold.

Taking up Charles Hermann's "graduated levels" of foreign policy change (Hermann 1990: 5–6), Germany's foreign deployment policy has seen two changes since the end of the Cold War. In the early 1990s, "program change" occurred, which refers to alterations in the methods and means employed by a country in international affairs. In the German case, this has related to the Bundeswehr's evolution into a viable tool of statecraft in international security beyond its original core task of territorial defense. Since the mid-1990s, "adjustment change" has occurred, which refers to a country's increased efforts in international politics without, however, altering the underlying method or means of its engagement. In the German case, the country has become one of the leading contributors to NATO and EU operations, several of which included peace enforcement activities. After providing some background on the case, the analysis proceeds along the three analytical steps of the veto player approach outlined above, first with respect to the program change of the early 1990s and then, briefly, for the adjustment change since the mid-1990s.

Background

From its inception in the mid-1950s onward, the main purpose of the Bundeswehr was to contribute to the territorial defense of the West against a possible attack from the Soviet Union. The end of the Cold War ushered in first changes in this respect.[2] While remaining disengaged for the most part, the now reunited Germany contributed not only financially but also militarily to the US-led war effort against the Iraqi occupation of Kuwait (1990–1991) (Szabo 2007: 354). In the following years, the Bundeswehr participated in a number of multinational conflict management missions, ranging from Cambodia to Somalia to the Balkans, that were conducted within the frameworks of the UN, NATO, and the Western European Union (WEU).

While the Bundeswehr thus increasingly became a tool of statecraft for purposes other than territorial defense, the constitutionality of those foreign deployments "out of area" (i.e., beyond the territory of NATO member states) was contested. As laid out in greater detail below, it took a ruling by the German Federal Constitutional Court (FCC) in 1994 to put the foreign deployments of the Bundeswehr on a firm legal basis. That court ruling completed the program change.

Within the parameters established by the 1994 ruling, Germany's military engagement has evolved further in the two decades since, which qualifies as "adjustment change." Indeed, Germany has become one of the main contributors to multiple military operations conducted within the frameworks of NATO (e.g., in Afghanistan and the Kosovo), the EU (e.g., in the Democratic Republic of Congo or off the coast of Somalia), and, to a lesser extent, the UN (e.g., off the Lebanese coast or in Mali). Overall, since the early 1990s Germany has deployed a total of around 380,000 soldiers to more than forty military operations (Bundeswehr 2016), which has incurred costs of around 20 billion euro.[3] The remainder of this section uses the veto player approach to explain how such change was possible.

Veto players in the early 1990s

Prior to the 1994 FCC ruling, two collective veto players existed: the federal government and, in some sense, the FCC itself. Deployment decisions lay firmly in the hands of the government. Formal approval on part of the German parliament, the Bundestag, was not required. Hence, no ex-ante veto point existed outside the executive branch that could have prevented the implementation of policy change initiated by the government. The FCC could come in only as a possible ex-post veto player, since it cannot become active by itself but only based on complaints lodged before it. Judging on the constitutionality of government deployment decisions,

---

[2] For an overview of major changes in Germany's foreign and security after the end of the Cold War, see Brummer and Oppermann (2016).

[3] Already in 2013, the federal government put the costs of foreign deployments at 17 billion euro (Deutscher Bundestag 2013: 10).

it could have found them in violation of the Basic Law (Grundgesetz), hence requiring the government to roll back change.

Policy preferences in the early 1990s

With the government being the key decision-maker, any change in Germany's approach to the use of the Bundeswehr must be linked to changes in the preferences of governmental actors. Such change was triggered by international and domestic pressure on the government as well as the aspirations of the government itself. Regarding the former, Germany's main allies expected it to take on a more active international role in the realm of security policy. A case in point was US President George H. W. Bush's vision of a "partnership in leadership" for the two countries (Hurst 1999). Similarly, Germany's European partners, above all France, wanted the country to shoulder more responsibility, albeit firmly rooted within the then newly established EU.

Turning to the domestic dimension, German decision makers considered increasing the country's commitment to the EU as well as its military contributions to the WEU and NATO as a viable strategy to assuage concerns that were held primarily by its European allies over a return to "Machtpolitik" on part of the reunited country—even if this meant becoming engaged (like other member states) in military operations conducted by the respective organization. Conversely, continued abstention from such missions would have "isolated" Germany from its allies, as Chancellor Helmut Kohl argued (Kohl 2007: 566). Besides, German decision-makers wanted to increase the country's status on the global level. Most prominently, increasing the country's contribution to international peacekeeping operations conducted through, or at least mandated by, the UN was considered as promoting the attainment of a permanent seat in the UN Security Council (Knapp 2005: 144). Last but not least, the German government was under pressure to change its policy and become more actively involved in conflict management because the country had become directly affected by conflicts in its vicinity. This was particularly true for the wars in the Balkans (1992–1995), from where a large number of refugees fled to Germany—more than 350,000 in 1992 alone (Alscher *et al.* 2015: 16). Overall, this combination of international and domestic factors paved the way for a shift in the preferences of the German government with respect to the use of the Bundeswehr as an instrument of foreign and security policy beyond the purpose of territorial defense.

As for the FCC, it might be somewhat misleading to discuss this institution's preferences as if it were a political actor. Still, through a number of rulings the court had developed a clearly defined position concerning the role of the government in foreign affairs, which was likely to influence its stance on the issue of foreign deployments of the Bundeswehr. Essentially, the court rulings assigned considerable leeway to the government in foreign policy. Two rulings serve as illustration. In the "Kalkar decision" of 1978 (BVerfGE 49, 89), the court referred to far-reaching competencies of the federal government in the realm of foreign policy decision making. The FCC held that if parliament objects to such decisions it could make use of its budgetary powers or its control competencies, while also making clear that the Basic Law did not assign decision competencies to the parliament in foreign affairs. Similarly, in the "Pershing decision" of 1984 (BVerfGE 68, 1) the FCC defined foreign policy as a core competence of the executive, which alone was seen as having the necessary organizational and political resources to adequately respond to changing international circumstances. Again, the court referred to the Bundestag's competencies to control the government in case it objects to the government's decisions. Thus, as long as its decisions were within the bounds established by the Basic Law, the government was free to change German foreign policy.

The non-use of veto power in the early 1990s

As stated before, the only ex-ante veto player that could have stopped the government from changing course were members of the Cabinet and/ or the government bureaucracy more broadly. And indeed, there was contestation within the Cabinet over the expansion of Germany's role beyond NATO territory. Cabinet members from the liberal FDP objected to Germany's contribution to surveillance flights over Yugoslavia by NATO AWACS aircraft since they perceived this out-of-area operation over a war zone as unconstitutional. The "compromise" on which the Cabinet agreed was that FDP ministers were deliberately outvoted by ministers from the conservative CDU/CSU—which was exceptional since the Cabinet usually seeks to reach consensus—while at the same time accepting that the FDP's parliamentary group would lodge a complaint before the FCC against the decision taken by its "own" government (Bierling 2014: 35). Thus, while opposition from within the Cabinet was not sufficient to block policy change directly, it could have led to a policy reversal (in the sense of requiring the rolling back of policy change) if the FCC had sided with the position of the FDP parliamentary group.

However, the court did not share the concerns of the FDP or of a number of other plaintiffs who had also lodged complaints against the Bundeswehr's participation in several military operations out of area. Rather, the FCC ruled that article 24, para. 2 of the Basic Law empowered Germany to enter into systems of "mutual collective security," which referred to the UN, NATO, and the WEU. The judges argued that through accession to such institutions Germany did not only agree to the resulting restrictions on its sovereignty but also to take over duties resulting from membership in these institutions, which might include participation in military operations conducted by the respective organizations. With this ruling, the program change in Germany's foreign policy was not only politically but also legally settled.

Establishing a new veto player constellation

Although the FCC rejected the complaints against the government's decision to use the Bundeswehr "out of area," it nonetheless curtailed the government's future room of maneuver. Its ruling comprised elements of co-operation and competition vis-à-vis the federal government in that it both strengthened the government's autonomy and established a new veto player to place limits on autonomous governmental action. Indeed, conceiving of the Bundeswehr as a "parliamentary army" (Parlamentsarmee), the judges ruled that future deployments would require the prior constitutive approval of the Bundestag. As result, the government continues to be the only institution that can formally propose the foreign deployment of the armed forces. It is still the government that defines the specific mandates of every deployment. The Bundestag can only vote those proposals up or down but cannot introduce any changes. However, while the government controls both the "if" and the "how" of any deployment, it now requires the consent of the Bundestag for actually sending out the troops.[4]

Thus, the FCC's ruling has altered the veto player constellation by establishing the Bundestag as a new collective veto player (next to the Cabinet and the FCC), and it has also changed the number of veto points. At first glance, the Bundestag qualifies as an institutional veto player since it needs to approve the proposed mandates by the government de jure. However, in Germany's parliamentary system the position of the Bundestag is essentially determined by political parties or, more precisely, by the parliamentary groups of those parties that make up the coalition government. The Bundestag as institutional veto player is thus superseded by a partisan veto player (Tsebelis 2000: 447) or rather (since coalitions in Germany typically consist of two parties) two partisan veto players.

As far as veto points are concerned, the FCC's ruling increased the number of institutional opportunities where veto players can block policy change. More specifically, the Bundestag can prevent policy change on two occasions. First, on an informal level the Bundestag can block change when government plans for deployments are discussed

---

[4] The practical details of the interaction between the federal government and the Bundestag were laid down in the Parliamentary Participation Act of 2005.

for instance in its committees or within the parliamentary groups of the coalition (Biermann 2004). While no formal votes are taken at this stage, strong resistance on part of the coalition parties might deter the government from further pursuing certain missions. Second, the Bundestag can formally resist change when the mandate is officially introduced into parliament for the required constitutive approval. As stated above, if the parliament votes a mandate down, Germany must not deploy its armed forces abroad.

Continuing policy change since the mid-1990s

Despite the increased number of veto players and veto points, which, all else being equal, would suggest that policy change becomes less likely, Germany's deployment policy has continued to change over time. While not representing as fundamental a shift as the one that was ushered in by the 1994 FCC ruling, Germany has gradually evolved from a bystander to one of the leading nations in both NATO and EU missions, including peace enforcement operations.

Returning to the distinction between international and domestic influences on government foreign policy, German decision-makers have been under pressure by its allies to further expand its international military engagement. The extent to which expectations have continued to grow is exemplified by the International Security Assistance Force (ISAF) operation. Whereas deploying the Bundeswehr to Afghanistan would have been inconceivable in the 1990s, Germany was the third largest troop contributor to ISAF (behind the United States and the United Kingdom) but still received harsh criticism from its allies for limiting its engagement to the initially more stable region of Northern Afghanistan and to Kabul (Saideman and Auerswald 2012). Similarly, Germany's non-contribution to the US-led invasion of Iraq and the UN-mandated and NATO-led operation "Odyssey Dawn" in Libya led to severe, albeit temporary frictions with its partners (Oppermann and Brummer 2014). In addition, Germany's participation in UN-mandated military operations has continued to be one of the main assets in its ongoing bid for a permanent seat in the UN Security Council.

Taking into consideration those pressures and ambitions, the preferences of successive German governments have pointed toward a continued evolution of Germany's deployment policy.[5] Following the

---

[5] This is not to suggest that pressures and/or ambitions have been constant or identical over the years. Still, we would contend that the different coalition governments have on a general level responded similarly to those external pressures and have also pursued similar ambitions for Germany as an international actor which translated into similar policy preferences that required further adjustments in the use of the Bundeswehr.

FCC ruling, though, the Bundestag could have blocked such (adjust-ment) change. Indeed, on more than 250 occasions the Bundestag has already had to vote on mandates introduced by the government to deploy the Bundeswehr abroad. But not once has a mandate been rejected. Therefore, the coalition parties in the Bundestag can be conceived not only as partisan but also as co-operative veto players that are expected not to block policy proposals for petty partisan reasons (Wagschal 1999). All else being equal, policy is likely to change (further) with the existence of co-operative veto players.

Conclusion

This chapter's core claim is that the three analytical steps of veto player approaches—identify veto points and veto players and establish the latter's policy preferences as well as their ability and incentives to use their veto power—are also applicable to foreign policy. Indeed, veto player approaches seem particularly promising for comparative foreign policy analysis since its analytical framework travels across different pol-itical systems and regime types. At the same time, veto player analyses of foreign policy decisions might be more challenging in empirical terms, since foreign policy-making relies less on formal acts than public policy-making which, in turn, means that veto points and players tend to be more ill-defined and less formal, and thus harder to identify. Similarly, veto players' policy preferences are likely to be less clearly defined and spelled out in foreign policy than in public policy. However, rather than calling into question the basic explanatory logic of veto player approaches or their transferability, those remarks merely point to certain shifts in emphasis and highlight specific methodological challenges for veto player studies when applied in the realm of foreign policy.

In this sense, the empirical illustration used in this chapter showed that there is nothing intrinsic to veto player approaches that would preclude their application in the domain of foreign policy. To the contrary, as far as their explanatory scope is concerned, the empirical discussion suggests that veto player perspectives promise to offer a systematic framework to analyze domestic constraints and drivers of foreign policy change as well as changes in the domestic set-up of foreign policy-making. In so doing, and contrary to punctuated equilibrium theory (see chapter 3 in this volume), the veto player perspective is capable of grasping gradual changes in foreign policy without, however, necessarily requiring a long-term perspective for change to materialize like the advocacy coalition framework (see chapter 4 in this volume).

More specifically, this chapter's use of the veto player approach against an empirical case highlighted, among other things, the potentially far-reaching but largely under-studied role of (constitutional) courts in foreign policy. It also showed that an increase in the number of veto players does not necessarily lead to policy stability. At the same time, the case might have been somewhat atypical for foreign policy since deployment decisions in Germany require formal approval by parliament. Future research should thus probe into the explanatory power of veto player approaches in more typical contexts of foreign policy-making which are characterized by less formal and/or more ill-defined veto players and veto points. Also, in order to realize the full potential of veto player studies in FPA, future research should employ comparative cross-country designs which ideally cover different political systems.

Finally, it is worth noting that a closer dialogue between veto player approaches and FPA should not only benefit the comparative study of foreign policy but also stands to further veto player research in Public Policy. Three points in particular come to mind. First, the second-image reversed perspective (Gourevitch 1978) in FPA would focus attention on top-down international impacts on the structure of veto points and veto player constellations. Second, concepts and approaches in foreign policy and international politics might help broadening the perspective of veto player approaches to include international veto points and veto players, such as, for example, international regimes and organizations. Finally, the use or non-use of veto power by individual actors, above all presidents, might be the result of idiosyncratic characteristics of individual office holders. Specific characteristics of leaders, like political beliefs or leadership traits, might render them more or less prone to block (or initiate) policy change. If this line of inquiry is pursued, the veto player perspective can be linked up with analytical constructs from FPA like the operational code approach (Walker *et al.* 2005) or leadership trait analysis (Hermann 2005).

References

Alons, Gerry C. (2007) Predicting a State's Foreign Policy: State Preferences between Domestic and International Constraints, *Foreign Policy Analysis* 3(3), 211–232.

Alscher, Stefan, Johannes Obergfell, and Stefanie Ricarda Roos (2015) *Migrationsprofil Westbalkan: Ursachen, Herausforderungen und Lösungsansätze,* Working Paper 63, Nürnberg: Bundesamt für Migration und Flüchtlinge.

Basinger, Scott J. and Hallerberg, Mark (2004) Remodeling the Competition for Capital: How Domestic Politics Erases the Race to the Bottom, *American Political Science Review* 98(2), 261–276.

Baum, Matthew A. and Philip B. K. Potter (2008) The Relationships Between Mass Media, Public Opinion, and Foreign Policy: Toward a Theoretical Synthesis, *Annual Review of Political Science* 11, 39–65.

Bierling, Stephan (2014) *Vormacht wider Willen: Deutsche Außenpolitik von der Wiedervereinigung bis zur Gegenwart*, Munich: C. H. Beck.

Biermann, Rafael (2004) Der Deutsche Bundestag und die Auslandseinsätze der Bundeswehr: Zur Gratwanderung zwischen exekutiver Prärogative und legislativer Mitwirkung, *Zeitschrift für Parlamentsfragen* 35(4), 607–626.

Bonoli, Giuliano (2000) *The Politics of Pension Reform: Institutions and Policy Change in Western Europe*, Cambridge: Cambridge University Press.

Boockmann, Bernhard (2006) Partisan Politics and Treaty Ratification: The Acceptance of International Labour Organisation Conventions by Industrialised Democracies, 1960–1996, *European Journal of Political Research* 45(1), 153–180.

Brummer, Klaus and Kai Oppermann (2016) Germany's Foreign Policy after the End of the Cold War: "Becoming Normal?". Oxford Handbooks Online, April 2016. Oxford University Press. DOI: 10.1093/oxfordhb/9780199935307.013.1.

Bundeswehr (2016) Überblick: Die Armee im Einsatz, 24 February 2016. Available at www.bundeswehr.de/portal/a/bwde/!ut/p/c4/04_SB8K8xLLM9MSSzPy8x Bz9CP3I5EyrpHK9pPKUVL3UzLzixNSSqlS90tSk1KKknMzkbCSmfkG2oyI Atx6Dow!!/ (last accessed October 12, 2016).

Choi, Seung-Whan and Yiagadeesen Samy (2008) Reexamining the Effect of Democratic Institutions on Inflows of Foreign Direct Investment in Developing Countries, *Foreign Policy Analysis* 4(1), 83–103.

Cunningham, David E. (2006) Veto Players and Civil War Duration, *American Journal of Political Science* 50(4), 875–892.

Deutscher Bundestag (2013) Antwort der Bundesregierung auf die Kleine Anfrage der Abgeordneten Wolfgang Gehrcke et al. und der Fraktion DIE LINKE, Drucksache 17/14491, August 6, 2013, Berlin.

Finke, Daniel, Thomas König, Sven-Oliver Proksch, and George Tsebelis (2012) *Reforming the European Union: Realizing the Impossible*, Princeton: Princeton University Press.

Franzese, Robert J. (2002) *Macroeconomic Policies of Developed Democracies*, Cambridge: Cambridge University Press.

Ganghof, Steffen (2003) Promises and Pitfalls of Veto Player Analysis, *Swiss Political Science Review* 9(2), 1–25.

George, Alexander L. and Andrew Bennett (2005) *Case Studies and Theory Development in the Social Sciences*, Cambridge, MA and London: MIT Press.

Gourevitch, Peter A. (1978) The Second Image Reversed: The International Sources of Domestic Politics, *International Organization* 32(4), 881–912.

Hall, Peter A. and Rosemary C. R. Taylor (1996) Political Science and the Three New Institutionalisms, *Political Studies* 44(5), 936–957.

Hallerberg, Mark (2011) Empirical Applications of Veto Player Analysis and Institutional Effectiveness, in Thomas König, George Tsebelis, and Marc Debus (eds.) *Reform Processes and Policy Change: Veto Players and Decision-Making in Modern Democracies*, New York: Springer, 21–42.

Hallerberg, Mark and Scott J. Basinger (1998) Internationalization and Changes in Tax Policy in OECD Countries: The Importance of Domestic Veto Players, *Comparative Political Studies* 31(3), 321–352.

Haverland, Markus (2000) National Adaptation to European Integration: The Importance of Institutional Veto Points, *Journal of Public Policy* 20(1), 83–103.

Hermann, Charles F. (1990) Changing Course: When Governments Choose to Redirect Foreign Policy, *International Studies Quarterly* 34(1), 3–21.

Hermann, Margaret G. (2001) How Decision Units Shape Foreign Policy: A Theoretical Framework, *International Studies Review* 3(2), 47–81.

Hermann, Margaret G. (2005) Assessing Leadership Style: Trait Analysis, in Jerrold M. Post (ed.) *The Psychological Assessment of Political Leaders: With Profiles of Saddam Hussein and Bill Clinton*, Ann Arbor: University of Michigan Press, 178–212.

Hill, Christopher (2016) *Foreign Policy in the Twenty-First Century*, 2nd edition, London: Palgrave.

Hurst, Steven (1999) *The Foreign Policy of the Bush Administration: In Search of a New World Order*, London and New York: Cassell.

Hurwitz, Jon and Mark Peffley (1987) How are Foreign Policy Attitudes Structured? A Hierarchical Model, *American Political Science Review* 81(4), 1099–1120.

Hymans, Jacques E. C. (2011) Veto Players, Nuclear Energy, and Nonproliferation, *International Security* 36(2), 154–189.

Immergut, Ellen M. (1992) Institutions, Veto Points, and Policy Results: A Comparative Analysis of Health Care, *Journal of Public Policy* 10(4), 391–416.

Jones, Christopher M. (2010) Bureaucratic Politics and Organizational Process Models, in Robert A. Denemark (ed.) *The International Studies Encyclopedia*, London: Blackwell, 151–168.

Knapp, Manfred (2005) Verpflichtung auf einen globalen Multilateralismus: Zur Außenpolitik Deutschlands gegenüber den Vereinten Nationen, in Klaus Dicke and Manuel Fröhlich (eds.) *Wege multilateraler Diplomatie: Politik, Handlungsmöglichkeiten und Entscheidungsstrukturen im UN-System*, Baden-Baden: Nomos, 126–154.

Kohl, Helmut (2007) *Erinnerungen 1990–1994*, Munich: Droemer.

Lupu, Yonatan (2015) Legislative Veto Players and the Effects of International Human Rights Agreements, *American Journal of Political Science* 59(3), 578–594.

MacIntyre, Andrew (2001) Institutions and Investors: The Politics of the Economic Crisis in Southeast Asia, *International Organization* 55(1), 81–122.

Mansfield, Edward D., Helen V. Milner, and Jon C. Pevehouse (2007) Vetoing Co-Operation: The Impact of Veto Players on Preferential Trading Arrangements, *British Journal of Political Science* 37(3), 403–432.

Mansfield, Edward D., Helen V. Milner, and Jon C. Pevehouse (2008) Democracy, Veto Players and the Depth of Regional Integration, *The World Economy* 31(1), 67–96.

Merkel, Wolfgang (2003) Institutions and Reform Policy: Three Case Studies on the Veto Player Theory, Centro de Estudios Avanzados en Ciencias Sociales, Working Paper 2003/186.

Moravcsik, Andrew (1997) Taking Preferences Seriously: A Liberal Theory of International Politics, *International Organization* 51(4), 513–553.

Oppermann, Kai (2008) Salience and Sanctions: A Principal-Agent Analysis of Domestic Win-Sets in Two-Level Games. The Case of British European Policy under the Blair Government, *Cambridge Review of International Affairs* 21(2), 179–197.

Oppermann, Kai (2013) The Politics of Discretionary Government Commitments to European Integration Referendums, *Journal of European Public Policy* 20(5), 684–701.

Oppermann, Kai and Klaus Brummer (2014) Patterns of Junior Partner Influence on the Foreign Policy of Coalition Governments, *British Journal of Politics and International Relations* 16(4), 555–571.

Peters, Dirk and Wolfgang Wagner (2011) Between Military Efficiency and Democratic Legitimacy: Mapping Parliamentary War Powers in Contemporary Democracies, 1989–2004, *Parliamentary Affairs* 64(1), 175–192.

Putnam, Robert D. (1988) Diplomacy and Domestic Politics: The Logic of Two-Level Games, *International Organization* 43(3), 427–460.

Rosenau, James N. ([1966] 2006) Pre-Theories and Theories of Foreign Policy, in James N. Rosenau, *The Study of World Politics. Volume 1: Theoretical and Methodological Challenges*, London and New York: Routledge, 171–199.

Saideman, Stephen M. and David P. Auerswald (2012) Comparing Caveats: Understanding the Sources of National Restrictions upon NATO's Mission in Afghanistan, *International Studies Quarterly* 56(1), 67–84.

Stoiber, Michael and Paul W. Thurner (2000) *Der Vergleich von Ratifikationsstrukturen der EU-Mitgliedsländer für Intergouvernementale Verträge: Eine Anwendung des Veto-Spieler Konzeptes*, Mannheimer Zentrum für Europäische Sozialforschung, Arbeitspapier Nr. 27.

Szabo, Stephen F. (2007) Vereinigte Staaten von Amerika: Politische und Sicherheitsbeziehungen, in Siegmar Schmidt, Gunther Hellmann, and Reinhard Wolf (eds.) *Handbuch zur deutschen Außenpolitik*, Wiesbaden: VS Verlag, 353–366.

Tsebelis, George (1995) Decision Making in Political Systems: Veto Players in Presidentialism, Parliamentarism, Multicameralism and Multipartyism, *British Journal of Political Science* 25(3), 289–325.

Tsebelis, George (1999) Veto Players and Law Production in Parliamentary Democracies: An Empirical Analysis, *American Political Science Review* 93(3), 591–608.

Tsebelis, George (2000) Veto Players and Institutional Analysis, *Governance* 13(4), 441–474.

Tsebelis, George (2002) *Veto Players: How Political Institutions Work*, Princeton: Princeton University Press.

Volkens, Andrea, Pola Lehmann, Theres Matthieß, Nicolas Merz, and Sven Regel (2016) The Manifesto Data Collection. Manifesto Project (MRG/CMP/MARPOR). Version 2016b. Berlin: Wissenschaftszentrum Berlin für Sozialforschung (WZB).

Volkerink, Bjørn and Jakob De Haan (2001) Fragmented Government Effects on Fiscal Policy: New Evidence, *Public Choice* 109(3/4), 221–242.

Wagschal, Uwe (1999) Blockieren Vetospieler Steuerreformen? *Politische Vierteljahresschrift* 40(4), 628–640.

Walker, Stephen G., Mark Schafer, and Michael D. Young (2005) Profiling the Operational Codes of Political Leaders, in Jerrold M. Post (ed.) *The Psychological Assessment of Political Leaders: With Profiles of Saddam Hussein and Bill Clinton*, Ann Arbor: University of Michigan Press, 215–245.

Wang, Yu and Shuai Jin (2013) Veto Players and Foreign Aid Provision, *Constitutional Political Economy* 24(1), 43–56.

Welch, David A. (2005) *Painful Choices: A Theory of Foreign Policy Change*, Princeton: Princeton University Press.

Zohlnhöfer, Reimut (2009) How Politics Matter When Policies Change: Understanding Policy Change as a Political Problem, *Journal of Comparative Policy Analysis: Research and Practice* 11(1), 97–115.

Part II

Structural perspectives

6

New institutionalism and foreign policy

Siegfried Schieder

As scholars in the field of Public Policy (PP) have pointed out, the new institutionalism (NI) in its rational, sociological, historical, and discursive variants is arguably one of the main theoretical frameworks for analyzing domestic institutions (Radaelli *et al.* 2012).[1] The claim that political institutions "matter" is not only central to the identity of the discipline of political science, but has also served "as a mantra for the social sciences for almost thirty years" (Gandhi and Ruiz-Rufino 2015: 1). While it is common to use institutional factors as independent variables to explain policy variation across countries and over time, there is still an unwarranted divide between NI, applied in PP and the field of Foreign Policy Analysis (FPA). Despite this striking division, the chapter on "Foreign Policy" in the magisterial *Handbook of Political Science* published in 1975 took it for granted that foreign policy belongs within the domain of PP rather than that of International Relations (IR) (Cohen and Harris 1975). More than forty years later, few foreign policy analysts would disagree that FPA is a sub-discipline of IR (Hellmann and Jørgensen 2015; Hill 2015).

However, this is not to say that public policy approaches to foreign policy such as NI enjoy an undisputed professional domicile within FPA. While foreign policy is explored from several theoretical perspectives in leading handbooks in the field, there is a notable lack of chapters on NI and foreign policy (Neack 2014; Smith *et al.* 2016). This is also the case if we look at the most frequently cited articles on foreign policy in leading journals. They contain, for instance, research on decision-making, bureaucratic politics, the various forms of liberalism, realism,

[1] I thank the editors and Franziska Petri for their helpful and constructive comments on earlier versions of this chapter.

and constructivism, as well as research on perceptions (Hudson 2005; Kaarbo 2015). Due to its primary actor-centered research focus, however, NI is clearly located outside of FPA's paradigmatic debates. In a similar vein, the chapter on "Foreign Policy" in the *Handbook of International Relations* touches rather casually on the NI as an FPA approach (Carlsnaes 2013: 309–315). Certainly, NI in its rational and sociological variants has been a powerful source of inspiration for IR theory. But the specific contributions of NI to the field of FPA have yet to be fully explored.

This chapter aims to show how NI can contribute for FPA. The next section briefly examines the rise of NI as the most successful paradigm in public policy analysis, scrutinizing the nature of institutions and the various streams of NI. Against this background, the following section examines the added value of NI for FPA. Then, the chapter discusses how NI in its historical variant can help to explain US foreign policy toward Russian interventions in Ukraine in 2014. The concluding section provides a synthesis of the new institutionalist research agenda and considers its merits and pitfalls when applied in the realm of foreign policy.

New institutionalism in political science

The study of institutions was one of the wellsprings of political science in the early twentieth century, although this approach was largely ousted by two theoretical schools based on more individualistic assumptions, namely behaviorism and rational choice (Binder *et al.* 2006). Both of these approaches, which gained prominence in the 1950s and 1960s, assume that individuals act autonomously, based on either socio-psychological characteristics or rational expectations. At the beginning of the 1980s, "a successful counter-reformation produced some return to the previous concern with formal (and informal) institutions of the public sector and the important role these structures play" (Peters 1999: 1). It was James March and Johan Olsen who coined the term "new institutionalism" in an article in the *American Political Science Review* entitled "The New Institutionalism: Organizational Factors in Political Life" (March and Olsen 1984).

"New" institutionalism is often contrasted with "old" or "classical" institutionalism, the latter being first articulated in the pragmatist writings of Thorstein Veblen and John Dewey and rooted in law and legal institutions. Although "new" institutionalism reflects many features of older studies of institutions, there are important differences between the two. According to Peters (1999: 6–12), "old" institutionalism is characterized by legalism, structuralism, holism, historicism, and normative analysis. The latter two elements in particular were out of sync with trends after World War II as the emerging behavioral and rational choice approaches took a radically anti-normative and anti-historical stance. New institutionalists began to focus on the political meanings, symbols, and cultures that constitute the regularity and durability underpinning the political institutions and its structures. Another initiative emerging from NI was a reaction to the methodological individualism, as manifested in rational-choice approaches. Hence, NI reinstates "methodological collectivism" (or "methodological institutionalism") by explaining economic actions in light of social units such as firms, classes, nations, and so on rather than individuals' preferences and choices. Nevertheless, the basic premise shared by both "old" and "new" forms of political thinking is that "institutions matter."

What are institutions?

On the basic level, institutions are simply rules. As such, they can be understood as formal organizational arrangements as well as informal regulatory systems in which actors such as individuals, organizations, or states are embedded, thus influencing their behavior (Thelen and Steinmo 1992: 2; Hall and Taylor 1996: 936). March and Olsen (2006: 3) assert that "an institution is a relatively enduring collection of rules and organized practices, embedded in structures of meaning and resources that are relatively invariant in the face of turnover of individuals and relatively resilient to the idiosyncratic preferences and expectations of individuals and changing external circumstances."

Depending on the degree of autonomy ascribed to them, the literature features a distinction between "thin" (such as systems of rules, decision-making procedures, or treaties) and "thick" institutions such as social practices, common discourses, or routine activities (Checkel 1999). On the basis of a "thin" understanding of the institution, Keohane (1989: 3) defines international institutions as "persistent and connected sets of rules (formal and informal) that prescribe behavioral roles, constrain activity, and shape expectations." This must be distinguished from a "thick" understanding of institutions. On this view institutions impact on actors not just by providing incentives for and setting limits to rational action but also by influencing their fundamental objectives and values.

Crucial here is the distinction between regulative and constitutive institutions (Kratochwil 1989). While in the case of the narrow definition of institutions actors' interests and identities are disregarded, in such a way that norms and rules play a merely regulative role, the broad definition works on the assumption that they also exercise a constitutive influence on actors' interests and social identities. From this perspective institutions exhibit both a cognitive and action-guiding dimension (Checkel 1999: 546). The norms and rules enshrined in institutions are based on ideas that have become entrenched within them. In this way institutions link the individual with society by laying down roles, defining functions, and providing collective stocks of knowledge, thus creating a framework within which political actions become meaningful and legitimate.

The varieties of new institutionalism

In a seminal article Hall and Taylor (1996) have distinguished between rational, historical and sociological institutionalism. Recently, Schmidt (2008, 2011) has proposed that a fourth variant, namely discursive institutionalism (or "constructivist institutionalism," see Hay 2006), provides theoretical leverage and can usefully supplement the three other strands. While this list could be expanded, for the endeavor to introduce NI to FPA, I join leading scholars in the field of PP such as Radaelli *et al.* (2012) and focus on rational, sociological, historical, and discursive institutionalism. Because the new institutionalist approaches are well known, I provide only brief sketches. I concentrate on the historical variant because this type of institutionalism is empirically illustrated in the final section on foreign policy.

Rational choice institutionalism (RI) is one of the most influential theoretical approaches in PP. RI not only triggered the claim that "we are all institutionalists now" (Pierson and Skocpol 2002: 706) in the 1990s, but also serves as a reference point for the three other institutionalisms. Although RI features some variation in outlook, it has four key characteristics (Hall and Taylor 1996: 944). First, rational choice institutionalists think of political institutions as a system of regularized behavior that reflects Pareto-optimal equilibria (Hall 2010: 204). They assume that the relevant actors have a set of fixed preferences and pursue their interests through rational calculations. This is what March and Olsen (1989: 14) refer to as the "logic of consequentiality." Second, rational institutionalists see politics as a series of collective action dilemmas. When actors try to maximize the attainment of their own preferences, this is likely to produce an outcome that is collectively sub-optimal. Institutions may help to overcome such collective action dilemmas. Third, RI emphasizes the role of strategic interaction in determining political outcomes. A given actor's behavior is not driven by impersonal historical forces but by a strategic calculus. Institutions help to structure such interactions by affecting the range of alternatives available. On the basis of this individualistic logic, fourth and finally, rational institutionalists typically assume that institutions are stable. Accordingly, institutional change happens only "when shocks exogenous to the system of institutions alter the context" (Hall 2010: 205).

In contrast to RI, *sociological institutionalism* (SI) emphasizes the structural dimension and is committed to a methodological holism

(Finnemore 1996b: 333). Three features of SI render it relatively distinct from the other variants of NI. First, SI defines institutions broadly to include "not just formal rules, procedures or norms, but the symbol systems, cognitive scripts, and moral templates that provide the 'frames of meaning' guiding human action" (Hall and Taylor 1996: 947). Such a broad definition of institutions breaks down the conceptual divide between "institutions" and "culture." Second, political institutions influence behavior not simply by specifying what one should do but also by specifying what one can imagine oneself doing in a given context. Finally, SI also takes a distinctive approach to the problem of explaining how institutional practices originate and change. Scholars of SI argue that "organizations often adopt a new institutional practice, not because it advances the means-ends efficiency of the organization but because it enhances the social legitimacy of the organization or its participants" (Hall and Taylor 1996: 949). In other words, actors are guided by the "logic of social appropriateness" (March and Olsen 1989: 160).

Within NI, the interplay between actors and institutions has long been regarded as either determined by actors (RI) or institutional structures (SI). Scholars of *historical institutionalism* (HI) who take temporality seriously assume a mediating position between RI and SI (Hall and Taylor 1996: 938; Steinmo 2008: 113). According to Pierson (1996: 126), HI is *"historical* because it recognizes that political development must be understood as a process that unfolds over time. It is *institutionalist* because it stresses that many of the contemporary implications of these temporary processes are embedded in institutions—whether these be formal rules, policy structures, or norms."

HI scholars have developed powerful tools for the study of politics (see Fioretos *et al.* 2016). The core concept of HI is "path dependency." A path begins at a point in time at which two alternative paths may be taken but just one is selected (Pierson 2000: 258). More precisely, path dependence means a three-stage process "that is triggered by a critical event leading to a critical juncture; is governed by a regime of positive, self-reinforcing feedback constituting a specific pattern of social practices, which gains more and more predominance against alternatives; and leads, at least potentially, in an organizational lock-in, understood as a corridor of limited scope of action that is strategically inefficient" (Sydow *et al.* 2009: 696).

As table 6.1 shows, the first stage of path dependency is characterized by a broad scope for action. Non-predictability (indeterminacy of outcome) and non-ergodicity (multiple equilibria) pertain before a process becomes path dependent. According to Sydow *et al.* (2009: 691), only major events create context-dependent decision-making windows that can trigger a "critical juncture." "Critical juncture" marks a point in time "at which an institution or practice was contingent or open to alternative

Table 6.1 Path dependency as three-stage process

	Stage I	Stage II	Stage III
Scope/range of action Path dependency	t_1 Open situation with no scope for action	t_2 Narrowing scope of action	t_3 Dominant decision pattern of action
	→	→	
	"Critical juncture" as the transition to stage II	"Lock-in" as the transition to stage III	
	Indeterminacy and multiple equilibria	Emergence of a path but still contingent	Reactive sequences and bound to a path

Source: Sydow *et al.* (2009), own compilation.

paths, and actors or exogenous events determined which path it would take" (Bennett and Checkel 2015: 16; Capoccia and Kelemen 2007). Therefore, a "critical juncture" indicates the transition from stage I to stage II. The second stage is characterized by a narrowing of the scope of action, which renders the path dependency process more and more irreversible. Although a process of self-reinforcing takes place, the path is still contingent (Sydow *et al.* 2009: 691). At the third stage, HI focuses on further constriction and the idea of "reactive sequences" as an event chain in which events following a trigger are a reaction to prior events. It is the transition from stage II to stage III "which eventually leads the whole setting into a lock-in" (Sydow *et al.* 2009: 694).

HI seems to be agnostic on the issue of the dominant mode of social action (see table 6.2). From a rationalist perspective, the path chosen is then self-reinforced and leads to a "lock-in" by a variety of forms of feedback such as "increasing returns," that is, a situation which makes the adoption of alternatives less attractive because the costs of reversal are very high (Pierson 2000). Whereas the rational model of path dependency is associated with the "logic of consequentiality," the normative path dependency is linked to the "logic of appropriateness." In contrast to the rational model of path dependence, normative paths emphasize normative "lock-in" effects. Consequently, "legitimation constitutes the primary mechanism of path reproduction rather than materialist 'increasing returns'" (Sarigil 2015: 226).

In addition to the three varieties of NI discussed above, *discursive institutionalism* (DI) defines institutions in light of the discourses prevailing within them (Schmidt 2008). According to the "logic of communication", ideas are the currency for discursive political processes and they can be categorized into two types: cognitive and normative. While

Table 6.2 Two models of path dependency

Model	Logic of social action	Mechanism of path reproduction
I. Rational	Consequentiality	Increasing returns (utilitarian "lock-in")
II. Normative	Appropriateness	Legitimation (normative "lock-in")

Source: Sarigil (2015), own compilation.

Table 6.3 Four new institutionalisms

	RI	SI	HI	DI
Object of explanation	Rational behavior and interest	Cultural norms and frames	Historical rules and regularities	Ideas and discourse
Logic of explanation	Calculation	Appro-priateness	Path-dependency	Communication
Problems of explanation	Economic deter-minism	Cultural deter-minism	Historical determinism	Ideational determinism
Ability to explain change	Static: continuity through fixed preferences	Static: continuity through cultural norms	Static: continuity through path-dependency	Dynamic: continuity/change through ideas and discourse

Source: Schmidt (2011) and Fioretos et al. (2016), own compilation.

cognitive discourses revolve around solutions to problems and scientifically grounded arguments, normative discourses appeal to norms and values in an attempt to trigger responses within society (Schmidt 2008: 314). This distinguishes DI from HI, which understands change merely as the outcome of exogenous crises or shocks. While Schmidt (2011: 51) puts forward solid arguments for classifying DI as "a distinctive approach that contributes to our understanding of political action in ways that rational choice, historical, and sociological Institutionalism cannot," other have questioned the distinctiveness of DI (see Bell 2011). Table 6.3 summarizes the central features of all four variants of NI.

The promise of new institutionalism for FPA

Due to its primary agent-based and psychologically oriented research focus (Kaarbo 2015), FPA appears at first sight less capable of linking NI to foreign policy. The only exception seems to be the field of European foreign policy, which has its own institutionalist tradition (Jørgensen *et al.* 2015). This section begins by discussing the development of NI in FPA. In the second part I consider the promise and pitfalls of applying NI to the realm of foreign policy.

Frontrunners and latecomers in the linkage of FPA and NI

Similar to the field of IR, in which institutionalist research has largely taken place under the aegis of both RI and SI, reflecting the rationalist-constructivist "divide" in the field (Rixen and Viola 2016: 6), the neo-liberal institutionalist perspective also offers an alternative account to FPA. The distinctiveness is that "neoliberal institutionalists view foreign policy-making as a process of constrained choice by purposive states" (Carlsnaes 2013: 309). Constraints are not primarily seen in terms of the configurations of power capabilities, but with reference to the provision of information and common rules in the form of international institutions.

FPA studies that have proceeded from this rational institutionalist perspective include a broad range of literature, all of which are essentially motivated to examine continuity and change in foreign policy (see Medick-Krakau 1999; Neack 2014). While the literature on foreign economic policy have adapted well to NI, the literature on foreign security policy has largely ignored the influence of political institutions (Ripsman 2005: 302). The most popular institutional theory in the field of security studies is the "democratic peace theory" (Bueno de Mesquita *et al.* 1999). A fertile approach within RI uses a principal-agent (PA) approach to analyze foreign policy. Inspired by RI, the PA approach has been widely used to study Congress's role in US foreign policy-making (see Lindsay 1994; Hawkins *et al.* 2006). Other scholars have discussed how a PA approach can shed light on the choice between multilateral and bilateral aid (Milner and Tingley 2013). More recently, the PA approach has also begun to flourish in EU foreign policy studies (see Delreux 2015).

Foreign policy theory from an SI perspective draws upon two research traditions (see Boekle *et al.* 2001: 115–123). On the one hand, SI emphasizes the importance of social norms as independent variables, which are shared within domestic society, to foreign policy. Representative studies include studies on the influence of the value-based expectations of behaviour shared by experts with respect to certain issues, while other scholars ascribe norms to the whole society. On the other hand, scholars emphasize the influence of norms that are shared by international institutions (Finnemore 1996a). Recent examples are studies of how the participation of China's foreign policy elites in international security institutions has socialized the country to accept practices and norms not congruent with their former foreign and security policy (Johnston 2008).

A SI centered research focus in FPA is often intertwined with the notion of identity to highlight the socially constructed nature of the state and its interests (Stark Urrestarazu 2015). The affinity with constructivist views in the study of IR is obvious (Risse 2000: 6). Representative studies are those on ideas and foreign policy (Goldstein and Keohane 1993) or on the culture of national security (Katzenstein 1996). Other seminal works include studies on the construction of national interests in US foreign policy (Nau 2002), on Russian and Soviet foreign policy (Hopf 2002), and on the comparison of "cultures of antimilitarism" in Japan and Germany (Berger 1998). Sociological (or normative) institutionalists also seek to explain the variation in the extent to which EU member-states co-operate on foreign policy matters (Thomas 2011; Delreux 2015). EU member-states are perceived as socialized actors whose EU foreign policy-making behavior is shaped by norms and rules operating at the EU level.

In contrast to RI and SI, both HI and DI are latecomers in the linkage of FPA and NI. As Mabee (2011: 28) has stated, much of the work in FPA has been "in the form of either rational choice institutionalism or in the form of more constructivist-oriented work that sees institutions as shared sets of identities (or rules) that govern social relations. Work by those using historical institutionalist forms of analysis has been much less prevalent in FPA." Major exceptions in FPA are Ikenberry (2001), Dannreuther (2010), and Mabee (2011). Ikenberry (2001) showed how rare historical junctures such as 1815, 1919, or 1945 gave powerful states extraordinary opportunities to shape world politics, whereas Dannreuther (2010) used concepts such as critical junctures, path dependence, and positive feedback to analyse the policy adopted by the United States, the Soviet Union, and the EU toward the Middle East Peace Process. Mabee (2011) has examined the evolution and path dependency of the National Security Council in the United States as a result of exogenous shocks such as World War II. Scholars examining EU foreign policy and external relations have employed HI more self-consciously (Delreux 2015: 158–162). The same is true with regard to DI. But apart from individual studies (Diez 1999; Carta and Morin 2014), a proper DI approach in FPA has only been developed recently (see Schmidt 2016).

Theorizing foreign policy via NI: promise and pitfalls

NI furnishes us with valuable insights into a number of central problems in FPA. However, we should not sweepingly import NI into the field of FPA (see Rixen and Viola 2016: 4–5). Not every institutionalist concept is transferable to FPA in the same way and some variants of NI are better suited to addressing foreign policy issues than others.

One major theoretical problem with new institutionalist approaches in FPA lies in the fact that only RI and SI include a proper theory of social action. Whereas both RI and SI are built on a rationalist and sociological theory of action, HI has largely been developed inductively from empirical observation. DI, meanwhile, is essentially an "umbrella concept" that combines insights from a vast range of approaches to the study of ideas, discourses, and institutions. Since no social theory that fails to include a theory of action can stand alone (Zürn 2016: 222), neither HI nor DI can be perceived as an independent institutionalist theory of foreign policy. It seems more plausible to regard HI (and perhaps DI as well) as a useful theoretical framework for analyzing foreign policies. As I will illustrate in the next section, especially HI offers pertinent tools for studying temporal processes and institutional dynamics in foreign policy.

NI can also enrich FPA in a broader empirical sense. As Haney (1995: 111) stated, NI can be especially useful to foreign policy analysts because "it focuses on both the formal and informal structures used in decision-making." While domestic policies are highly institutionalist, much of what constitutes foreign policy is far less institutionalized. Foreign policy issues are often decided by power rather than laws and courts. But this does not mean that institutions are not important and that NI can therefore contribute nothing to FPA. What it means is that institutions tend to be less formal and hierarchical than their counterparts in the domestic realm. The premise of "weaker" institutions in the realm of foreign policy (i.e., diplomacy, defense, and development co-operation) might explain to some extent why the different variants of NI face challenges when it comes to the study of foreign policy.

For a long time foreign policy was mainly focused on security issues and economic relations. Today, it has to deal with a much broader range of issues, while a growing number of bilateral and multilateral agreements and international institutions have risen to prominence. The external environment of foreign policy has thus reached a level of "thickness" that makes it plausible to approach it through the prism of NI. However, not all the concepts generated by NI can be applied to FPA in the same way. For example, RI thinks of foreign policy as a process of decision-making in which actors pursue their interests through rational calculations, and emphasizes the role of strategic interaction in conducting relations with other countries. RI scholars focus on the effect of formal institutional structures, such as agenda-setting and voting rules, and on policy-making processes and their outcomes. The premise of a "thin" understanding of institutions is one reason why RI has been widely applied to research on foreign policy.

A "thick" understanding of institutions might limit the application of SI to FPA. Institutions at the domestic and foreign policy level do not have the commonality (the extent to which a norm is widely shared by actors) and specificity (how precisely the norm defines permissible or inadmissible behavior) to be ascribed the causal force of norms, a core claim of SI. International norms are seldom unambiguous or undisputed. Norms in the foreign policy domain can be garnered from international law, the legal acts of international organizations, and the final acts of international conferences, which are thus weaker than domestic norms derived from the constitutional and legal order of a given society. Given the more limited validity of international norms, security and defense policy might represent a special case for SI. However, under certain circumstances the domestic and international norms produce a convergent expectation about appropriate behavior in foreign policy, like Germany's decision to keep its armed forces integrated into NATO's military structure after the end of the Cold War (Boekle *et al.* 2001).

A similar argument can be made about path dependency, which depends upon certain "stickiness." HI's original object of study was the welfare state and many would argue that foreign policy is about as far away from the politics of the welfare state as it is possible to get (Zürn 2016: 203). In fact, while foreign policy as a practice might be more weakly institutionalized in terms of enforcement capacities, its path dependence and "lock-in" effects should not be underestimated, especially when legislatures have to ratify international treaties or agreements or vote on participation in military interventions (Keohane *et al.* 2009). Nevertheless, to leave a given policy path (either because of decision-makers' expectations of utility or because the norms that constitute the path have become inappropriate) is easier in the realm of foreign policy than in public policy: the latter typically proceeds through laws, whereas a broad range of foreign policy behavior takes place without any such legislative involvement, instead consisting of executive orders, negotiations, or government responses to international crises.

While public policy and foreign policy vary in their degree of institutionalization, all four strands of NI deal with institutional stability and change—concepts that are also at the core of FPA (Hill 2015). From the perspective of RI, foreign policy change occurs only when exogenous shocks or international crises alter the specific context or situation. SI also faces problems when confronted with institutional change because it tends to regard institutions as relatively inert, that is, they resist efforts to change foreign policy. HI has also grappled with the problem of change in foreign policy, but traditionally it has stressed continuity over change. In contrast, DI offers plausible explanations of institutional change featuring interpretive agents operating in relatively fluid ideational and discursive foreign policy contexts. More recent contributions by NI scholars reject a simple dichotomy between stability and change (Mahoney and Thelen 2010). This is particularly the case with HI, which emphasizes the dynamics of institutional development and path dependency (Pierson

2015). The concern with when and how historical processes shape institutional outcomes is akin to FPA: it gives us tools of temporal analysis that enable us to assess the legacies of founding moments in foreign policy, the consequences of new foreign policy ideas, and the unintended consequences of foreign policy decisions.

Yet, attempts to bridge the gap between NI and FPA entail certain pitfalls. These are familiar from the field of PP in which NI is normally at home (Radaelli *et al.* 2012: 539–541). First, because institutional characteristics of an economic, historical, cultural, and ideational kind are believed to determine foreign policy outcomes, all four variants of NI tend toward "institutional determinism." Because foreign policy-making takes place in a highly contested political arena and is surrounded by institutional dynamics that unfold uniquely for every policy area over time, fixed institutional characteristics cannot provide convincing explanations of policy decisions and non-decisions. Even HI, which focuses on the temporal dimension and unintended consequences, might be an inadequate means of explaining foreign policy, which is often ill-structured and evolves in a non-linear manner.

Second, NI is subdivided into a number of variants corresponding to different understandings of what an institution is. Radaelli *et al.* (2012: 540) call this pitfall "drop in the box." The problem does not lie in using typologies, but in the assumptions made about institutional variables and policy outcomes. Radaelli *et al.* (2012: 541) remind us that "ideal types" in the Weberian sense "are useful for classification, but do not provide causal explanations of policy outcomes." As discussed above, the majority of FPA literature looks at one variant of NI. Only a few studies have explicitly explored the potential for combining insights from the different variants of NI as a promising way of enriching future research in FPA (see, for example, Ikenberry 2001).

"Theoretical conjecture" that fails to identify a foundational mechanism is the third pitfall. The insight that "institutions matter" does not qualify as theory if all we get is institutional variation associated with policy variation. More often than not, new institutionalist studies "lack the mechanisms through which the institutional setting explains policy outcomes" (Radaelli *et al.* 2012: 543). To put it in "FPA" terms, the use of NI can only cross-fertilize the analysis of foreign policy if NI carefully clarifies the causal or constitutive chain linking institution-level variables and foreign policy outcomes, necessarily passing through the behavior of policy actors. This pitfall might originate in the argument put forward by NI scholars that the structure of a state's political institutions shapes the decision-making context faced by policy-makers. Furthermore, theoretical arguments about institutions are often used in studies of foreign policy to situate it at the level of the country, instead of looking at policy-level variables which may better explain foreign policy. This means that institutionalist analysis leads us to track down the wrong independent variables.

The path to US sanctions on Russia: a historical institutionalist perspective

Explaining US foreign policy on Russia's 2014 invasion of Ukraine in light of HI deserves special attention for both empirical and theoretical reasons. Empirically, Russia's annexation of Crimea and the following expansion of the conflict to the Eastern Ukraine caused the biggest crisis in the relations between Russia and the West since the end of the Cold War. Dealing with the Ukraine crisis is also theoretically puzzling, particularly when it comes to the sanctions that the United States imposed on Russia. As FPA scholars have argued, US foreign policy toward Russia in response to the Ukraine crisis can neither be fully explained by realism nor by liberal approaches, the main traditional FPA approaches (see Böller and Werle 2016).

Against this backdrop, new institutionalist approaches might be better suited to explaining US foreign policy toward Russian interventions in Ukraine. From an RI perspective, "the basic paradox at the heart of the sanctions debate is that policy-makers continue to use sanctions with increasing frequency, while scholars continue to deny the utility of such tools of foreign policy" (Baldwin 2000: 81). Indeed, the West's more severe restrictions have failed to force Russia to withdraw from Crimea and end its financial and military support for pro-Russian separatists in the eastern part of Ukraine (Ashford 2016: 116). SI would hypothesize that sanctions are appropriate even if they are unsuccessful. However, SI fails to explain why the Obama administration not only blamed and sanctioned Russia for violating the sovereignty and territorial integrity of Ukraine but sought to step up NATO's defensive posture and relied on coercive instruments.

In assessing the explanatory power of NI, I hold that HI provides the best explanation of the assertive US foreign policy response to Russia over the Ukraine crisis. HI's strengths lie in its "mid-range causal tools concerning context, embeddedness, and temporality" (Nexon 2012: 2). A further reason why I use HI here is that a historical institutionalist framework can be based on both rational and normative accounts of social action (Hall 2010). Drawing on the theoretical insights outlined above, this section hypothesizes a three-stage process of path dependence in the US sanctions policy toward Russia, starting with critical events, which themselves transform into a self-reinforcing process that leads to a critical juncture, and triggers a "lock-in." To illustrate the added value of HI to FPA, I will adopt the notion of the "normative path" as a distinct model of path dependency.

The first stage: toward path dependency in the Ukraine crisis

More than any other bilateral relationship, US–Russian relations are dependent on structural factors, which also affect the path of US responses to the Russian invasion of Ukraine in 2014 (Rudolf 2016: 9–12). First, the unique US–Russian relationship is bound up with mutually assured destruction, the consequence of which is permanent nuclear rivalry. Second, economic interdependence between the United States and Russia is far less significant than other bilateral relations, and the sanctions imposed on Russia further restrict economic co-operation and exchanges with the country. Third and finally, since the post-Soviet space is among the most challenging problems for US foreign policy, US–Russian relations are characterized by geopolitical competition.

These three elements of structural path dependency with respect to a former enemy are also reflected in the domestic politics of Washington's Russia policy (Stent 2014). In the quarter century since the implosion of the former Soviet Union, interaction between the United States and the Russian Federation has followed a familiar cycle, namely "presidents enter office believing that relations are adrift, so they seek to renew ties and enhance cooperation. But over time tensions rise, engagement ebbs, and critics declare that the initial approach was naïve" (Chollet 2016: 161). Neither President Bill Clinton nor President George W. Bush was able to escape this cycle; Obama's experience followed the same rhythm.

Against this backdrop, the Obama administration made no secret of its frustration with Russia (Chollet 2016: 64–66). When it comes to the Ukraine crisis, even after the first Executive Order 13660 on March 6, 2014, it was by no means obvious that Washington would implement an economic sanctions regime in response to Russian aggression toward Ukraine. In the wake of the violent protests in Kiev's Maidan Square, the US government initially imposed travel restrictions on members of the former Yanukovych government. Even in reaction to the occupation of Crimea by Russian soldiers without military insignia in mid-February 2014, Washington merely implemented diplomatic measures, cancelling meetings with Russian leaders under the auspices of the US–Russia Bilateral Presidential Commission. It was only in the wake of the Russian's annexation of Crimea at the end of the first stage that a path dependency was created, which entails a narrowing of possible outcomes.

The transition to the second stage: Russia's annexation of Crimea as a "critical juncture"

Russia's invasion of Ukraine, the illicit referendum in Crimea on March 16 and the subsequent incorporation of Crimea by the Russian Federation on March 18, 2014 were disrupting ties between Moscow and Washington. The overwhelming majority vote by Crimea in favor of accession to Russia has not only brought the Ukrainian crisis to a "critical juncture," it also indicates the beginning of a self-reinforcing process at the second stage of path dependency.

That a path was evolving becomes apparent if we consider Obama's strategic approach to the Ukraine crisis (Chollet 2016: 164–171). In light of the "national emergency" declared in the first Executive Order, the Obama administration announced on March 17 following the illicit referendum in Crimea and on March 20 following the formal annexation of Crimea two more Executive Orders (13661 and 13662), which gradually expanded the range of targets of the US sanctions regime (US Department of the Treasury 2016). At the same time, however, President Obama wanted to avoid confrontation with Russia since Washington has no "vital interests" in Ukraine (Obama 2016). This might be one reason why the Obama administration opted to impose targeted sanctions instead of opting for a strategy of deterrence. Although the Obama administration supported the government in Kiev both politically and economically, it held off supplying lethal defensive weapons as demanded by Ukraine's interim government and unanimously approved by the US Congress to stop Russian aggression (Rudolf 2016: 19).

From a historical institutionalist perspective it is important to note that the United States imposed far-reaching sanctions on Russia in close coordination with the EU: "coordination effects" are considered an important self-reinforcing mechanism that contributes to the development of path dependence. Normative paths are linked to the norm-based logic of appropriateness, which means that the US sanctions imposed on Russia are primarily guided by rules and norms rather than by material interests or expectations. To justify the imposition of sanctions, Obama framed Russia's action in the Ukraine as a violation of core international norms, especially the non-use of force and the principle of territorial integrity, which is embodied in Article 2(4) of the UN Charter. At the same time, Russia was portrayed as an outcast within the international community. As a signatory to the 1994 Budapest Memorandum, the United States was unequivocally committed to Ukrainian territorial integrity (Böller and Werle 2016: 330).

Due to the low costs of the sanctions regime imposed on Russia—the US–Russian economic relations are hardly important enough to produce negative externalities for the US economy—Washington accepted new sanctions as an appropriate and legitimate reaction to Moscow's violations in the Ukraine crisis, especially in light of Russian backing for armed separatists in Eastern Ukraine. What is more, the normative path of the US sanctions policy with respect to Russia has developed increasing path inefficiency. As long as the sanctions regime was limited, the ambivalent target of early choices might be reconciled. But in a continuous self-reinforcing process, in which sanctions were increasingly institutionalized and internalized in response to Russian misbehavior, the target of early choices of sanctions is becoming more in conflict. This conflict became apparent with the downing of the Malaysia Airlines flight MH-17 over Eastern Ukraine in July 17, 2014 which triggered a "lock-in" effect on US foreign policy toward Russia.

The transition to the third stage: the downing of MH-17 as a normative "lock-in"

Prior to the downing of MH-17 over Ukraine, both the United States and the EU were lagging in their imposition of sanctions in the form of trade and financial restrictions on Russia. But the downing of MH-17 by a missile launched from the separatist-controlled territory, killing 298 passengers and crew, resulted in the transition to the third stage and led to a normative "lock-in" in that it raised expectations about tougher sanctions. On July 29, 2014, President Obama initiated economic sanctions targeting powerful interests in Russia's financial, energy, and military dual-use export sectors. Given the new circumstances, the president's decision received bipartisan support in the US Congress, which has been a strong advocate of assisting Ukraine and supporter of sanctions on Russia (Ashford 2016: 114). If the downing of MH-17 had been a singular event, it probably would not have been sufficient to provoke the extension of sectoral economic sanctions on Russia. But in fact such sanctions were extended in a joint effort with the EU, which made their bite far more painful.

The timing and sequencing of events played a key role in a policy process that had become path dependent and created a "lock-in" effect. As President Obama (2014) stated, "if Russia continues on its current path, the cost on Russia will continue to grow." However, the "lock-in" effect rendered sanctions potentially inefficient because Putin's Russia was very unlikely to change any time soon. The United States therefore needed an approach that would endure. In addition to punishing and sanctioning Russia and condemning pro-Russian forces in Ukraine for violating the ceasefire agreed in Minsk 2015, Obama devised a strategy to reassure the United States' European partners, chiefly through military power (Chollet 2016: 166–167). At the summit in Wales in September 2014, NATO agreed a "Readiness Action Plan" to strengthen the defense of its members against a resurgent Russia and pledged to reverse the decline in military spending. Two years later, Obama announced at the NATO summit in Warsaw the deployment of 1,000 more US troops in Poland to bolster NATO's eastern flank. The US government also called on the US Congress to support a "European Reassurance Initiative" of up to $1 billion. In 2016, the Pentagon put Russia at the top of its list of national security threats and decided to quadruple military spending in Europe from $789 million to $3.4 billion (Chollet 2016: 168).

Given the past sequence of events and decisions, the US government is likely to deliberately leave the path of sanctions against Russia over Ukraine crisis only due to an exogenous shock or Russia's willingness to implement the Minsk agreement. Much like rational paths, a normative path is "sticky" and hypothesizes stability over change because norms tend to reinforce the status quo (Sarigil 2015: 233). While President Donald Trump has already said he would consider eliminating some sanctions, several members of the US Congress reminded President Trump that there is bipartisan support for blocking such a move and threaten to work with colleagues to codify sanctions against Russia into law (*Washington Post* 2017). To be sure, the Trump administration could remove the sanction regime because they were initiated by Obama's Executive Orders. Given Trump's emphasis on striking a "great deal" for the United States with Russia, it is unlikely the Trump administration could simply lift all sanctions without securing something in return from Moscow.

Conclusion

This chapter has argued that NI can contribute much to the analysis of foreign policy. While not all four NIs can stand alone in the institutionalist camp because HI and DI lack a proper theory of action, NI provides FPA with a set of conceptual mechanisms and tools for understanding and explaining foreign policy. As evident in the discussion of the potential to apply NI in general and HI in particular to foreign policy, FPA can learn from NI's focus on dynamic processes and sources of change.

Indeed, the preceding analysis of the US foreign policy reaction to Russia's incursion into Ukraine in 2014 suggests that HI promises to provide systematic tools for the temporal analysis of foreign policy. My intention here is not to imply that HI provides the best theory for FPA, but to demonstrate that HI is helpful as it highlights the importance of path dependency, critical junctures, and "lock-in" effects. We have seen evidence of the normative logic of path dependency: the more assertive US response to Russia's 2014 intervention in Ukraine was influenced by the power and widely shared character of international norms, which Moscow had violated. Since legitimation constitutes the primary mechanism of path reproduction, the United States and EU have agreed to gradually impose and maintain sanctions against Russia as a normative appropriate reaction to Moscow's infringements with respect to Ukraine.

However, NI as an approach to the study of foreign policy entails certain pitfalls. We found that NI's understanding of foreign policy is hindered by pitfalls concerning a lack of mechanisms or scope conditions through which the institutional setting explains foreign policy outcomes, a prevailing institutional determinism and the tendency to operate via typologies dividing NI into a number of separate understandings of what an institution is. Having said that, in the wake of the "institutionalist turn" political science has shifted away from the study of power. This might be the reason why new institutionalist scholars have recently argued for bringing the power back into politics. For example, Pierson (2015: 133) pursues the idea that the distribution of power itself may be path-dependent. Thinking about power relationships as path-dependent is not a new idea. Nevertheless, systematic arguments about power dynamics hold much promise, especially if we apply them to the realm of foreign policy, in which the degree of institutionalization is lower and power is still of prime importance.

References

Ashford, Emma (2016) Not-So-Smart Sanctions: The Failure of Western Restrictions against Russia, *Foreign Affairs* 95(1), 114–123.

Baldwin, David A. (2000) The Sanctions Debate and the Logic of Choice, *International Security* 24(3), 80–107.

Bell, Stephen (2011) Do We Really Need a New "Constructivist Institutionalism"?, *British Journal of Political Science* 41(4), 883–906.

Bennett, Andrew and Jeffrey T. Checkel (2015) Process Tracing: From Philosophical Roots to Best Practices, in Andrew Bennett and Jeffrey T. Checkel (eds.) *Process Tracing: From Metaphor to Analytic Tool*, Cambridge: Cambridge University Press, 3–38.

Berger, Thomas U. (1998) *Cultures of Antimilitarism: National Security in Germany and Japan*, Baltimore: Johns Hopkins University Press.

Binder, Sarah, R. A. W. Rhodes, and Bert A. Rockman (eds.) (2006) *The Oxford Handbook of Political Institutions*, New York: Oxford University Press.

Boekle, Henning, Volker Rittberger, and Wolfgang Wagner (2001) Constructivist Foreign Policy Theory, in Volker Rittberger (ed.) *German Foreign Policy since Unification: Theories and Case Studies*, Manchester: Manchester University Press, 105–137.

Böller, Florian, and Sebastian Werle (2016) Fencing the Bear? Explaining US Foreign Policy towards Russian Interventions, *Contemporary Security Policy* 37(3), 319–340.

Bueno de Mesquita, Bruce, James Morrow, and Randolph M. Siverson (1999) An Institutional Explanation of the Democratic Peace, *American Political Science Review* 93(4), 791–807.

Capoccia, Giovanni and Daniel R. Kelemen (2007) The Study of Critical Junctures: Theory, Narrative, and Counterfactuals in Historical Institutionalism, *World Politics* 59(3), 341–369.

Carlsnaes, Walter (2013) Foreign Policy, in Walter Carlsnaes, Thomas Risse, and Beth A. Simmons (eds.) *Handbook of International Relations*, London: Sage, 298–325.

Carta, Caterina and Jean-Frédéric Morin (eds.) (2014) *EU Foreign Policy through the Lens of Discourse Analysis: Making Sense of Diversity*, Farnham: Ashgate.

Checkel, Jeffrey T. (1999) Social Constructivism and European Integration, *Journal of European Public Policy* 6(4), 545–560.

Chollet, Derek (2016) *The Long Game: How Obama Defied Washington and Redefined America's Role in the World*, New York: Public Affairs.

Cohen, Bernard and Scott A. Harris (1975) Foreign Policy, in Fred I. Greenstein and Polsby W. Nelson (eds.) *Handbook of Political Science, Vol. 6: Policies and Policymaking*, Reading, MA: Addison-Wesley, 381–438.

Dannreuther, Roland (2010) Understanding the Middle East Peace Process: A Historical Institutionalist Approach, *European Journal of International Relations* 17(2), 187–208.

Delreux, Tom (2015) Bureaucratic Politics, New Institutionalism and Principal-Agent Models, in Knud E. Jørgensen, Aasne Kalland Aarstad, Edith Drieskens, Katie Laatikainen, and Ben Tonra (eds.) *The SAGE Handbook of European Foreign Policy*, London: Sage, 152–165.

Diez, Thomas (1999) *Die EU lesen: Diskursive Knotenpunkte in der britischen Europadebatte*, Opladen: Leske und Budrich.

Finnemore, Martha (1996a) *National Interest in International Society*, Ithaca, NY: Cornell University Press.

Finnemore, Martha (1996b) Norms, Culture, and World Politics: Insights from Sociology's Institutionalism, *International Organization* 50(2), 325–347.

Fioretos, Orfeo, Tulia G. Falleti, and Adam Sheingate (eds.) (2016) *The Oxford Handbook of Historical Institutionalism*, Oxford: Oxford University Press.

Gandhi, Jenniger and Rubén Ruiz-Rufino (2015) Introduction, in Jenniger Gandhi and Rubén Ruiz-Rufino (eds.) *Routledge Handbook of Comparative. Political Institutions*, Abingdon: Routledge, 1–10.

Goldstein, Judith and Robert O. Keohane (eds.) (1993) *Ideas and Foreign Policy. Beliefs, Institutions and Political Change*, London: Cornell University Press.

Hall, Peter A. (2010) Historical Institutionalism in Rationalist and Sociological Perspective, in James Mahoney and Kathleen Thelen (eds.) *Explaining Institutional Change*, Cambridge: Cambridge University Press, 204–224.

Hall, Peter A. and Rosemary C. Taylor (1996) Political Science and the Three New Institutionalisms, *Political Studies* 44(5), 936–957.

Haney, Patrick J. (1995) Structure and Process in the Analysis of Foreign Policy Crises, in Laura Neack, Jeanne A. K. Hey, and Patrick J. Haney (eds.) *Foreign Policy Analysis: Continuity and Change in Its Second Generation*, Englewood Cliffs: Prentice Hall, 99–116.

Hawkins, Darren G., David A. Lake, Daniel L. Nielson, and Michael J. Tierney (eds.) (2006) *Delegation and Agency in International Organizations*, Cambridge: Cambridge University Press.

Hay, Colin (2006) Constructivist Institutionalism, in Sarah Binder, R. A. W. Rhodes, and Bert A. Rockman (eds.) *The Oxford Handbook of Political Institutions*, New York: Oxford University Press, 56–74.

Hellmann, Gunther and Knud E. Jørgensen (eds.) (2015) *Theorizing Foreign Policy in a Globalized World*, Houndmills: Palgrave.

Hill, Christopher (2015) *Foreign Policy in the Twenty-First Century*, Basingstoke: Palgrave.

Hopf, Ted (2002) *Social Construction of International Politics: Identities and Foreign Policies, Moscow, 1955 and 1999*, Ithaca, NY: Cornell University Press.

Hudson, Valerie M. (2005) Foreign Policy Analysis: Actor-Specific Theory and the Ground of International Relations, *Foreign Policy Analysis* 1(1), 1–30.

Ikenberry, John G. (2001) *After Victory: Institutions, Strategic Restraint, and the Rebuilding of Order After Major Wars*, Princeton: Princeton University Press.

Johnston, Alastair I. (2008) *Social States: China in International Institutions, 1980–2000*, Princeton: Princeton University Press.

Jørgensen, Knud E., Aasne Kalland Aarstad, Edith Drieskens, Katie Laatikainen, and Ben Tonra (eds.) (2015) *The SAGE Handbook of European Foreign Policy*, London: Sage.

Kaarbo, Juliet (2015) A Foreign Policy Analysis Perspective on the Domestic Politics Turn in IR Theory, *International Studies Review* 17(2), 189–216.

Katzenstein, Peter J. (ed.) (1996) *The Culture of National Security: Norms and Identity in World Politics*, New York: Columbia University Press.

Keohane, Robert O. (1989) *International Institutions and State Power: Essays in International Relations Theory*, Boulder: Westview.

Keohane, Robert O., Stephen Macedo, and Andrew Moravcsik (2009) Democracy-Enhancing Multilateralism, *International Organization* 63(1), 1–31.

Kratochwil, Friedrich (1989) *Rules, Norms, and Decisions: On the Conditions of Practical and Legal Reasoning in Internatinnal Relations and Domestic Affairs*, Cambridge: Cambridge University Press.

Lindsay, James M. (1994) Congress, Foreign Policy, and the New Institutionalism, *International Studies Quarterly* 38(2), 281–304.

Mabee, Bryan (2011) Historical Institutionalism and Foreign Policy Analysis: The Origins of the National Security Council Revisited, *Foreign Policy Analysis* 7(1), 27–44.

Mahoney, James and Kathleen Thelen (2010) A Theory of Gradual Institutional Change, in James Mahoney and Kathleen Thelen (eds.) *Explaining Institutional Change*, Cambridge: Cambridge University Press, 1–37.

March, James G. and Johann P. Olsen (1984) The New Institutionalism: Organizational Factors in Political Life, *American Political Science Review* 78(3), 734–749.

March, James G. and Johann P. Olsen (1989) *Rediscovering Institutions*, New York: Free Press.

March, James G. and Johann P. Olsen (2006) Elaborating the "New Institutionalism," in Sarah Binder, R. A. W. Rhodes, and Bert A. Rockman (eds.) *The Oxford Handbook of Political Institutions*, New York: Oxford University Press, 3–20.

Medick-Krakau, Monika (ed.) (1999) *Außenpolitischer Wandel in theoretischer und vergleichender Perspektive: Die USA und die Bundesrepublik Deutschland*, Baden-Baden: Nomos.

Milner, Helen V. and Dustin Tingley (2013) The Choice for Multilateralism: Foreign Aid and American Foreign Policy, *Review of International Organizations* 8(3), 313–341.

Nau, Henry (2002) *At Home Abroad: Identity and Power in American Foreign Policy*, London: Cornell University Press.

Neack, Laura (2014) *The New Foreign Policy: Complex Interactions, Competing Interests*, 3rd edition, Boulder: Rowman & Littlefield.

New institutionalism 137

Nexon, Daniel (2012) Historical Institutionalism and International Relations, available at www.e-ir.info (last accessed December 20, 2016).

Obama, Barack (2014) Statement by the President on Ukraine on July 29, 2014, available at www.whitehouse.gov (last accessed December 6, 2016).

Obama, Barack (2016) The Obama Doctrine, available at www.theatlantic.com (last accessed December 17, 2016).

Peters, B. Guy (1999) *Institutional Theory in Political Science: The "New Institutionalism,"* London and New York: Pinter.

Pierson, Paul (1996) The Path to European Integration: A Historical Institutionalist Analysis, *Comparative Political Studies* 29(2), 123–163.

Pierson, Paul (2000) Increasing Returns, Path Dependence, and the Study of Politics, *American Political Science Review* 94(2), 251–267.

Pierson, Paul (2015) Power and Path Dependence, in James Mahoney and Kathleen Thelen (eds.) *Advances in Comparative-Historical Analysis*, Cambridge: Cambridge University Press, 123–146.

Pierson, Paul and Theda Skocpol (2002) Historical Institutionalism in Contemporary Political Science, in Ira Katznelson and Helen V. Milner (eds.) *Political Science: The State of the Discipline*, New York: Norton, 693–721.

Radaelli, Claudio M., Bruno Dente, and Samuele Dossi (2012) Recasting Institutionalism: Institutional Analysis and Public Policy, *European Political Science* 11(4), 537–550.

Ripsman, Norrin M. (2005) Moving Beyond (or Beneath) the Democratic Peace Theory: Intermediate-Level Institutions and Foreign Security Policy, in Andrè Lecours (ed.) *New Institutionalism: Theory and Analysis*, Toronto: Toronto University Press, 301–318.

Risse, Thomas (2000) Let's Argue! Communicative Action in World Politics, *International Organization* 54(1), 1–39.

Rixen, Thomas and Lora A. Viola (2016) Historical Institutionalism and International Relations: Towards Explaining Change and Stability in International Institutions, in Thomas Rixen, Lora A. Viola, and Michael Zürn (eds.) *Historical Institutionalism and International Relations Explaining Institutional Development in World Politics*, Oxford: Oxford University Press, 3–34.

Rudolf, Peter (2016) *Amerikanische Russland-Politik und europäische Sicherheitsordnung*, Berlin: Stiftung Wissenschaft und Politik.

Sarigil, Zeki (2015) Showing the Path to Path Dependence: The Habitual Path, *European Political Science Review* 7(2), 221–242.

Schmidt, Vivien A. (2008) Discursive Institutionalism: The Explanatory Power of Ideas and Discourse, *Annual Review of Political Science* 11, 303–326.

Schmidt, Vivien A. (2011) Reconciling Ideas and Institutions through Discursive Institutionalism, in Daniel Béland and Robert H. Cox (eds.) *Ideas and Politics in Social Science Research*, Oxford: Oxford University Press, 47–64.

Schmidt, Vivien A. (2016) The Roots of Neo-Liberal Resilience: Explaining Continuity and Change in Background Ideas in Europe's Political Economy, *British Journal of Politics and International Relations* 18(2), 318–334.

Smith, Steve, Amelia Hadfield, and Tim Dunne (eds.) (2016) *Foreign Policy. Theories, Actors and Cases*, Oxford: Oxford University Press.

Stark Urrestarazu, Ursula (2015) "Identity" in International Relations and Foreign Policy, in Gunther Hellmann and Knud E. Jørgensen (eds.) *Theorizing Foreign Policy in a Globalized World*, Basingstoke: Palgrave, 126–149.

Steinmo, Sven (2008) Historical Institutionalism, in Donatella Della Porta and Michael Keating (eds.) *Approaches in the Social Sciences*, Cambridge: Cambridge University Press, 113–138.

Stent, Angela (2014) *The Limits of Partnership: U.S.-Russian Relations in the Twenty-First Century*, Princeton: Princeton University Press.

Sydow, Jörg, Georg Schreyögg, and Jochen Koch (2009) Organizational Path Dependence: Opening the Black Box, *Academy of Management Review* 34(4), 689–709.

Thelen, Kathleen and Sven Steinmo (1992) Historical Institutionalism in Comparative Politics, in Sven Steinmo, Kathleen Thelen, and Frank Longstreth (eds.) *Structuring Politics*, Cambridge: Cambridge University Press, 1–32.

Thomas, Daniel C. (ed.) (2011) *Making EU Foreign Policy National Preferences, European Norms and Common Policies*, Basingstoke: Palgrave.

US Department of the Treasury (2016) Ukraine-/Russia-Related Sanctions, available at www.treasury.gov (last accessed January 7, 2017).

Washington Post (2017) Not all Republicans on Board with Democrat's Bill to Sanction Russia, available at www.washingtonpost.com (last accessed January 10, 2017).

Zürn, Michel (2016) Historical Institutionalism and International Relations: Strange Bedfellows? in Thomas Rixen, Lora A. Viola, and Michael Zürn (eds.) *Historical Institutionalism and International Relations Explaining Institutional Development in World Politics*, Oxford: Oxford University Press, 199–227.

7

The network approach and foreign policy

Christopher Ansell and Jacob Torfing

This chapter aims to explore the relevance of the increasingly fashionable network approach for studying the formulation, implementation, and diffusion of foreign policy. Traditionally, foreign policy-making has been viewed as a prerogative of an executive branch of government that unilaterally defines the national interest and pursues it through strategic action in contexts characterized by intense rivalry, constant crisis, and dynamic conflicts (Allison 1969). However, the gradual decentering of government—a combined effect of the denationalization of statehood, the de-stratification of politics, and the internationalization of policy-making (Jessop 2002)—tends to enhance the dependence of national governments on a plethora of state and non-state actors when it comes to defining the national interest, developing foreign policy strategies, and executing these in an anarchic, yet increasingly regulated, world. The securitization of a growing number of policy areas, such as climate change, trade agreements, and disease control, further contributes to the decentering and pluralization of foreign policy-making, although the government tends to play a prominent role in securitized policy fields (Buzan *et al.* 1998). Understanding the pluricentric interactions through which foreign policy is made, implemented, and diffused is essential and the network approach may be helpful in this regard as it captures the structured interactions between state and/or non-state actors.

Today, there is a growing interest in networks of all kinds. Increasingly, we talk about the role of social networks for our general well-being, the impact of professional networks on career development, the value chains connecting contractors and sub-contractors in economic networks, transport networks moving people and goods around the globe, and digital networks enhancing the speed of communication and data processing. We even talk about terror networks and network-centric warfare (Cebrowski and Garstka 1998). The networks that we shall focus on in this chapter link public and private actors in a negotiated interaction that contributes to public policy-making and governance of society and the economy. We shall refer to this type of network as "policy networks" or "governance networks" and our claim is that the study of policy and governance networks is useful for understanding and analyzing foreign policy-making.

The plan of this chapter is the following. The next section defines the network concept, sets out the core features of the network approach, and explains how and why it has emerged as an alternative lens for understanding policy-making in dispersed and interactive settings that defy description in terms of the traditional hierarchy–market dichotomy. It then compares different theories and methods for understanding policy and governance networks and discusses how these networks can be instrumental for enhancing knowledge sharing, improving inter-organizational and cross-sector coordination, and solving wicked and unruly problems in ways that both increase effectiveness and democratic legitimacy. This section also explores core insights of network research, such as the need for network management or meta-governance. The following section describes how and why the network approach is applicable to foreign policy-making and assesses the scope conditions and merits and limits of applying the approach. The network approach has been associated with collaborative governance in relatively stable, co-operative, high trust settings in which power is dispersed among a large number of actors. Therefore, it may be deemed of less relevance in foreign policy-making where power is concentrated in the executive branch and where security-related conflicts and crisis situations predominate. However, as we shall see, these are not necessarily limiting factors for the use of the network approach. In fact, the network approach is useful for analyzing how states formulate, implement, and diffuse foreign policy in response to domestic interests and global problems and events. The next section investigates how the network approach has been applied in foreign policy-making. Using a Venn diagram, we distinguish different types of policy and governance networks at the domestic and global levels in order to identify those networks that have a direct bearing on foreign policy-making. After this brief mapping of network types, we provide a more extended example of how the network approach is applicable to core concerns of foreign policy. The example illustrates the role of networks in facilitating political co-operation to prevent nuclear proliferation. The concluding section summarizes the argument and suggests avenues for future research.

The network approach to policy-making and governance

In the field of public policy and regulation, governance has traditionally been associated with formal and legal steering processes orchestrated and controlled by public authorities and government officials at different levels. However, the unilateral action of government is increasingly supplemented and supplanted by multilateral action involving a plethora of public and private actors. This recognition has triggered a growing interest in "interactive forms of governance" (Kooiman 1993), defined as the complex processes through which a plurality of social and political actors with diverging interests interact in order to formulate, promote, and realize common objectives by means of mobilizing, exchanging, and deploying a range of ideas, rules, and resources (Torfing *et al.* 2012).

Interactive governance can take different forms and has been studied variously as "corporatist arrangements," "advocacy coalitions," and "epistemic communities." Many scholars have paid special attention to the interactive forms of governance taking place in pluricentric networks (Kickert *et al.* 1997; Van Kersbergen and Warden 2004; Sørensen and Torfing 2007a). Social Network Analysis (SNA) defines networks as the presence of relations and non-relations between different nodes that can be states, organizations, persons, or things (Scott 2012). While this definition portrays networks as relational patterns that evolve over time, Policy Network Analysis (PNA) has been more interested in the collaborative processes through which the actors in a network exchange knowledge, coordinate action, and attempt to solve policy problems through negotiation and joint action (Ansell and Gash 2008). Both approaches tend to adopt a relational and processual stance toward understanding social phenomena (Emirbayer 1997).

SNA emerged within sociology out of the long-standing interest in studying the relationship between social actors, but it was not developed as a systematic method until after the 1930s where graph theory was introduced in the analysis of patterns of ties (Freeman 2004). PNA developed within political science and public administration in response to the discovery of policy subsystems in the US Congress (Heclo 1978) and the critique of corporatist theory in Europe for failing to appreciate the broad set of public and private actors involved in public policy-making and regulation (Jordan 1990; Marsh and Rhodes 1992). SNA and PNA developed in splendid isolation from each other (Marcussen and Olsen 2007), but the insights gained from the quantitative studies of the impact of network structures within SNA and the qualitative studies of the relationship between institutional designs, network interaction, and negotiated outcomes within PNA are increasingly combined and integrated in the growing research on interactive governance (Ansell and Torfing 2016).

The new research on interactive forms of governance is particularly interested in how networks of social and political actors contribute to the production and development of public governance. Governance networks are defined as: (1) a relatively stable, horizontal articulation of interdependent, but operationally autonomous actors from the public and/or private for-profit and non-profit sector; (2) who interact with one another through ongoing negotiations; (3) which take place within a relatively institutionalized framework; (4) facilitate self-regulation in the shadow of hierarchy; and (5) contribute to the production of public purpose in the broad sense of public values, visions, plans, standards, regulations, and concrete decisions (Sørensen and Torfing 2007a).

It follows from this definition that networks have a relative endurance in time and space and that they are formed out of a mutual recognition of the need to exchange or pool knowledge, resources, and ideas. The network actors retain their operational autonomy, but realize that they cannot single-handedly solve the problem or challenge at hand and, therefore, must engage in horizontal interaction with one another in order to establish a common ground for creative problem-solving. The relations in the network are not horizontal in the sense that the participants have an equal amount of resources, but only in the sense that no one can settle a dispute by pulling rank and referring to their formal authority. The actors interact and settle disputes through negotiations that may either take the form of hard-nosed bargaining or involve joint deliberation through which problems are defined and solutions developed through an open-ended inquiry. The network actors all have a different rule and resource base, and in the beginning there will be no common constitution. However, over time, the interaction will become institutionalized as a contingent set of rules, norms, values, and ideas will become taken for granted and regulate the behavior of the actors in the network. The rule-bound negotiations will be self-regulated, but the self-regulated network will tend to operate in the shadow of hierarchy as public authorities will frame the networked interaction and threaten to take over if the network fails to provide an acceptable solution and generate desirable outcomes. Governance networks thus have a bounded autonomy that they can use in the production of public purpose in a broad sense of the term.

There are many different types of governance networks, but no well-established typology. Many different kinds of distinctions have been drawn to distinguish different features of networks: some are formal whereas others are informal; some are mandated from above while others are self-grown from below; some are relatively large and inclusive whereas others are small and exclusive; some are star-shaped with communication flowing from the center to the periphery, whereas others are diamond-shaped and characterized by all-to-all communication; and some are engaged in knowledge-sharing and policy-making whereas others focus on policy implementation and policy diffusion (Sørensen and Torfing 2007a). Networks also differ in terms of whether they are operating at a single scale or at multiple scales. They may also cut across scales to form a multilevel governance system, or be subject to a process of scaling whereby they are moved to a higher or lower scale in response to changes in the problem or task at hand (Ansell and Torfing 2015). Last but not least, network management may either be provided by a lead actor (either a government agency or a "third-party" facilitator), a plenary meeting of all the members of the network, or a Network Administrative Organization established by a core group of network actors (Kenis and Provan 2007).

The core features of the network approach can be summarized in five basic claims. The first claim is that mutual dependence between social and political actors is the key driver in the formation of networks and helps to keep the network actors together despite the emergence of conflicts. Social and political actors are willing to pool or surrender their sovereignty and engage in co-created policy-making when they realize that none of them have the knowledge, resources, and ideas to solve complex problems and challenges on their own (Kooiman 1993, 2003). The network actors are linked through relations of mutual dependency that encourage them to exchange or share relevant resources (Kickert *et al.* 1997; Rhodes 1997a). Conflicts may emerge because the actors have different interests, worldviews, and opinions, but the network actors will try to mitigate or solve the conflicts rather than just leave the network because the ability to solve the problem depends on continued resource exchange. The network actors will only leave the network if the negotiated solution appears to be worse than no solution, and even then they might want to stay in the network in order to try to veto the solution or fight for compensation from damaging effects (Gray 1989).

The second claim is that networked policy-making means that political power becomes positional rather than attributional (Kahler 2009). While the standard political science approach tends to see political power as a function of the individual resources and capacities of the actors and explain these in terms of the underlying socio-economic structures and cultural disparities, the network approach claims that it is often the relational position of the actors in interactive policy arenas that determines their relative power (Padgett and Ansell 1993). Hence, the relational power of a network actor may stem either from being well-connected to other actors who are otherwise weakly connected, or from having a high degree of centrality defined by the number of links to other actors (Knoke 1994). The positional view of power in networks supplements the traditional attributional view of power that, nevertheless, continues to be important in order to understand the ability of actors to exploit their relational position in the network to influence key decisions (White 1992).

The third claim is that antecedent conditions and the development of relations of trust determine whether the network actors will collaborate and find a joint solution. Starting conditions are found to be important for the actors to engage in joint problem solving (Ansell and Gash 2008). The system context is also important, including legal frameworks, political culture, and traditions of and experiences with multi-actor collaboration (Emerson *et al.* 2012). Other factors that spur collaboration are high costs of adversarial legal strategies, absence of alternative arenas where actors can pursue their goals unilaterally, and large resource imbalances that may tempt strong actors to go it alone (Gray 1989). If there is a pre-history of antagonism between the network actors, efforts to build trust are a crucial condition for successful collaboration (Klijn *et al.* 2010). Trust building may be pursued either through the expansion of informal social contacts that allow the actors to get to know each other on a personal basis or through the organization of joint fact-finding missions that permit the actors to establish a common reference point in terms of a joint description of the problem and its context (Koppenjan and Klijn 2004).

The fourth claim is that processes of institutionalization help to stabilize the ongoing negotiations in networked arenas by enhancing the clarity and acceptance of the underlying rules, norms, and values, but that too much institutionalization may prevent the emergence of the flexibility gain associated with network governance (Provan and Kenis 2008; Torfing *et al.* 2012). Institutionalization helps to lower the transaction costs of networking through the routinization of interaction, and the normative and ideational aspects of the institutionalization process create a common set of norms, values, and ideas that help to foster a sense of belonging to a community of like-minded actors and facilitate communication and mutual learning. However, the degree of institutionalization can become too high and prevent the network from flexibly adjusting to new events and changing contexts which is often cited as one of the main advantages of governance networks (Milward and Provan 2006). In sum, it appears that successful collaboration in networks depends on striking a balance between institutionalization and deinstitutionalization.

The final claim is that the perennial risk of network failure necessitates some kind of network management (Jessop 2002). There is no guarantee that networks arise spontaneously when they are needed, and there is always a danger that conflicts become destructive and that political dynamics will make networks spin out of control and produce solutions that are either too expensive or politically unacceptable. Hence, some kind of network management is necessary in order to convene the actors, design the collaborative arena, mediate conflicts, and give direction to the problem-solving process through a combination of framing and active intervention (Kickert *et al.* 1997; Agranoff and McGuire 2001). Network management is a big challenge for many government officials who have been brought up with the idea of leading their own organization and employees in order to achieve a pre-defined result. When serving as network managers they are called upon to lead a broad range of public and private actors that are constantly negotiating problems, goals, and solutions and may come up with new and innovative ideas that disrupt established practices. Since network management aims to govern more or less self-governing networks it is often referred to as meta-governance, which is defined as the attempt to influence the process and outcomes of collaborative network governance without reverting too much to hierarchical forms of command and control (Jessop 2002; Sørensen and Torfing 2009; Torfing *et al.* 2012). The tools for meta-governing networks include institutional design, goal and framework steering, process management, and direct participation in the decision-making process.

These five claims capture the core of the network approach that aims to understand how public policies are made and governance outcomes are produced in complex, dispersed, and rhizomatic settings that defy description in terms of the traditional hierarchy–market dichotomy. The network approach allows us to understand the structural, institutional, and political conditions for a plurality of interdependent actors to come together and produce a particular set of outcomes through trust-based collaboration in a world of shared power where nobody is in control. Figure 7.1 illustrates the core argument of the network approach as expressed in the five basic claims.

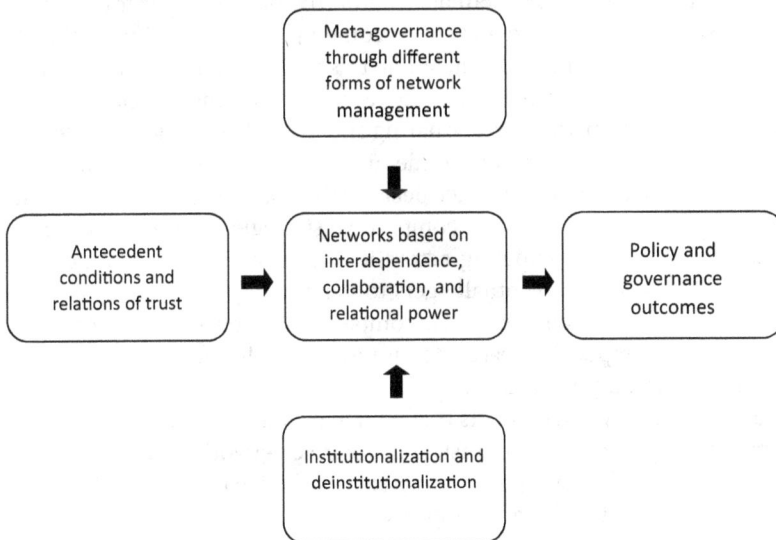

Figure 7.1 Illustration of the core argument of the network approach

According to Jessop (2002), the network approach becomes increasingly relevant as the political powers associated with the nation state are displaced upwards to international and supranational institutions, downwards to regional and local levels, and outwards to new cross-border regions. At the same time, governments seem to have lost their monopoly on policy-making as a growing number of non-state actors are involved in initiating, formulating, and implementing policies. Last but not least, policy-making is becoming internationalized as new policy ideas are increasingly being uploaded to and downloaded from international and supra-national institutions. As a result, policy-making is taking place in a multilevel and multi-actor world with many hands and many eyes, thus generating an urgent need for knowledge-sharing, coordination, and collaboration between actors from different countries, sectors, and levels. Neither the classical model of hierarchical government based on unicentric control and imperative command, nor the alternative market model based on multi-centric competition, captures the complex and pluricentric interactions through which public policy is made and executed and this explains the increasing interest in the network approach (Kersbergen and Waarden 2004).

The network approach has particular relevance for solving wicked and unruly problems (Ansell and Bartenberger 2016). Roberts (2000) compares authoritative, competitive, and collaborative strategies and concludes that collaboration in networks is superior to hierarchical authority and market-based competition when it comes to spurring creative problem solving. Authoritative strategies authorize a particular group of decision-makers to define the problem at hand on the basis of their formal position or expertise and urge them to come up with a matching solution that is implemented top-down. While this is a fast and efficient decision method, the solution might miss the target because the decision-makers fail to benefit from knowledge-sharing and mutual learning with relevant and affected actors. In addition, the hierarchical imposition of the solution might meet fierce resistance because there is little ownership over it. These problems are solved by competitive strategies that tend to engage a large number of competing actors in a zero-sum game in which the winner takes all and eventually gets to define the problem and its solution. While the advantage is that competition involves a broader range of actors, prompts the search for innovative solutions and challenges institutionalized power monopolies, a lot of resources are nevertheless wasted on rivalry and conflicts that tend to prohibit the exchange of ideas among competitors. By contrast, collaborative network-strategies permit the exchange of knowledge, competences, and ideas and thus facilitate mutual learning that helps to improve the understanding of the problem, develop an innovative solution, and generate ownership over its implementation (Roberts 2000; Weber and Khademian 2008).

Although the network approach can be summarized in a handful of core claims supported by the majority of network theorists, there is no commonly accepted theory of policy and governance networks. As argued elsewhere (Sørensen and Torfing 2007a), it is possible to identify four different theories of policy and governance networks that tend to subscribe to different strands of the new institutionalism (Peters 2013). Let us briefly consider the four theories in turn, beginning with the two main approaches in the study of governance networks: *interdependence theory* and *governability theory*. Both theories tend to view social and political action as driven by institutionally conditioned calculations of rational actors, but they differ in their view on the prospect for overcoming conflicts and facilitating collaboration among multiple stakeholders with diverging interests.

Interdependence theory is firmly anchored in historical institutionalism (Kickert *et al.* 1997; Rhodes 1997a; Jessop 1998). It defines governance networks as an inter-organizational medium for interest mediation between interdependent—but conflicting—actors, each of which has a rule and resource base of their own. Governance networks are formed as a result of strategic calculations of self-interested collective actors who choose to interact because the presence of mutual resource dependencies makes it rational to exchange or share resources. The formation of governance networks enables the actors to find joint solutions to joint problems and counteracts the increasing institutional fragmentation caused by New Public Management reforms that prevents public and private actors from benefiting from the exchange and pooling of relevant resources. Networks are formed through incremental and contingent processes, but are often recruited as vehicles of public policy-making and governance by public authorities (Rhodes 1997b). The network actors pursue different interests by engaging in political conflicts and power struggles, but they are held together by their mutual interdependence and the gradual development of common rules, norms, values, and perceptions, which facilitate trust-based learning that over time will tend to modify and transform the interests and objectives of the public and private actors. The codification of the "rules of the game" and the transformation of interests helps to contain and regulate conflicts between the actors, but does not eliminate them. Conflicts constantly threaten to disrupt the joint search for solutions and hard-nosed bargaining and unstable and contested compromise formation is the order of the day.

Governability theory combines rational choice institutionalism with a systems theoretical view of societal development (Mayntz 1993a, 1993b; Scharpf 1994; Kooiman 2003). It defines governance networks as arenas for horizontal coordination between autonomous actors who interact in and through different negotiation games. The formation of governance networks is seen as a functional response to the increasing societal complexity, differentiation, and dynamism that undermine the ability to govern society efficiently through the traditional means of hierarchy and market. Governance networks are viewed as game-like structures that facilitate horizontal coordination among sectoral and organizational systems, and they are held together by the anticipated gains from the exchange and pooling of resources and the development of mutual trust. A proactive creation of incentive structures may help to overcome collective action problems and mitigate conflicts. The result is either "negative coordination" where the actors aim to steer free of conflicts by avoiding particular problems or issues, or "positive coordination" based on the development of joint problem definitions and common solutions through mutual engagement and substantive discussions (Scharpf 1994). Conflicts will persist, but there is a good prospect for producing joint solutions with broad, if not unanimous, support.

Theories of normative integration perceive governance networks as institutionalized fields of interaction that bring together relevant and affected actors who become normatively integrated by the emerging rules, norms, values, and perceptions that together define a particular logic of appropriate action (Powell and DiMaggio 1991; March and Olsen 1995). Governance networks are regarded as a way of organizing and structuring organizational fields (Powell and DiMaggio 1991) and as a normative response to the twin problems of over-integration of social agency, which is typically found in bureaucratic settings, and under-integration of social agency, which often emerges in market-based environments (March and Olsen 1995). They are formed through a bottom-up process whereby tentative and provisional contacts, which are established due to the recognition of interdependence, are positively evaluated and extended on the basis of institutional logics of appropriateness that over time are modified and integrated through mutual learning and pragmatic adjustments. The proliferation of governance networks in organizational fields may also be further accelerated by isomorphic pressures that establish network types of governance as a legitimate and "fashionable" way of organizing resource exchange (Powell and DiMaggio 1991). Network actors interact on the basis of a shared logic of appropriate action, but that does not preclude the rise of conflicts. However, there seems to be considerable scope for civilizing conflicts through the dissemination of norms of solidarity and agonistic respect and the construction of democratic identities (March and Olsen 1995: 48–89).

Governmentality theory (Foucault 1991; Rose and Miller 1992; Dean 1999) implicitly defines governance networks as an attempt by an increasingly reflexive, facilitating, and regulatory state to govern by means of mobilizing and shaping the free actions of actors who are connected by the formation of interactive policy arenas. Citizens, community groups, NGOs, interest organizations, private enterprises, and public agencies are encouraged to regulate themselves and their mutual interaction in a particular area. However, their self-regulated governance practices take place within an institutional framework of regulatory norms, performance standards, and calculative practices that ensures conformity with overall policy objectives. From this perspective, the formation of governance networks can be interpreted as a political response to the failure of neoliberalism to realize its key goal of "less state and more market": market-based governance and service provision has grown, but so has the amount of market-enhancing and market-controlling state regulation. More market and more bureaucratic state regulation seem to go hand in hand. The inherent problems of neoliberalism have stimulated the formulation of a new governmentality program referred to as "advanced liberal government," which aims to displace governmental tasks to local, regional, and national networks where the resources and energies of social and political actors are mobilized and given a particular direction in order to achieve particular policy objectives (Dean 1999; Triantafillou 2007). Governance networks are constructed and framed by particular governing technologies and narratives that aim to recruit social actors as vehicles for the exercise of power. However, these social actors might resist and oppose the normalizing power strategies to which they are subjected and the result is the proliferation of conflicts and struggles.

As shown in table 7.1, the four theories of policy and governance networks differ in their perception of the nature of social and political action and in their view of the role of power and conflicts in public governance. Given the predominance of actor-centered theories of instrumental action in international politics and the inherent conception of the geopolitical system as a potentially anarchic order, interdependency theory seems to be an obvious starting point for analyzing the role of networks in foreign policy-making.

Table 7.1 Theoretical overview of the four main network theories

	Action is based on calculation (logic of consequentiality)	Action is based on rule-following (logic of appropriateness)
Social system is basically conflict-ridden	*Interdependency theory* (Historical institutionalism)	*Governmentality theory* (Discourse institutionalism)
Social system is potentially consensual	*Governability theory* (Rational choice institutionalism)	*Normative integration theory* (Sociological institutionalism)

Policy and governance networks can be analyzed both as relational structures and as institutionalized arenas for multi-actor collaboration. The first aspect can be studied by drawing on the sophisticated quantitative techniques of SNA, whereas the latter aspect can be analyzed by drawing on a broad range of qualitative methods associated with PNA.

SNA provides a variety of software packages that use relational data about ties to analyze the patterns of interaction, calculate a variety of quantitative measures, and produce graphs that depict the relational structure of a network. The quantitative measures can help to establish the density of the network defined as the number of direct ties relative to the total number of possible ties; the relative centrality of the actors in terms of how well and closely connected they are; the distance between the actors in terms of the number of links that are needed to connect them; and the network closure in terms of the completeness of relational triads. Visualization of networks using illustrative graphs can help to determine the overall shape of the network, identify unconnected clusters of well-connected actors (structural holes) and actors functioning as brokers who aim to provide a bridge between relevant clusters and cliques.

The quantitative measures and graphs produced by SNA emphasize the structure over the content of network relations. They give priority to analyzing patterns of relationships, but say less about the qualitative dimensions of relational exchange. By contrast, PNA analyzes the form and character of the collaborative interaction among the network actors, the results in terms of stalemate, compromises, and decisions, and the impact in terms of innovative solutions, effective governance, or democratic legitimacy (Kenis 2016). PNA is also interested in the effect that institutional design and network management may have on network performance and the achievement of particular results and impacts (Kickert *et al.* 1997). Case studies are the preferred methodology and data is collected through the deployment of a variety of qualitative data collection techniques. The study of documents such as policy reports, agendas, and minutes from meetings, case files, and media coverage can help to identify the key network actors, analyze the political framing of problems and solutions, and detect changes in the substantive and procedural norms that are governing the networked interactions (Esmark and Triantafillou 2007). However, official documents may be heavily censored and they do not reveal the experiences and perceptions of the actors, the patterns of interaction, and the informal aspects of network governance. Document studies must therefore be supplemented with other methods such as qualitative interviews and observational studies.

The advantage of qualitative interviews based on either reputational or representative sampling is that you can ask about almost everything and often get pretty reliable answers. Hence, qualitative interviews can help to establish the factual history of the network, the formal and informal interactions, and the actors' perception of each other, the collaborative process, and the actual results (Zølner *et al.* 2007). The downside of qualitative interviews is that there is always a risk of ex-post rationalization. The actors that are interviewed may tend to paint a far too rosy picture of events. Observation studies can solve this problem by offering a direct and contemporaneous way of studying formal and informal interactions in policy and governance networks. Non-participatory observation of meetings and other important network gatherings facilitates first-hand studies of interactions, power games, and internal and external exclusions (Sørensen and Torfing 2007b). Shadowing of individual actors between the meetings in the network may help to establish a fuller picture of the informal interactions that often take place in the days leading up to or following a network meeting. However, shadowing is extremely resource demanding and may therefore be replaced with diary writing. Some of the network actors might be persuaded, or paid, to keep a diary or to write a logbook that records events in the network and perhaps offer a subjective account of these events (Sørensen and Torfing 2007b). These different methods each have their particular strengths and weaknesses and mixing the methods is often a good idea.

The relevance of the network approach for studying competition, crisis, and conflict

The network approach has been widely used to investigate public policy-making and governance at the local, regional, national, and global level and in a variety of different policy areas. However, a number of objections might be raised against the relevance of the network approach in studies of foreign policy-making. First, foreign policy-making is considered among the most statist of policy areas. National governments play a privileged role in defining and pursuing the national interest and political executives jealously guard their policy-making prerogatives. After all, foreign policy-making is an area of high politics where the responsibility for success and failure ultimately lies with government. Therefore, government officials will be disinclined to share power with a broader network of actors where responsibility and accountability are diffuse. Second, foreign policy is often made in an atmosphere of crisis that demands swift action. Effective decisions under these conditions often call for hierarchical decision-making based on clear chains of command. By contrast, decision-making in networks requires lengthy deliberation and is often a messy process. Third, foreign policy-making is about pursuing national interests, and as realists have long pointed out, it is fundamentally conflictual. Security concerns are rooted in a military logic of defending the nation and its sovereignty from foreign threats. This conflictual and defensive stance is not conducive to building trust and collaboration in networks. Finally, the issues pertaining to national security that involve relations to foreign powers require a high degree of secrecy and seclusion. Decision-making must take place behind closed doors with limited participation and publicity. It is difficult to achieve these conditions in broad networks where it is difficult to contain information and influence.

Although these are all reasonable objections, we do not think that they rule out the potential applicability of the network approach. In fact, there are plausible counter-arguments that attest to the relevance of the network approach even in the realm of foreign policy. First, in response to the objection that states jealously guard their policy prerogatives in foreign policy, we would point to countertrends that have partially decentered the statist approach to foreign policy-making and increased the relevance of more networked approaches (Metzl 2001; Eilstrup-Sangiovanni 2005; Krahmann 2005; Mérand *et al.* 2011). States must now operate in complex inter-organizational fields that include many new public and private institutions operating at different political levels (Keck and Sikkink 2014). States may retain sovereign power but they cannot be effective by exercising their power unilaterally. To achieve their objectives they must negotiate with and build alliances with other states, international and supra-national organizations, and strong non-state actors. This decentering is spurred by the securitization of policy areas, such as trade, climate change, disease control, resource management, etc., where other state and non-state actors have crucial interests (Buzan *et al.* 1998; Stern 2003). Often there are long traditions of public–private negotiation in these policy sectors. This decentering encourages states to shift their leadership strategy to one of meta-governing emerging foreign policy networks. In so doing they can benefit from slackening the reins while maintaining some degree of control. New social media and the internet may change public opinion, create new forms of social mobilization, and produce new public demands on states for accountability and inclusion in foreign policy-making. Policy networks often connect public opinion and foreign policy-makers (Risse-Kappen 1991).

Second, in response to the objection that foreign policy-making requires swift executive decision, we submit that such decisions will often have to be tested through consultation with actors in relatively permanent networks in order to draw on their expertise and secure their support. While networks may take time to make consensual decisions, their flexibility allows rapid structural adaption to new events and developments. Moreover, once decisions are taken, they must be implemented, and here governments can benefit from mobilizing broad networks of state and non-state actors. As such, states may also use networks to expand their reach into policy areas and geographical regions that would otherwise be difficult to access.

Third, in response to the objection that foreign policy is conflictual and hence ill-suited to network collaboration, we would argue for many foreign policy issues it is too costly to resolve conflicting interest through confrontational strategies. Collaboration through the formation of partnerships and coalitions can help to produce win-win situations that avoid risky confrontations, disgruntled losers, and zero-sum outcomes. Hence, we should not forget that foreign policy is inherently about diplomacy and diplomacy requires networking (Metzl 2001).

Fourth, in response to the objection that foreign policy requires secrecy and seclusion, we note that these demands are not incompatible with the network approach. The network approach clearly recognizes that secrecy and seclusion can facilitate collaborative outcomes, which would not be produced if the content of the negotiations were to be reported in the media (Naurin 2007). In addition, there are clear examples from foreign policy-making, such as the Oslo Agreement, where the network actors were capable of keeping sensitive information to themselves (Torfing *et al.* 2012).

The network approach helps to capture how foreign policies are shaped and reshaped through networked interactions that encompass multiple actors operating at multiple levels. These networks can be analyzed as arenas for policy formulation, as instruments for policy implementation, as structures of policy communication, or as outcomes of the policy process. As an *arena*, networks provide forums that allow dispersed actors to come together to deliberate and negotiate foreign policy content. The recognition of mutual dependency prompts actors to participate in networked arenas and reach working compromises despite differences in perspectives and interests. As an *instrument* for executing foreign policy, networks facilitate coordination and alignment and help to mobilize distributed knowledge, resources, and capacities. As a *structure* of interaction, networks represent patterns of communication, resource exchange, or co-operation that can be analyzed using the techniques of social network analysis (Kahler 2015).[1] Finally, networks can also be an *outcome* of foreign policy processes as recurring social and organizational contacts become partially institutionalized. These emerging networks build trust and social capital that may be valuable in subsequent foreign policy situations.

Taking a network approach provides a framework to capture the pluricentric character of foreign policy and the importance of ongoing negotiations between state and non-state actors operating at different political or geographical scales (McKeown 2016). The network approach also calls our attention to the way that interdependence is managed

---

[1] Kahler (2015) distinguishes between a "network as structure" versus a "network as actor" perspective in international relations.

through the building of sustainable multilateral relationships that are often not well represented by formal international organizations (Morse and Keohane 2014). While not all networks are informal, the network approach permits us to see the interplay between formal institutions and informal social relationships (Samii 2006; McKeown 2016). Network governance also offers a different interpretation of power that emphasizes the actors' relational position in networks in addition to their resources and capabilities (Carpenter 2011; Kahler 2015; Avant and Westerwinter 2016). Finally, the network approach helps us appreciate the way states pursue foreign policy objectives by acting as meta-governors that convene, orchestrate, and give direction to networks. In short, the network approach rejects the standard realist alternative between anarchy and hierarchy and thus provides a particular strategy for conceptualizing complex interdependence (Keohane and Nye 2001; Maoz 2010; Kahler 2015; Avant and Westerwinter 2016).

Social network analysis can be an effective tool for representing and analyzing this complex interdependence and has been increasingly utilized to study international relations (Hafner-Burton *et al.* 2009; Maoz 2010; Avant and Westerwinter 2016). A number of examples relevant to foreign policy-making can be noted. SNA has been used to visualize the complex relationships among advocacy groups and international institutions and to identify actors who have positional power to set policy agendas (Carpenter 2011; Mérand *et al.* 2011; Carpenter *et al.* 2014). It has also been used to study complex patterns of international co-operation and conflict (Maoz *et al.* 2007), transnational secrurity (Avant and Westerwinter 2016), contributions to UN peacekeeping operations (Ward and Dorussen 2016), multilateral negotiations (Money 1998), and new and old media reporting on foreign policy matters (Kim *et al.* 2007; Zeitzoff *et al.* 2015).

The network approach tends to be more useful when power is widely shared. By contrast, when power is exercised unilaterally or hierarchically, actors will not form or work through networks to achieve their goals. Generally, actors must recognize their interdependence with other actors for power to be shared and for the network approach to be relevant. Power-sharing is more likely when foreign policy actors lack sufficient knowledge or resources, when there is a need for coordination or alignment, and when these actors must search for novel solutions to complex problems. Power-sharing is less likely when foreign policy actors are overridingly concerned with sovereign power and state authority and when the task is to implement policy in a standardized or routinized fashion. Studies show that implementation in network settings can be problematic due to the lack of clear rules and division of labor (O'Toole 1997).

Applied to foreign policy, the network approach focuses on the relational dynamics between foreign policy actors and on the consequences of these dynamics. The network approach is perhaps best at representing a meso-level of analysis that examines the relationship between organizations or key decision-makers. For this reason, it is perhaps less attuned to what goes on at either the macro- or micro-levels. For instance, the network approach has a blind spot when it comes to explaining the big socio-economic or political system transformations that set the key parameters of foreign policy (see, however, Maoz 2010). Likewise, the network approach may be inclined to overlook the micro-dynamics taking place within organizations that make foreign policy—although network analysis has been used to investigate micro-level social interaction (see Krackhardt 1992). Finally, by downplaying pure zero-sum conflict situations, the network approach exhibits a collaboration bias.

Empirical application of the network approach in foreign policy

The remainder of this chapter briefly examines some of the existing applications of the network approach in foreign policy-making. To do this, we first create a framework that helps us to locate foreign policy networks within the larger field of policy and governance networks. In doing this, we point to several studies that already apply the network approach to foreign policy. We then present a short case study of how the network approach can be useful in understanding foreign policy-making at its core. The case illustrates the value of applying the network approach to nuclear non-proliferation.

Policy and governance networks are frequently analyzed at the domestic or at the global/transnational level. Only some of these networks are relevant to foreign policy-making. The Venn diagram shown in figure 7.2 illustrates the partial overlap between, on the one hand, domestic and global/transnational policy and governance networks, and on the other hand, those networks pertaining to foreign policy.

The Venn diagram identifies seven different types of policy and governance networks. We briefly describe each of these types and point to exemplary studies, while focusing our attention on the types relevant to foreign policy-making.

Type 1: Policy communities and issue networks engaged in national or sub-national policy-making, which bring together a variety of domestic policy actors to address policy issues that are not directly related to foreign policy.

Classic examples include networks for water management, infrastructure, and employment policy (Marcussen and Torfing 2007). While these domestic networks are primarily involved in policy-making, other domestic networks are involved in policy implementation and delivery

Global and transnational policy and
governance networks

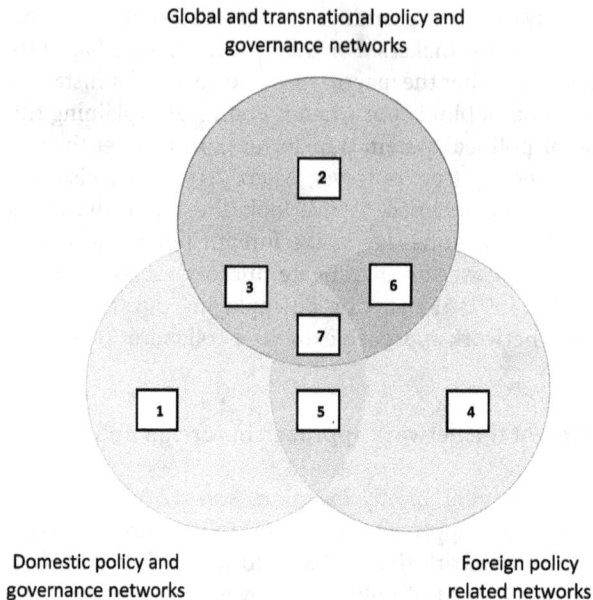

Domestic policy and
governance networks

Foreign policy
related networks

Figure 7.2 The field of policy and governance networks

(Provan and Milward 1995). These networks are often composed of public agencies, service providers, interest organizations, and civil society associations and citizen groups.

> *Type 2: Global/transnational public policy networks dealing with non-foreign policy issues.*

In the late 1990s, scholars began to notice the proliferation of global public policy networks (Reinicke 1999–2000). Many of these networks were "cross-sectoral," bringing together national governments, international organizations, private corporations, and civil society organizations. They developed to deal with challenging transboundary problems that do not respect national borders, such as pollution, infectious disease, human trafficking, and overfishing (Stone 2008). Two specific versions of these networks include transnational advocacy networks that bring private and civil society together around a specific cause (Metzl 2001) and intergovernmental networks that bring together government officials in a particular policy area, e.g., financial regulation, environmental protection, or policing (Slaughter 2009; Woods and Martinez-Diaz 2009).

> *Type 3: Policy and governance networks not directly related to foreign policy, but bringing together domestic, transnational, and perhaps even global actors to engage in multilevel policy coordination.*

Many scholars have noted the importance of multilevel policy and governance networks in the European Union (Hooghe 1996; Levi-Faur 2011). An important example is the EU's Open Method of Coordination (OMC), where multilevel networks are involved in setting, implementing, and monitoring voluntary standards and benchmarks in specific policy areas. Employment policy is one notable area where the OMC operates (Sørensen *et al.* 2015).

Type 4: Intra-governmental networks engaged in foreign policy-making.

National government agencies may often work together in networks to deal with specific foreign policy issues without involving other domestic actors or global/transnational actors (Metzl 2001). For example, foreign policy, military and intelligence agencies routinely work together when dealing with global terrorism threats. Indeed, studies show that failure to provide effective interagency coordination can lead to disastrous outcomes when it comes to preventing terrorism (Zegart 2009).

Type 5: Domestic policy and governance networks aiming to influence the content and direction of foreign policy.

As policy areas such as trade, climate change, humanitarian relief become increasingly seen as a part of foreign policy, domestic policy networks will lobby foreign policy-makers to advocate for specific goals. This advocacy tends to politicize foreign policy-making. Business interests, labor unions, religious groups, and think tanks are all known to engage in lobbying aimed to influence foreign policy (Jacobs and Page 2005; Mearsheimer and Walt 2006). Another example is when particular ethnic or national groups try to influence foreign policy through establishing a web of relationships between their associations and different government agencies. The influence of Cuban exiles on the US government's policy toward Cuba is a case in point (Haney and Vanderbush 1999).

Type 6: Global and transnational policy and governance networks that deal directly with foreign policy issues.

Many global or transnational networks operate as "epistemic communities" (Haas 1992) or knowledge-based networks. These epistemic communities may directly influence foreign policy. For example, Evangelista (1995) found that despite Soviet wariness, a transnational epistemic community of scientists and arms control policy-makers successfully influenced Soviet defense policy. While many transnational policy networks are oriented to knowledge production or sharing, others are better described as global advocacy networks through which global

NGOs aim "to persuade, pressure, and to gain leverage over much more powerful organizations and governments" (Keck and Sikkink 2014: 2). A transnational advocacy network, for example, successfully diffused new global norms opposing land mines (Price 1998).

Transnational intergovernmental networks that influence foreign policy are also visible. One example is "Friends" or "Contact" groups, which have been described as "ad hoc, informal, issue-specific minicoalitions of states or intergovernmental organizations that become involved in and provide support for resolving conflicts and implementing peace agreements" (Whitfield 2007: 9). One important example is the G20, the international forum designed to negotiate and coordinate policy between the nineteen largest national economies and the EU (Woods and Martinez-Diaz 2009). Mobilized in response to the global financial crisis in 2008, the G20 creates a framework for economic diplomacy by bringing together national leaders in annual global summits. The G20 and its predecessors, the G5 and G7, are sometimes referred to as the "informals," a reference to the fact that they are relatively informal mechanisms of negotiation and communication between their members (Alexandroff and Brean 2015). As Diane Stone (2015) notes, the G20 is not an international organization and was not established by treaty. It has no permanent secretariat. Instead, summits are organized by the host country on a rotating basis. However, the work of preparing the summits is serious business and falls largely on senior diplomats known colloquially as the "sherpas."

Type 7: Multilevel policy and governance networks engaged in foreign policy-making.

A number of scholars have noted the importance of networks and network governance in the EU's Common Foreign and Security Policy (CFSP) (Smith 2004; Krahmann 2005; Cross 2011; Mérand *et al.* 2011; Bicchi 2013). Over time, a number of formal information networks have been created to support European foreign policy (Bicchi 2013). Bicchi and Carta (2012), for instance, describe the importance of the COREU, a formalized network of information-sharing among member-states and EU institutions on foreign policy and security matters. This information-sharing network links together twenty-seven European Correspondents located in member-state capitals with the twenty-seven Permanent Representatives in Brussels. They argue that COREU now has a "vast array of functions" and has led to a deepening of European co-operation on foreign policy (Bicchi and Carta 2012). The development of COREU reflects EU treaty obligations that require member-states to share relevant foreign policy information.

Many of the networks described for the EU's CFSP are what Cross (2011, 2013) calls "knowledge-based networks." Over time, she argues, these networks have created processes of "thick diplomacy" (Cross 2011: 216). As she writes: "The most powerful networks are those with the richest backgrounds of historical professionalization as well as those whose motivations derive from their expert knowledge rather than from some other factor" (2011: 218). For example, one of the most influential knowledge-based networks in the CFSP is the network of professional diplomats on the Committee of Permanent Representatives (Coreper). Beyond strong professionalization, she argues that the influence of knowledge-based networks depends on the frequency and quality of their interaction and on their ability to establish strong norms to guide their actions. She finds that Coreper's norms have had a particularly important impact on internal security integration in the EU. She also notes that Coreper serves as a linchpin for other epistemic communities in the foreign policy domain. Mérand *et al.* (2011) analyze the social networks of co-operation among groups involved in the EU's Common Security and Defense Policy. They found that Brussels-based diplomats in the Political and Security Committee play a prominent gatekeeping role in these networks. Wunderlich (2012) uses SNA to map the communication linkages in European external migration policy.

Other networks operate more like advocacy coalitions. Elgström (2016) finds that EU foreign policy is strongly influenced by policy networks of member-states who tend to share particular perspectives—they are "like-minded." These networks tend to be open and informal. For example, he describes the Nordic network in Brussels (Denmark, Finland, and Sweden) as being in "very frequent, almost daily, contact by phone or email" though "very seldom meet[ing] eye-to-eye as a separate group" (Elgström 2016: 8). He argues that these networks tend to work by advocating particular norms. The Nordic network, for example, has been a major advocate for gender equality in EU development policies. He also finds that these networks are crucial in policy negotiations and he describes a pattern of "concentric negotiation" where "new normative ideas are first anchored in an inner circle of network participants and only then promoted to a wider circle of Member States, inside and outside the network" (Elgström 2016: 12).

The typology that we have constructed and presented above helps us to identify four types of policy and governance networks that play a role in foreign policy-making. However, the examples that we have supplied in relation to types 4–7 have not really demonstrated the value of the network approach in relation to what is traditionally considered as the core of foreign policy, namely the question of war, weapons and world peace. As we noted above, it is possible to acknowledge the usefulness of the network approach for many policy domains, while rejecting its applicability to areas where security concerns are paramount. For this reason, our first criteria in selecting a case for more in-depth investigation was that it should sit squarely in the security field. We selected the field of non-proliferation, mainly because we found a number of authors describing the relevance of networks in this policy domain (Lipson 2005; Lennon 2006). Our preliminary perusal of this literature, however, led us to formulate additional criteria. A number of these non-proliferation networks are largely technical in nature, while others are forums for discussion of non-proliferation policy. To make the strongest case for the applicability of networks at the heart of security policy, we wanted a case that demonstrated both policy-making and policy implementation. Finally, reasoning that a national non-proliferation policy network (type 4 above) would not provide as compelling of an example, we searched for a case that was clearly transnational in character (types 6 or 7). Taking these criteria together, we eventually settled on the case of the Proliferation Security Initiative (PSI).

Based on the network approach, we expect the formation of the PSI to be driven by actors' recognition of their interdependence in the face of a particular problem. The resulting pattern of interaction will be non-hierarchical and will combine formal and informal characteristics. Both public and private actors will co-operate in this emerging network. We also anticipate that actors with a central position in the network and the political and organizational capacity for network management will take the lead in the Initiative and serve as meta-governors of the network. We also hypothesize that the success of the Initiative will depend on the prior history of collaboration and its ability to develop and sustain trust among its members and to institutionalize clear and transparent norms and procedures.

A number of scholars have described the PSI as an important example of a transgovernmental network in the security field (Gulati 2013; Eilstrup-Sangiovanni 2015). The PSI was initiated by US President George Bush in 2003 in response to a high-profile failure to prevent the movement of weapons of mass destruction (Winner 2005; Koch 2012). Dunne provides a succinct summary of the initiative: "The Proliferation Security Initiative (PSI) is a means to secure the political commitment of states, and promote their practical cooperation, to counter the transfer of weapons of mass destruction (WMD), their delivery systems and related materials to and from states and non-state actors of proliferation concern. It was conceived as a response to a growing threat from the proliferation of WMD and their means of delivery, and a perceived gap in the global non-proliferation system" (Dunne 2013: vii). The problem of nuclear non-proliferation creates significant mutual interdependence among states. None of them are capable of solving the problem unilaterally.

While the goal of non-proliferation enjoys widespread support, the laws and norms pertaining to the interdiction of maritime shipments are far more tenuous. Thus, the network provides an informal political mechanism to address a difficult problem not yet adequately addressed by formal treaty. Antecedent conditions were favorable: the PSI began as a small core group of trusted US allies. Building on this relationship of mutual trust, the PSI has since grown to a network of 105 states (Proliferation Security Initiative website n.d.).

Interaction in the PSI is not based on a formal treaty and it resists many if not most of the trappings of international organizations. In the rhetoric of the United States, it is an "activity not an organization" (Gulati 2013: 1). Instead, it tries to work with and reinforce existing national and international laws. It has no secretariat and functions through staff support and funding provided by the United States. Gulati describes it as an "informal architecture of co-operation" (2013: 69). Although its technical working groups meet regularly, the PSI as a whole does not have a formal meeting structure and it has no formalized rules of decision-making. It has established a Statement of Interdiction Principles (SIP) to promote political co-operation and encourage best practices. However, these SIPs are relatively vague (Dunne 2013) and according to Koch are notable primarily by what they do not include: "There is no mention of any organizational structure. No groups of member state representatives are created or explicitly envisaged, at senior or expert level, or in any area—diplomatic, military, law enforcement, or intelligence. There is no provision for a central secretariat or staff. No schedule or other system is set up for PSI meetings or training exercises" (Koch 2012: 18).

States become participants (as opposed to "members") of the PSI by endorsing its principles. Although international organizations and NGOs do not directly participate, Gulati (2013) notes that the PSI increasingly coordinates with the private sector and this public–private interaction is likely to intensify in the future. The Initiative tends to operate under a relatively high degree of operational secrecy, both to maintain control over interdictions and to avoid political controversy. Much of the informal co-operation in the PSI takes place between "sub-state" actors—that is, among experts operating in national security-related agencies. These meetings are organized through the "Operational Experts Working Group," which was created at the PSI's second meeting. These meetings exchange information and plan and conduct training practices. As of 2012, forty-nine multinational exercises had been held (Durkalec 2012).

Although there have been attempts to institutionalize the PSI and give it a more formal legal basis, it has largely remained an informal arrangement (Durkalec 2012). This informality is seen as an advantage in addressing the thorny legal and political concerns at the heart of the non-proliferation issue, though the "club-like" quality of the PSI has been criticized (Müller *et al.* 2014). Gulati (2013) argues that the PSI has enabled the United States and other network participants to respond effectively to proliferation challenges while avoiding the tricky legal and political constraints of a more formal regime. These potential constraints could include both political conflicts between states about the approach to non-proliferation and domestic political barriers. Establishing a PSI-like mechanism on a formal treaty basis would likely run into significant domestic opposition in the United States.

Although Koch (2012) and Durkalec (2012) note the difficulty of assessing the contribution and success of PSI in preventing shipments of WMDs (in part because of the secrecy of its operations), it has generally been seen as a flexible and effective mechanism for rapid response to potential WMD threats. Already by 2006, it claimed to have contributed to thirty successful interdictions, a number that grew to about fifty by 2009 (Durkalec 2012: 18). The high-profile interdiction of the German ship *BBC China*, which was carrying equipment for the Pakistani scientist A. Q. Khan's illicit nuclear network, was achieved through the co-operation of the United States, the United Kingdom, Germany, and Italy. Koch (2012) uses this case as an example of how it is difficult to isolate the effect of the PSI, since it is possible that this co-operation would have been achieved without the network.

Non-proliferation is an established international security regime that includes international organizations like the International Atomic Energy Agency and NATO. A number of technical transgovernmental networks operate in this regime, such as the Nuclear Suppliers Group and the Zangger Committee (Lipson 2005). However, Gulati (2013) argues that the PSI is distinctive because it serves a political as well as a technical role. Moreover, he argues that it goes beyond playing a subsidiary role to the existing treaty and intergovernmental organization (IGO) regime structure and instead "acts as a functional substitute for IGO/treaty based cooperation over a highly salient issue" (2013: 49). He also argues that the PSI has "catalyse[d] a shift in the long-held norm regarding the use of force and interdiction on the high seas" (2013: 93). Finally, he shows that the PSI has also served a role of engaging with and to some degree promoting other non-proliferation networks, making it a "network of networks."

The United States is clearly the meta-governor of this transnational network. Gulati describes it as the "quasi-imperial manager" (Gulati 2013: 6). Rather than acting as "hegemon," the United States plays this meta-governor role by facilitating interaction among state and non-state actors, often operating through soft law arrangements. Essentially, it steers this policy area by encouraging states to endorse the SIP and to sign bilateral ship boarding agreements.

We can summarize this case by evaluating it according to the five claims made above about policy network analysis. The first claim was that mutual interdependence is the driver of policy networks. In the case of PSI, the network emerged after a high-profile maritime interdiction failure illuminated this interdependence by demonstrating the insufficiency of addressing the problem unilaterally or via existing international agreements. The second claim is that positional power (as opposed to strictly attributional power) becomes important in policy networks. This claim is somewhat harder to judge given the available information, but we note that the United States, as the initiator of the PSI, has sought to work through its existing alliances. Its capacity to encourage members to sign bilateral ship-boarding agreements is perhaps an expression of this positional power. The expansion of the network from a core of close-knit allies is also an example of the third claim—that networks build on antecedent conditions and relations of trust. The fourth claim is that the ongoing negotiations inherent in networks will become institutionalized over time. The PSI has resisted attempts to give it a formal treaty basis. Nevertheless, the ongoing meetings of the PSI's Operational Experts Working Group and its impressive number of training exercises and interdictions suggest an important degree of institutionalization. Finally, the fifth claim was that networks require a degree of network management or "meta-governance." The United States clearly plays this role of meta-governor of the PSI.

Conclusion

This chapter has summarized the increasingly popular network approach and demonstrated how it can be applied to foreign policy. The network approach has been developed to understanding policy-making and inter-active governance at the local, regional, national, and even supra-national levels, but there have been few reflections on its applicability in the field of foreign policy, which tends to be dominated by statist approaches. We argue that the network approach is applicable in foreign policy-making despite the fact that this policy area is dominated by concerns about sovereignty, executive authority, and by conflict. To illustrate the different ways the network approach may be applied, the chapter presents a typology that identifies four specific types of networks involved in foreign policy-making. In order to demonstrate the relevance of the network approach, we present a brief case study of a network that lies at the heart of foreign policy—the PSI. This example illustrates how the United States has acted as a meta-governor in forming and orchestrating a transnational network of states and other actors engaged in preventing the proliferation of weapons of mass destruction. This non-proliferation network has facilitated successful international co-operation at a political and operational level in an area where formal treaty-based co-operation has serious limitations.

Further development of the network approach has a number of important advantages for the study of foreign policy. As the world becomes more pluricentric, both within nations and at the global level, the network approach provides a framework for understanding the kinds of policy dynamics that are likely to become more prominent. Social network analysis is particularly good at representing the complexity inherent in pluricentric policy domains. As a result of the political constraints imposed by sovereignty, the ongoing basis of transnational negotiations, and the incentives to use backchannels, foreign policy-making is also characterized by an admixture of formality and informality. The network approach is good at describing such situations, as our analysis of PSI suggests. A network approach also does a good job capturing the dynamics associated with multilevel and transboundary policy processes and it can accommodate the increasingly important role that NGOs and other private actors in foreign policy.

On the one hand, the network approach is already well-developed theoretically and methodologically and, on the other hand, there are already a number of empirical studies that explicitly apply a network approach in the field of foreign policy. However, what we still lack are answers to a number of research questions that can help us to more fully understand the value of a network approach in this field. Addressing four critical questions can refine the network approach in the future. First, what are the conditions in foreign policy that push states and non-state actors to adopt network strategies? Second, what are the institutional design issues associated with foreign policy networks? Why do actors adopt one type of foreign policy network rather than another and which types of network are more appropriate for formulating, implementing or diffusing foreign policy? Third, how are policy and governance networks affecting the outcomes of foreign policy-making? Fourth, how can networks be managed or meta-governed to improve the processes and outcomes of foreign policy-making? Finally, how can we ensure the democratic accountability of foreign policy networks? Answering these questions can make an important contribution to Foreign Policy Analysis.

References

Agranoff, Robert and Michael McGuire (2001) Big Questions in Public Network Management Research. *Journal of Public Administration Research and Theory* 11(3), 295–326.

Alexandroff, Alan and Donald Brean (2015) Global Summitry: Its Meaning and Scope Part One, *Global Summitry* 1(1), 1–26.

Allison, Graham (1969) Conceptual Models and the Cuban Missile Crisis, *American Political Science Review* 63(3), 689–718.

Ansell, Christopher and Martin Bartenberger (2016) Tackling Unruly Public Problems, in Christopher Ansell, Jarle Trondal, and Morten Øgård (eds.) *Governance in Turbulent Times*, Oxford: Oxford University Press, 107–136.

Ansell, Christopher and Alison Gash (2008) Collaborative Governance in Theory and Practice, *Journal of Public Administration Research and Theory* 18(4), 543–571.

Ansell, Christopher and Jacob Torfing (2015) How Does Collaborative Governance Scale? *Policy & Politics* 43(3), 315–329.

Ansell, Christopher and Jacob Torfing (eds.) (2016) *Handbook on Theories of Governance*, Cheltenham: Edward Elgar.

Avant, Deborah and Oliver Westerwinter (eds.) (2016) *The New Power Politics: Networks and Transnational Security Governance*, Oxford: Oxford University Press.

Bicchi, Federica (2013) Information Exchanges, Diplomatic Networks and the Construction of European Knowledge in European Union Foreign Policy, *Cooperation and Conflict* 49(2), 239–259.

Bicchi, Federica and Caterina Carta (2012) The COREU Network and the Circulation of Information within EU Foreign Policy, *Journal of European Integration* 34(5), 465–484.

Buzan, Barry, Ole Wæver, and Jaap de Wilde (1998) *Security: A New Framework for Analysis*, Boulder: Lynne Rienner.

Carpenter, Charli (2011) Vetting the Advocacy Agenda: Network Centrality and the Paradox of Weapons Norms, *International Organization* 65(1), 69–102.

Carpenter, Charli, Sirin Duygulu, Alexander Montgomery, and Anna Rapp (2014) Explaining the Advocacy Agenda: Insights from the Human Security Network, *International Organization* 68(2), 449–470.

Cebrowski, Arthur and John Garstka (1998) Network-Centric Warfare: Its Origin and Future, *US Naval Institute Proceedings* 124(1), 28–35.

Cross, Mai'a K. Davis (2011) *Security Integration in Europe: How Knowledge-Based Networks are Transforming the European Union*, Ann Arbor: University of Michigan.

Cross, Mai'a K. Davis (2013) A European Trans-Governmental Intelligence Network and the Role of IntCen, *Perspectives on European Politics and Society* 14(3): 388–402.

Dean, Mitchell (1999) *Governmentality: Power and Rule in Modern Society*, London: Sage.

Dunne, Aaron (2013) *The Proliferation Security Initiative: Legal Considerations and Operational Realities*, Stockholm: SIPRI.

Durkalec, Jacek (2012) *The Proliferation Security Initiative: Evolution and Future Prospects*, EU Non-Proliferation Consortium, Non-proliferation papers 16.

Eilstrup-Sangiovanni, Mette (2005) Transnational Networks and New Security Threats, *Cambridge Review of International Affairs* 18(1), 7–13.

Eilstrup-Sangiovanni, Mette (2015) Varieties of Cooperation: Governance Networks in International Security, in Miles Kahler (ed.) *Networked Politics: Agency, Power, and Governance*, Ithaca, NY: Cornell University Pres, 194–227.

Elgström, Ole (2016) Norm Advocacy Networks: Nordic and Like-Minded Countries in EU Gender and Development Policy, *Cooperation and Conflict* 52(2), 224–240.

Emerson, Kirk, Tina Nabatchi, and Stephen Balogh (2012) An Integrative Framework for Collaborative Governance, *Journal of Public Administration Research and Theory* 22(1), 1–29.

Emirbayer, Mustafa (1997) Manifesto for a Relational Sociology, *American Journal of Sociology* 103(2), 281–317.

Esmark, Anders and Peter Triantafillou (2007) Document Analysis of Network Topography and Network Programmes, in Peter Bogason and Mette Zølner (eds.) *Methods in Democratic Network Governance*, Basingstoke: Palgrave Macmillan, 99–124.

Evangelista, Matthew (1995) The Paradox of State Strength: Transnational Relations, Domestic Structures, and Security Policy in Russia and the Soviet Union, *International Organization* 49(1), 1–38.

Foucault, Michel (1991) Governmentality, in Graham Burchell, Colin Gordon, and Peter Miller (eds.) *The Foucault Effect: Studies in Governmentality*, Chicago: University of Chicago Press, 87–104.

Freeman, Linton (2004) *The Development of Social Network Analysis: A Study in the Sociology of Science*, Vancouver: Empirical Press.

Gray, Barbara (1989) *Collaborating: Finding Common Ground for Multiparty Problems*, San Francisco: Jossey-Bass.

Gulati, Pallavi (2013) *Regime Evolution and the Non-Proliferation Regime: The Proliferation Security Initiative as a Case Study of Transgovernmental Networking*, University of Denver, *Electronic Theses and Dissertations*.

Haas, Peter (1992) Introduction: Epistemic Communities and International Policy Coordination, *International Organization* 46(1), 1–35.

Hafner-Burton, Emilie Miles Kahler, and Alexander Montgomery (2009) Network Analysis for International Relations, *International Organization* 63(3), 559–592.

Haney, Patrick and Walt Vanderbush (1999) The Role of Ethnic Interest Groups in US Foreign Policy: The Case of the Cuban American National Foundation, *International Studies Quarterly* 43(2), 341–361.

Heclo, Hugh (1978) Issue Networks and the Executive Establishment, in Anthony King (ed.) *The New American Political System*, Washington, DC: American Enterprise Institute for Public Policy Research, 87–124.

Hooghe, Lisbet. (1996) *Cohesion Policy and European Integration: Building Multi-Level Governance*, Oxford: Oxford University Press.

Jacobs, Lawrence and Benjamin Page (2005) Who Influences US Foreign Policy? *American Political Science Review* 99(1), 107–123.

Jessop, Bob (1998) The Rise of Governance and the Risks of Failure: The Case of Economic Development, *International Social Science Journal* 155, 29–45.

Jessop, Bob (2002) *The Future of the Capitalist State*, Cambridge: Polity Press.

Jordan, Grant (1990) Sub-Governments, Policy Communities and Networks Refilling the Old Bottles? *Journal of Theoretical Politics* 2(3), 319–338.

Kahler, Miles (ed.) (2009) *Networked Politics: Agency, Power, and Governance*, Ithaca, NY: Cornell University Press.

Kahler, Miles (ed.) (2015) *Networked Politics: Agency, Power, and Governance*, Ithaca, NY: Cornell University Press.

Keck, Margaret and Kathryn Sikkink (2014) *Activists Beyond Borders: Advocacy Networks in International Politics*, Ithaca, NY: Cornell University Press.

Kenis, Patrick (2016) Network, in Christopher Ansell and Jacob Torfing (eds.) *Handbook on Theories of Governance*, Cheltenham: Edward Elgar, 149–157.

Kenis, Patrick and Keith Provan (2007) Modes of Network Governance: Structure, Management, and Effectiveness, *Journal of Public Administration Research and Theory* 18(2), 229–252.

Keohane, Robert and Joseph Nye (2001) *Power and Interdependence*, New York: Longman.

Kersbergen, Kees Van and Frans Van Waarden (2004) "Governance" as a Bridge Between Disciplines: Cross-Disciplinary Inspiration Regarding Shifts in Governance and Problems of Governability, Accountability and Legitimacy, *European Journal of Political Research* 43(2), 143–171.

Kickert, Walter, Erik-Hans Klijn, and Joop Koppenjan (eds.) (1997) *Managing Complex Networks*, London: Sage.

Kim, Jang, Tuo-Yu Su, and Junhao Hong (2007) The Influence of Geopolitics and Foreign Policy on the US and Canadian Media: An Analysis of Newspaper Coverage of Sudan's Darfur Conflict, *The Harvard International Journal of Press/Politics* 12(3), 87–95.

Klijn, Erik-Hans, Jurian Edelenbos, and Bram Steijn (2010) Trust in Governance Networks: Its Impacts on Outcomes, *Administration & Society* 42(2), 193–221.

Knoke, David (1994) *Political Networks: The Structural Perspective*, Cambridge: Cambridge University Press.

Koch, Susan (2012) *Proliferation Security Initiative: Origins and Evolution*, Washington, DC: Center for the Study of Weapons of Mass Destruction.

Kooiman, Jan (ed.) (1993) *Modern Governance*, London: Sage.

Kooiman, Jan (2003) *Governing as Governance*, London: Sage.

Koppenjan, Joop and Erik-Hans Klijn (2004) *Managing Uncertainties in Networks*, London: Routledge.

Krackhardt, David (1992) The Strength of Strong Ties: The Importance of *Philos* in Organizations, in Nitin Nohria and Robert Eccles (eds.) *Networks and Organizations*, Cambridge, MA: Harvard Business School Press, 216–239.

Krahmann, Elke (2005) Security Governance and Networks: New Theoretical Perspectives in Transatlantic Security, *Cambridge Review of International Affairs* 18(1), 15–30.

Lennon, Alexander (2006) *Why Do We Do Track Two? Transnational Security Policy Networks and US Nuclear Nonproliferation Policy*, doctoral dissertation. University of Maryland, College Park.

Levi-Faur, David (2011) Regulatory Networks and Regulatory Agencification: Towards a Single European Regulatory Space, *Journal of European Public Policy* 18(6), 810–829.

Lipson, Michael (2005) Transgovernmental Networks and Nonproliferation: International Security and the Future of Global Governance, *International Journal* 61(1), 179–198.

Maoz, Zeev (2010) *Networks of Nations: The Evolution, Structure, and Impact of International Networks, 1816–2001*, Cambridge: Cambridge University Press.

Maoz, Zeev, Ranan Kuperman, Lesley Terris, and Ilan Talmud (2007) What is the Enemy of My Enemy? Causes and Consequences of Imbalanced International Relations, 1816–2001, *Journal of Politics* 69(1), 100–115.

March, James and Johan Olsen (1995) *Democratic Governance*, New York: The Free Press.

Marcussen, Martin and Hans Olsen (2007) Transcending Analytical Cliquishness with Second-Generation Governance Network Analysis, in Martin Marcussen and Jacob Torfing (eds.) *Democratic Network Governance in Europe*, Basingstoke: Palgrave Macmillan, 273–292.

Marcussen, Martin and Jacob Torfing (eds.) (2007) *Democratic Network Governance in Europe*, Basingstoke: Palgrave Macmillan.

Marsh, David and Roderick Rhodes (eds.) (1992) *Policy Networks in British Government*, Oxford: Clarendon Press.

Mayntz, Renate (1993a) Modernization and the Logic of Interorganizational Networks, in John Child, Michel Crozier, and Renate Mayntz (eds.) *Societal Change between Markets and Organization*, Aldershot: Avebury, 3–18.

Mayntz, Renate (1993b) Governing Failure and the Problem of Governability: Some Comments on a Theoretical Paradigm, in Jan Kooiman (ed.) *Modern Governance*, London: Sage, 9–20.

McKeown, Timothy (2016) A Different Two-Level Game: Foreign Policy Officials' Personal Networks and Coordinated Policy Innovation, *Review of International Political Economy* 23(1), 93–122.

Mearsheimer, John and Stephen Walt (2006) The Israel Lobby and US Foreign Policy, *Middle East Policy* 13(3), 29–87.

Mérand, Frederic, Stephanie Hofmann, and Bastien Irondelle (2011) Governance and State Power: A Network Analysis of European Security, *Journal of Common Market Studies* 49(1), 121–147.

Metzl, Jamie (2001) Network Diplomacy: Politics and Diplomacy, *Georgetown Journal of International Affairs* 3(2), 77–87.

Milward, Brinton and Keith Provan (2006) A Manager's Guide to Choosing and Using Networks, Networks and Partnerships Series, IBM Center for Business and Government.

Money, Bruce (1998) International Multilateral Negotiations and Social Networks, *Journal of International Business Studies* 29(4), 695–710.

Morse, Julia and Robert Keohane. (2014) Contested Multilateralism, *The Review of International Organizations* 9(4), 385–412.

Müller, Harald, Carmen Wunderlich, Marco Fey, Klaus-Peter Ricke, and Annette Schaper (2014) *Non-Proliferation Clubs vs. the NPT*, Stockholm: Strålsäkerhetsmyndigheten.

Naurin, Daniel (2007) *Deliberation Behind Closed Doors: Transparency and Lobbying in the European Union*, Colchester: ECPR Press.

O'Toole, Lawrence (1997) Implementing Public Innovations in Network Settings, *Administration & Society* 29(2), 115–138.

Padgett, John F. and Christopher K. Ansell (1993) Robust Action and the Rise of the Medici, 1400–1434, *American Journal of Sociology* 98(6), 1259–1319.

Peters, B. Guy (2013) *Institutional Theory in Political Science: The New Institutionalism*, 3rd edition, New York: Continuum.

Powell, Walter and Paul J. DiMaggio (eds.) (1991) *The New Institutionalism in Organizational Analysis*, Chicago: University of Chicago Press.

Price, Richard (1998) Reversing the Gun Sights: Transnational Civil Society Targets Land Mines, *International Organization* 52(3), 613–644.

Proliferation Security Initiative website (n.d.) www.psi-online.info/Vertretung/ psi/en/03-endorsing-states/0-PSI-endorsing-states.html (last accessed January 10, 2017).

Provan, Keith G. and Patrick Kenis (2008) Modes of Network Governance: Structure, Management, and Effectiveness, *Journal of Public Administration Research and Theory* 18(2), 229–252.

Provan, Keith A. and H. Brinton Milward (1995) A Preliminary Theory of Interorganizational Network Effectiveness: A Comparative Study of Four Community Mental Health Systems, *Administrative Science Quarterly* 40(1), 1–33.

Reinicke, Wolfgang (1999–2000) The Other World Wide Web: Global Public Policy Networks, *Foreign Policy* 144, 44–57.

Rhodes, Roderick (1997a) *Understanding Governance*, Buckingham: Open University Press.

Rhodes, Roderick (1997b) Foreword, in Walter Kickert, Erik-Hans Klijn, and Joop Koppenjan (eds.) *Managing Complex Networks: Strategies for the Public Sector*, London: Sage, 11–15.

Risse-Kappen, Thomas (1991) Public Opinion, Domestic Structure, and Foreign Policy in Liberal Democracies, *World Politics* 43(4), 479–512.

Roberts, Nancy (2000) Wicked Problems and Network Approaches to Resolution, *International Public Management Review* 1(1), 1–19.

Rose, Nicholas and Peter Miller (1992) Political Power beyond the State: Problematics of Government, *British Journal of Sociology* 43(2), 173–205.

Samii, Abbas (2006) The Iranian Nuclear Issue and Informal Networks, *Naval War College Review* 59(1), article 5.

Scharpf, Fritz (1994) Games Real Actors could Play: Positive and Negative Coordination in Embedded Negotiations, *Journal of Theoretical Politics* 6(1), 27–53.

Scott, John (2012) *Social Network Analysis*, London: Sage.

Slaughter, Anne-Marie (2009) *A New World Order*, Princeton: Princeton University Press.

Smith, Michael (2004) Institutionalization, Policy Adaptation and European Foreign Policy Cooperation, *European Journal of International Relations* 10(1), 95–136.

Sørensen, Eva and Jacob Torfing (2007a) *Theories of Democratic Network Governance*, Basingstoke: Palgrave Macmillan.

Sørensen, Eva and Jacob Torfing (2007b) Studying Local Network Exclusion through Observation and Diaries, in Peter Bogason and Mette Zølner (eds.) *Methods in Democratic Network Governance*, Basingstoke: Palgrave Macmillan, 148–178.

Sørensen, Eva and Jacob Torfing (2009) Making Governance Networks Effective and Democratic through Metagovernance, *Public Administration* 87(2), 234–258.

Sørensen, Eva, Peter Triantafillou, and Bodil Damgaard (2015) Governing EU Employment Policy: Does Collaborative Governance Scale Up?, *Policy & Politics* 43(3), 331–347.

Stern, Eric (2003) Crisis Studies and Foreign Policy Analysis: Insights, Synergies, and Challenges, *International Studies Review* 5(2), 155–202.

Stone, Deborah (2008) Global Public Policy, Transnational Policy Communities, and their Networks, *Policy Studies Journal* 36(1), 19–38.

Stone, Deborah (2015) The Group of 20 Transnational Policy Community: Governance Networks, Policy Analysis and Think Tanks, *International Review of Administrative Sciences* 81(4), 793–811.

Torfing, Jacob, B. Guy Peters, Jon Pierre, and Eva Sørensen (2012) *Interactive Governance: Advancing the Paradigm*, Oxford: Oxford University Press.

Triantafillou, Peter (2007) Governing the Formation and Mobilization of Governance Networks, in Eva Sørensen and Jacob Torfing (eds.) *Theories of Democratic Network Governance*, Basingstoke: Palgrave Macmillan, 183–198.

Van Kersbergen, Kees and Frans van Waarden (2004) Governance as a Bridge between Disciplines: Cross-Disciplinary Inspiration Regarding Shifts in Governance and Problems of Governability, Accountability and Legitimacy, *European Journal of Political Research* 43(2), 143–171.

Ward, Hugh and Han Dorussen (2016) Standing Alongside Your Friends: Network Centrality and Providing Troops to UN Peacekeeping Operations, *Journal of Peace Research* 53(3), 392–408.

Weber, Edward and Anne Khademian (2008) Wicked Problems, Knowledge Challenges, and Collaborative Capacity Builders in Network Settings, *Public Administration Review* 68(2), 334–349.

White, Harrison C. (1992) *Identity and Control: A Structural Theory of Social Action*, Princeton: Princeton University Press.

Whitfield, Teresa (2007) *Friends Indeed? The United Nations, Groups of Friends, and the Resolution of Conflict*, Washington, DC: US Institute of Peace Press.

Winner, Andrew (2005) The Proliferation Security Initiative: The New Face of Interdiction, *Washington Quarterly* 28(2), 129–143.

Woods, Ngaire and Leonardo Martinez-Diaz (eds.) (2009) *Networks of Influence? Developing Countries in a Networked Global Order*, Oxford: Oxford University Press.

Wunderlich, Daniel (2012) Europeanization through the Grapevine: Communication Gaps and the Role of International Organizations in Implementation Networks of EU External Migration Policy, *Journal of European Integration* 34(5), 485–503.

Zegart, Amy (2009) *Spying Blind: The CIA, the FBI, and the Origins of 9/11*, Princeton: Princeton University Press.

Zeitzoff, Thomas, John Kelly, and Gilad Lotan (2015) Using Social Media to Measure Foreign Policy Dynamics: An Empirical Analysis of the Iranian–Israeli Confrontation (2012–13), *Journal of Peace Research* 52(3), 368–383.

Zølner, Mette, Iben Rasmussen, and Allan Hansen (2007) Qualitative Interviews: Studying Network Narratives, in Mette Zølner and Peter Bogason (eds.) *Methods in Democratic Network Governance*, Basingstoke: Palgrave Macmillan, 125–147.

8

Policy diffusion and transfer meet foreign policy

Katja Biedenkopf and Alexander Mattelaer

Policy diffusion describes a process through which policies spread from one governmental jurisdiction to multiple other jurisdictions, whereas policy transfer focuses on individual transfers of a policy from one jurisdiction to another. Policy diffusion could be characterized as a set of policy transfers. Diffusion generally focuses on structure and finding patterns, while transfer tends to concentrate on agency and individual cases (Biedenkopf *et al.* 2017: 92–93). A defining feature of both policy diffusion and transfer is the causal interconnection between individual policy decisions in contrast to the coincidental but causally unconnected adoption of similar policies. Policy decisions in different countries can be connected through conceptually different causal mechanisms, generally differentiated as emulation, learning, and competition (Dolowitz and Marsh 2000; Simmons and Elkins 2004; Marsh and Sharman 2009; Gilardi 2012).

The analytical lens of interdependent policy decisions and mutual influence among foreign policy-makers can add a useful angle to Foreign Policy Analysis (FPA). While some strands of FPA include international drivers and constraints of the foreign policy-making process in their analytic models, an explicit application of policy diffusion and transfer concepts is a rare find. Yet, those approaches could mutually enrich each other since policy-makers do not devise their policies in a vacuum. Ideas and influences can stem from domestic sources and previous own experiences but, in a number of cases, they interact with ideas and influences that originate from external sources. Since FPA explores various factors that can explain foreign policy processes and outcomes (Hudson 2005: 3), including aspects extracted from policy diffusion and transfer literature can complement and enrich the analysis.

Policy diffusion and transfer can be linked to foreign policy in two ways. First, they can be seen as an instrument of foreign policy and, second, they can provide an analytical lens for explaining certain foreign policy choices. When countries purposefully support and foster the diffusion and transfer of their own policy through activities such as diplomatic outreach, the provision of policy-related information, using market access as incentive (Vogel 1997), and capacity building (Biedenkopf *et al.* 2017), it can be considered external governance and an instrument of foreign policy (Biedenkopf and Dupont 2013: 190–192). Those aspects are not discussed in this chapter since they relate to the content of foreign policy rather than explaining decisions on what kind of foreign policy to pursue, and why. The focus of this chapter is thus on policy diffusion and transfer as independent variable in the analysis of foreign policy choices.

The following section outlines policy diffusion and transfer as public policy approaches, which is followed by a proposal for ways in which these two concepts could enrich FPA. The fourth section illustrates the application of a policy diffusion lens to foreign policy decisions, namely the case of planning doctrine for military crisis response operations. It explores the historical origins of NATO's operational planning doctrine and how it has diffused to other international organizations such as the EU and the UN. The concluding section provides some reflections on the contribution and limitations of integrating policy diffusion and transfer in FPA.

Policy diffusion and transfer

Policy diffusion and transfer can occur through distinctive mechanisms that describe different sequences of events; explaining how one policy can affect the adoption of policies in other jurisdictions (Braun and Gilardi 2006: 299; Checkel 2008: 115). The main diffusion mechanisms are learning, emulation, and competition. Various conditions can render diffusion and transfer more or less likely but often these are case-specific. They include the policy's degree of politicization, the intensity and type of interaction among policy-makers from different jurisdictions, and cultural, historical, and institutional factors. Since those factors can be foreign policy specific, they are discussed in the third section that proposes ways to combine policy diffusion and transfer with FPA.

The concept of diffusion is not confined to political science and international relations. Sociologists, anthropologists, and economists, among others, have studied the diffusion of various kinds of innovations such as new technologies and educational practices (Hägerstrand 1967;

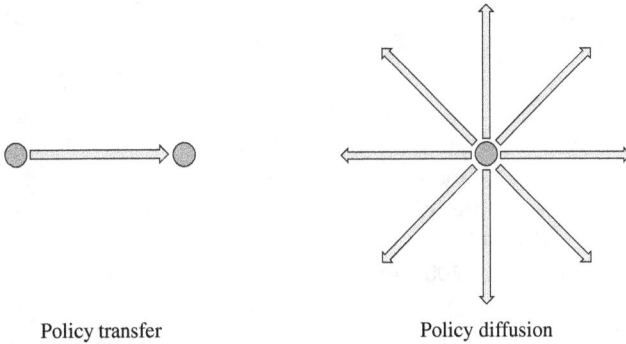

Policy transfer   Policy diffusion

Figure 8.1 Policy transfer and diffusion

Brown 1969; Rogers 1995). Under the label of *Galton's Problem*,[1] the interaction among jurisdictions and mutual policy influence initially was characterized as a complication for comparative political studies (Naroll 1965; Braun and Gilardi 2006: 299). The explicit analysis of inter-jurisdictional diffusion processes slowly emerged in the early 1970s (Walker 1969: 890–892; Gray 1973; Eyestone 1977). Initial policy diffusion studies analyzed the spread of policies among states in the United States, searching for diffusion patterns and explanatory state-level factors (Clark 1985; Savage 1985). The geographical scope of policy diffusion studies expanded over the course of time. The explicit and separate focus on policy transfer gained currency in the 1980s when comparative politics scholars criticized policy diffusion studies' focus on process rather than the substance of the diffused policy (Clark 1985: 65; Dolowitz and Marsh 1996: 345). In political science and international relations, policy diffusion research surged in the 1990s (Graham *et al.* 2013).

A terminology of different but related concepts emerged over the course of time with policy transfer, policy diffusion, policy learning, and policy convergence at their core. Policy transfer centers on the transfer of a policy from one individual jurisdiction to another one. Policy diffusion studies a set of transfers from one source to a multitude of jurisdictions. Figure 8.1 illustrates the difference between policy transfer and diffusion. Policy learning refers to the revision and updating of an actor's knowledge about a given policy. It is a separate strand of literature (see chapter 9 in this volume) but also one of the diffusion and transfer mechanisms when the source of learning is another country's policy. Policy convergence

---

[1] In the late nineteenth century, Sir Francis Galton criticized a study that claimed that different cultures independently follow the same sequence of development. He stressed that cross-cultural borrowing could have resulted in the similarities rather than inde-pendent developments (Marsh and Sharman 2009: 273).

focuses on increasing or decreasing similarities among policies in different jurisdictions and can be the result of diffusion and transfer but also of unrelated policy developments (Holzinger *et al.* 2007: 13–17).

Both the policy transfer literature and the diffusion literature identify a varying number of mechanisms by which policy can spread from one jurisdiction to others. Some studies go into greater detail and make finer distinctions between the different mechanisms than others (for examples, see Lazer 2001: 476–482; Checkel 2005: 808–813; Braun and Gilardi 2006: 306–312; Lazer 2006: 457–466; Simmons *et al.* 2006: 789–801). Yet, a growing convergence on three broad mechanisms has emerged: learning, emulation, and competition. Some studies additionally include the fourth mechanism of coercion, which is the imposition of policy change by one jurisdiction on another (Marsh and Sharman 2009: 271–272; Gilardi 2012: 460–461). The three other mechanisms are voluntary processes (Tews 2005: 65). The different mechanisms are based on different ontologies, actor motivations, and logics of action. While emulation can be attributed to social constructivist approaches, learning and competition are based on (bounded) rational actor models. What all mechanisms have in common is that they ultimately shape the policy positions of policy-makers so that they adopt a policy choice similar to another jurisdiction's policy.

The variation among policy diffusion studies with regard to their conceptualization and labeling of the mechanisms renders a clear overview of existing literature and a comparison of findings difficult. Especially learning and emulation have been conceptualized in numerous variations and definitions. A significant share of studies, however, differentiates these two mechanisms based on their logic of action (Shipan and Volden 2008: 842–843; Gilardi 2012: 461–469). Learning is considered a (bounded) rational action in which actors analyze an external policy to draw lessons from it. They act based on a logic that gauges the possible consequences of adopting a certain policy. Emulation, by contrast, is defined as a policy decision based on the perception that adopting an external policy is the appropriate course of action. Diffusion or transfer occurs thus based on a policy's socially constructed characteristics. Table 8.1 summarizes the three mechanisms, which are outlined in more detail in the following subsections.

Learning

Learning is the updating of beliefs and knowledge based on the analysis of a policy or practice. It can be both a policy diffusion and transfer mechanism as well as a public policy approach in its own right. The main conceptual difference between the two is their scope of application. Learning as a diffusion and transfer mechanism is limited to learning

Table 8.1 Diffusion and transfer mechanisms

Mechanism	Description
Learning	A policy provides positive and negative experiences from which external policy-makers draw lessons for their own policy (logic of consequences).
Emulation	A policy is taken over by external policy-makers because they consider it a legitimate and appropriate measure (logic of appropriateness).
Competition	A policy changes the cost and benefit structures of adopting a similar policy in another jurisdiction (logic of consequences).

from policies that have been adopted externally, while the public policy approach mostly focuses on learning from own domestic experiences. As discussed in detail in chapter 9 of this volume, learning from a country's own or another country's historical experience is an approach that has been applied to foreign policy. This chapter exclusively discusses learning as a policy diffusion and transfer mechanism.

While the term learning has widely been used in a range of studies, its definition can differ significantly (for examples of different applications see Simon 1965: 72–73; Meseguer 2005; Dolowitz 2009: 323; Knill and Tosun 2009: 877–878). At its core, learning describes the process in which actors revise their beliefs and update their knowledge based on the analysis of another jurisdiction's policy. The depth and intensity of actors' analysis can vary. Although some authors label the updating of beliefs based on the conviction that a given external policy is appropriate *social learning* (Levy 1994: 286; Checkel 2001: 561–562; Schimmelfennig and Sedelmeier 2004: 667–668; Dolowitz 2009: 323; Knill and Tosun 2009: 877–878), this is conceptualized here, as in many other studies (see for example Zürn and Checkel 2005: 1052; Simmons *et al.* 2006: 799–801; Shipan and Volden 2008: 842–843; Gilardi 2012: 461–469), a separate mechanism, namely emulation (see the following subsection), since it is based on a logic of appropriateness rather than a logic of consequences (March and Olsen 1989).

The learning mechanism is triggered by the dissemination of information about a given policy to actors in other jurisdictions that have not (yet) adopted a similar policy. Actors in possible follower jurisdictions can draw lessons from the provided information, which can lead to the revision of behavior, strategies, and policy positions (Meseguer 2005: 73; Gilardi 2012: 463–466), which can in turn lead to actors' decisions to pursue policy change in their own country that is informed by the lessons learned from abroad. Learning adds more complexity to an actor's construction of arguments (Etheredge 1985) and reduces uncertainties about a certain policy option and its consequences (Levy 1994: 290). Learning essentially takes place at the individual level. For it to lead to policy change, which would be learning at the level of a jurisdiction, sufficient and central policy-makers need to change their beliefs so as to garner the necessary political support. Institutional and political constraints can impede the transmission of individual level learning into collective learning at the level of a country or another type of jurisdiction.

Most actors in most incidents draw lessons in a bounded manner. Fully rational learning presupposes complete knowledge of all exact consequences of each possible alternative while bounded learning acknowledges that actors operate in a limited environment of given premises that they accept as basis for their choices and do not search for complete knowledge (Simon 1965). Actors are not aware of all information available and they do not attempt to gather all existing information given their resources limitations such as time, staff, and cognitive capacity. Actors also do not weigh all information equally. Given their prior beliefs and ideologies they weigh some pieces of information more than others, and choose to draw lessons from this particular subset of information.

Learning from other countries' foreign policies seems a plausible course of events that can contribute to explaining a country's foreign policy choice. Learning from others' experiences can reduce uncertainties with regard to the possible effect of a foreign policy and provide ideas, especially in a situation in which a country has taken the principled decision to change its existing policy and is in search for the optimal new policy design.

Emulation

Like the learning mechanism, the emulation mechanism also is activated when actors become aware of another jurisdiction's policy. Yet the logic on which they base their action differs. They deem a particular external policy a legitimate and appropriate measure (March and Olsen 1989: 160–162). The concept of emulation is distinct from the concept of learning because it does not involve the (bounded) rational analysis of the external policy (logic of consequences), but rather the advocating of a similar policy based on the normative perception that it is particularly appropriate (logic of appropriateness).

A range of different terminologies can be found that can be subsumed under the concept of emulation (for examples of different terminologies see DiMaggio and Powell 1983: 150–154; Braun and Gilardi 2006: 299–300; Shipan and Volden 2008: 842–843). Emulation often occurs based on common norms (Finnemore and Sikkink 1998: 891) that are created through the socialization and regular interaction among actors, leading to their similar assessment of a policy and its appropriateness (Simmons and Elkins 2004: 799–801; Polillo and Guillén 2005: 1777). Once a policy has spread widely it often automatically is considered appropriate (Finnemore and Sikkink 1998: 893–905; Johnston 2001: 492–495; Checkel 2005: 804). International peers can reward the adoption of a policy with their recognition of the respective country as part of their group (Braun and Gilardi 2006: 311–312). Emulation can also occur without necessarily sharing the same norms. In this case, the motivation is based on the high esteem and perceived success of another jurisdiction (Finnemore and Sikkink 1998: 906; Polillo and Guillén 2005: 1778–1779; Shipan and Volden 2008: 842–843), which generally results from the fit of the policy and its perceived output with aims of the actors and jurisdictions that emulate it.

Emulation seems a plausible mechanism to contribute to explaining foreign policy choices since the community of foreign policy-makers is relatively well connected through a number of international organizations such as the United Nations and NATO. Among the involved actors, socialization effects that can lead to policy choices based on shared perceptions of appropriateness seem likely to occur.

Competition

The competition mechanism is triggered by the alteration of the costs and benefits of introducing policy similar to another country's policy. Actors adjust their behavior, strategies, and policy positions to this altered situation. One country's policy can alter the costs and benefits of introducing similar measures in another country (Lavenex and Uçarer 2004: 421; Elkins and Simmons 2005: 39–42; Braun and Gilardi 2006: 308–309). For example, the compliance costs for multinational businesses with measures similar to another country's policy can be considerably lowered, which can make it politically easier for policy-makers to adopt a similar measure rather than a radically different one.

A number of different terms are used in academic literature to describe the competition mechanism (for examples of different terms see Vogel 1997; Lazer 2001: 476–482; Simmons and Elkins 2004: 173; Braun and Gilardi 2006: 308–309; Lazer 2006: 457–466; Simmons et al. 2006: 792–795). Policy can diffuse and be transferred based on the competition between two or more jurisdictions to attract internationally mobile capital and businesses. Policy in one jurisdiction can aim at rendering its domestic conditions more attractive for capital and businesses and through this can exert competitive pressure to introduce a similar policy in other jurisdictions with which it is in direct competition (Lazer 2001: 476; Braun and Gilardi 2006: 308–309). This mechanism is often associated with a race to the bottom. Yet, interconnection can also lead to a race to the top when a certain policy decision in one country makes it more attractive or easier to adopt a similar policy in another country (Vogel 1997: 556–557; Drezner 2001: 75–76). This could for example be the case in the area of purchasing military equipment. One country's purchasing decision can have implications for others in terms of equipment compatibility in case collaboration is considered and the costs of developing and producing the equipment might be lowered with larger orders.

The competition mechanism differs from explicitly coercive measures such as trade sanctions, conditionality, and (the threat of) the use of force. Although these coercive measures can also change the costs and benefits of introducing policy similar to another country's policy, they differ in their nature. Coercive measures change costs and benefits purposefully through a conscious action by the country adopting it. In the competition mechanism, however, policy introduces requirements that apply within a given country and the change to costs and benefit structures in other countries often merely is a by-product of the policy decision.

The competition mechanism seems somewhat less applicable to the realm of foreign policy than to policies that aim at regulating market activities or environmental and social regulation but it cannot entirely be discarded. For example, the decision to enact sanctions on another country can be deemed too economically costly by one country acting unilaterally but a similar policy decision by a large economy can alter cost–benefit calculations by other countries and thereby influence their foreign policy decision to impose sanctions.

Horizontal and vertical diffusion and transfer

Policy diffusion and transfer studies often analyze processes among jurisdictions of the same level of governance, which in many cases are nation states. This is termed horizontal diffusion and transfer. Yet, policy can also diffuse and be transferred across levels of governance, for example, from a sub-national entity to a country or from a country via sub-national jurisdictions or international organizations to another country. Figure 8.2 illustrates horizontal diffusion/transfer as well as a vertical diffusion/transfer process via an international organization.

International organizations such as NATO and the EU can provide fora in which policy-makers and officials interact on a regular basis. Mutual influence on each other over the course of time can approximate their norms, ideas, and concepts, leading to shared norms through socialization (Checkel 2005; Alecu de Flers and Müller 2012: 25). This can provide the basis for emulation. Actors can try to influence the discourse and action within an international organization according to their own foreign policy preferences, and thereby influence peers and their policies.

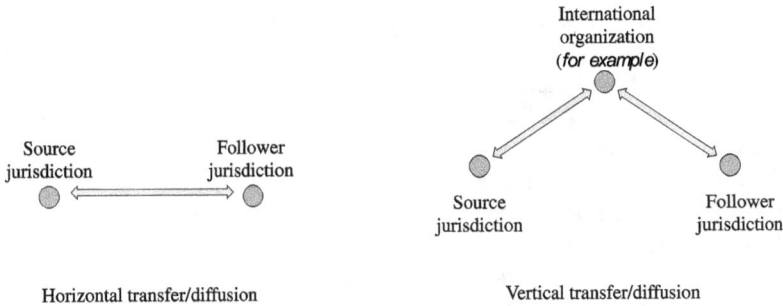

Figure 8.2 Horizontal and vertical transfer/diffusion

They can, at the same time, try to diffuse their policies and receive policies that are diffused from other sources.

Interaction within international organizations can also foster learning in addition to or in lieu of emulation. International organizations can raise awareness of an external policy and provide analysis to enable foreign policy-makers to learn from certain foreign policy experiences. In addition to formal organizations, formal and informal networks can also foster emulation and learning (see chapter 7 in this volume).

The domain of foreign policy is characterized by a number of international organizations in which certain foreign policy-makers interact closely and frequently. This includes the already mentioned UN, NATO, and EU. This suggests that policy diffusion and transfer, in particular, through the emulation and learning mechanisms seem likely. The following section further delves into the mutual enrichment between FPA and policy diffusion/transfer approaches.

Policy diffusion and transfer in the realm of foreign policy

Policy diffusion and transfer can be useful approaches for studying foreign policy change since domestic policy-making has increasingly become entangled with international policies and politics. Growing collaboration within international organizations and networks increases foreign policy-makers' exposure to policies adopted elsewhere. Foreign policy-makers often need to balance external normative and other pressures with domestic concerns and politics. From this follows that, while in many cases FPA primarily investigates how the domestic politics and decision-making parameters affect foreign policy-makers' choices within a given country, external influences cannot entirely be separated from those decisions. For this reason, policy diffusion and transfer concepts seem to bear the potential to enrich and complement existing accounts of FPA.

External policy is most likely one of many factors that can explain a certain foreign policy decision and outcome. In such complex areas as foreign policy, conjunctural causality seems to help explain decisions. By no means do we argue that policy diffusion and transfer can explain foreign policy singlehandedly. We rather propose to add to the multifaceted FPA toolbox an additional element. In combination with other domestic factors, policy diffusion and transfer can contribute to explaining certain foreign policy decisions.

Despite the possibilities for cross-fertilization between FPA and policy diffusion and transfer approaches, this combination has so far been applied only to a limited extent in existing studies. It seems obvious that foreign policy is made in response to developments outside a country's borders. War is declared or arms are built up in response to another country's (perceived) aggression or armament. Yet, the influence of one country's foreign policy settings and concepts on other countries through diffusion or transfer has not received much academic attention so far. A diffusion and transfer angle goes far beyond reacting to a country's policy decisions and focuses on a different level of policy than the definition and redefinition of national interest. It includes learning from another country's foreign policy, emulating it based on normative grounds or taking similar decisions due to interdependence, as outlined in the previous section.

In recent years, some scholars have pointed to the cross-fertilization potential of FPA and international relations concepts. Kaarbo (2015) argues that domestic and decision-making factors and conceptions of agency are undertheorized and underdeveloped in contemporary international relations (IR) theory. She proposes to integrate FPA insights in IR approaches, which is the mirror-reverse of this chapter's plea. Thies and Breuning (2012) also address the potential of combining FPA and IR concepts. Their proposal revolves around role theory and stipulates that national role conceptions can exert effects on countries' foreign policy since it depends on a country's perception of its role in the international setting.

The field in which most FPA-type studies can be found that can be considered part of the diffusion and transfer studies family is Europeanization, which analyses ways in which member-states of the EU construct roles and procedures and internalize norms and expectations in response to EU policy-making (Tonra 2001; Wong 2007). The EU involves relatively close co-operation among its member-states. It therefore seems a likely case for socialization leading to changes in national foreign policy (Checkel 2005; Rieker 2006; Alecu de Flers and Müller 2012). Europeanization in the area of foreign policy differs from some other EU policy areas in which substantial competences have been transferred to the EU level. In EU foreign policy there is no clear vertical chain of command through which policy change could be coerced. Influence from the EU level to the member-states rather occurs voluntarily (Alecu de Flers and Müller 2012: 21). This brings it very close to policy diffusion and transfer, which in many conceptualizations excludes coercive mechanisms.

Europeanization scholars have analyzed the effects of European integration on individual EU member-states such as France (Rieker 2006) or a small set of countries such as Hungary, Romania, and Slovakia (Denca 2009). As part of the Europeanization literature, scholars also have investigated the influence of the EU on non-EU countries' foreign policy such as Turkey (Terzi 2016). The potential of combining FPA and policy diffusion and transfer approaches in a way that considers diffusion or transfer as one factor of a set of interacting domestic and external variables is addressed to a lesser extent in Europeanization studies. They mostly are relatively EU-focused and take the EU's influence on member-state foreign policy as their dependent variable. Studies that strive to explain a certain national foreign policy output as the dependent variable in which Europeanization is one of a set of factors exist but seem less prominent.

The EU is by far not the only organization in which foreign policy-makers interact on a regular basis. Nonetheless, research on the diffusion and transfer of policies and concepts through those other organizations seem relatively scarce. The role of international organizations in providing, diffusing, and transferring new information in general has been studied, but its application to the specific field of foreign policy seems less prevalent. Research on epistemic communities that spread policy options among themselves and try to influence others has been well established (Adler 1992; Haas 1992) and the role of epistemic communities and networks in EU foreign and security policy has, for example, been subject to Cross' (2011, 2015a, 2015b) work (see chapter 7 in this volume). However, those studies do not address the entire range of mechanisms that are included in the policy diffusion and transfer approaches and do not always make conceptual distinctions with regard to the mechanisms which are as clear as those made in the diffusion and transfer literature. Those strands of literature can be seen as mutually reinforcing and complementary.

An explicit focus on diffusion can be found in a few foreign policy studies. Yet the subject of diffusion are, for example, war or norms. The diffusion of war, rather than policy, has been subject to a number of studies (see, for example, Levy 2011; Vasquez *et al.* 2011). The diffusion of international norms, which is closely related to policy diffusion, has also been subject to a number of studies in the FPA field, including the (non) ratification of the 1948 Genocide Convention (Greenhill and Strausz 2014) and the failure of entrepreneurs to advocate for foreign policy change (Breuning 2013) as well as successful impact of international norms on foreign policy (Breuning 2011). Such norm diffusion studies can be found in foreign policy areas such as development co-operation (Hook 2008) and the prevention of sexual violence in conflict (Davies and True 2017). Explicit policy diffusion or transfer studies seem rare.

Policy diffusion and transfer approaches appear nonetheless useful for analyzing foreign policy decisions since the community of foreign policy-makers seems internationally relatively well connected, which can create a conducive environment for policy diffusion and transfer. Interaction within international organizations such as NATO and the UN can lead to socialization that can foster emulation. These and other organizations provide analysis and information about policies and practices, which can foster learning (especially when such organizations also feature an educational system, as in the case of the NATO Defense College in Rome and the NATO School in Oberammergau). The foreign policy community is also characterized by formal and informal networks, which can fulfill similar functions as international organizations in spurring policy diffusion and transfer. The competition mechanism seems somewhat less pertinent for the field of foreign policy but it can nonetheless explain some incidents of foreign policy choices. For example, Most and Starr (1980) observe changes in the risks and opportunities of one nation caused by the entry into a war of another nation.

In FPA, the making and changing of foreign policy is traced back to people who act individually or in groups. It largely focuses on political leaders and foreign policy-makers (Hudson 2005: 1–3). This actor-centered approach fits well with policy transfer studies. While quantitative policy diffusion studies often take countries as their unit of analysis, a number of qualitative diffusion and, in particular, transfer studies delve into the detail of decision-making processes in an attempt to isolate the precise details of the mechanism(s) at play. Not countries but individuals learn, emulate, and take decisions based on altered cost–benefit calculations. The mechanisms occur thus at the level of individuals who then decide to pursue certain policy goals. This can result in the adoption or change of foreign policy, depending on domestic policy-making parameters. The diffusion and transfer mechanisms can provide a (partial) explanation for a foreign policy-maker's motivation to pursue a certain policy and the content and form of this policy. The respective policy-maker's success in pursuing the policy can most likely be explained by one or a combination of the other public policy approaches discussed in this volume since those approaches include domestic dynamics that can elucidate the reasons and processes of adopting policy.

Foreign policy has some specific traits that differentiate it from public policy. Most prominently, foreign policy tends to be made to a lesser extent through formal legislative acts. A number of decisions such as the ratification of international treaties and the approval of budgets are, of course, taken by the legislature but a host of decisions are taken in forums that are less visible to the public. Foreign policy is made in the form of activities such as diplomatic outreach, negotiations, and military planning in which the role of the executive is more privileged than in most public policy areas. This has implications not only for the making of foreign policy but also for its empirical analysis. Information about the unfolding of certain decision processes can be more difficult to obtain. This can pose challenges for an in-depth analysis that traces every step of how an external policy might have influenced foreign policy-makers. This is, however, a common challenge to analyzing foreign policy and not specific to diffusion and transfer studies.

Different sets of scope conditions under which foreign policy diffusion and transfer seems more likely can be identified. They relate to the inter-action among foreign policy-makers, the degree of politicization of the respective foreign policy, and the similarity of the countries among which the foreign policy diffuses or is transferred. Foreign policy diffusion and transfer seems more likely when foreign policy-makers frequently interact with each other, over a longer period of time and to a relatively high degree of intensity (Alecu de Flers and Müller 2012). These factors enable socialization and foster the exchange of lessons and knowledge that can spur learning. Foreign policy diffusion and transfer can also occur without direct interaction among actors but it makes it less likely since this situation provides for fewer opportunities to become aware of certain policies. For the competition mechanism, interaction among foreign policy-makers seems less important.

Less politicized policies seem to be more likely to diffuse and be transferred (Alecu de Flers and Müller 2012) since their lower degree of contestation makes it easier for those foreign policy-makers who have learned, emulated, or are influenced by altered cost–benefit calculations to pursue and push for their preferred policy option. The implementation of a foreign policy seems in many cases to be facilitated when the source and the adopting countries have similar cultures, histories, and institutions. This makes it easier to fit a policy that originates from abroad into a country's system and set of already existing foreign policies. While this section pondered the enrichment of FPA with policy diffusion and transfer approaches in general terms, the following section showcases a concrete example.

The diffusion of planning doctrine for crisis response operations

This section provides an illustration of how policy diffusion concepts can contribute to the analysis of foreign policy. It focuses on the case of the diffusion of operational planning doctrine. The codification of NATO planning doctrine can be seen as a product of learning over time and space. Putting this body of ideas to the test in various crisis response operations in recent years, furthermore, led to the horizontal and vertical diffusion of key operational planning concepts from NATO to other international organizations and individual countries through a process of emulation. This short qualitative single case study thus highlights two distinct ways in which different diffusion mechanisms have been at play and can explain the relative similarity of concepts across different organizations and countries in the areas of operational planning doctrine. It also emphasizes some of the scope conditions that can foster and hamper diffusion.

Learning and the origins of operational planning concepts

The process of designing military operations and campaigns—what is referred to as *operational art*—can be said to rely on two types of input. The first is the creativity of the operation commander and his/her planning team. Human imagination makes operational planning an art rather than a science: individual intelligence trumps the mere application of procedures. The second source of input is the contribution made by operational doctrine. This assumes the form of conceptual planning tools that enable the design process without putting an unreasonable burden on planners in terms of imagination. Essentially, doctrine substitutes collective wisdom for individual creativity. Ideally, both aspects of operational art therefore go hand in hand.

This section shows that many conceptual planning tools have deep historical roots. As these have been codified in NATO planning doctrine, their influence can hardly be overstated—they represent the bread and butter of operational planners across the Western world. Planning doctrine can be understood as the product of a learning process in which ideas and concepts from historical experience get analyzed, fine-tuned, and adapted to the present context. As a detailed account of operation design concepts lies outside the scope of this analysis, the focus here is limited to four interlinked key concepts: centers of gravity, decisive points, lines of operations, and end-states. Despite having their foundations in the nineteenth century, these concepts retained a continuing interest in the US military community, which ultimately succeeded in establishing these as Alliance norms.

Much ink has already been spilt over the concept of center of gravity (COG) (see for example Echevarria 2002; Eikmeier 2004, 2010; Strange and Iron 2004; Vego 2007). In general terms, COG analysis is a military methodology for determining the strengths and weaknesses of all conflict parties. The COG concept was originally coined by Clausewitz

who defined it as "the hub of all power and movement, on which everything depends" (Clausewitz 1976: 595–596). In NATO doctrine, centers
of gravity are defined as those characteristics, capabilities, or locations
from which an actor derives its freedom of action, physical strength,
or will to fight (AAP-6 2010). The COG concept serves as the basis for
more elaborate analytical frameworks such as the one popularized by
Joe Strange (1996). While there exists much discussion on how the COG
concept should be precisely defined and whether it can be salami-sliced
into different levels of analysis, COG analysis remains a highly popular
methodology to understand how an actor can be thrown off balance and
forced to collapse. A concept originally coined in the age of Napoleonic
warfare was thus continuously re-learned among various foreign policy-
makers to the point at which it became the foundational anchor point of
NATO operational planning doctrine.

After analyzing the centers of gravity of the conflict parties the next
step is to visualize an operation design by means of decisive points and
lines of operations—both concepts popularized by Clausewitz's contemporary Antoine-Henri Jomini.[2] An operation design provides the general outline of how an operation should develop. A decisive point is a
geographic place, specific event, critical factor or function that allows
one to gain an advantage over one's adversary: it is a point from which
a COG can be threatened. Usually, these decisive points can be logically
deduced from the capabilities, requirements, and vulnerabilities already
identified in the COG analysis. A line of operations, furthermore, links
such decisive points in temporal, spatial, or functional terms on a path to
the adversary's COG.

The underlying assumption is that the neutralization of this COG will
in turn bring about the defeat of the adversary and as such the desired
end-state, i.e., the situation wherein the mission objectives have been
achieved. Typically, how an operation should work toward its objectives can be visualized by several lines of operations connecting decisive
points, which can be grouped into different phases in time. These lines all
converge toward an adversary's COG and the attainment of the end-state.

It must of course be admitted that the doctrinal template for operation design sketched above is highly simplified. The point, however,
is to suggest that those concepts that are most central to NATO operational planning doctrine individually have a genealogy reaching back to
Clausewitz and his contemporaries. Over the past two centuries, these
ideas of Prussian and Napoleonic origin have migrated through various

---

[2] The notion of a line of operations was originally coined in 1781 by Henry Lloyd (one of
Frederick the Great's generals theorizing about the Seven Years War) but it was Jomini
who broadened the concept beyond its original logistical meaning into a key concept of
campaign design. See Coxwell (1995) for discussion.

military establishments, a learning process in which defense academies across the Western world played a prominent part. Ultimately, they crystallized in US doctrinal thinking, which in turn provided the basis for exporting them once more into NATO doctrine as common norms.

During the first decades of the Alliance's existence, the standardization efforts undertaken in the Alliance were only put to test in exercise and deterrence settings. The end of the Cold War, however, ushered in a new era in which these planning tools were put to practice and correspondingly migrated into other institutional frameworks. So here we have an example of one state uploading policy ideas that it acquired through learning to an international organization, from where these ideas achieved a much broader dissemination through emulation.

The emulation of NATO planning doctrine

The effort that had been invested into military standardization and the development of allied joint doctrine eventually paid off. NATO proved to be a better-equipped platform for planning and conducting complex multinational crisis response operations than the UN. The need for American support in managing a problem occurring in Europe's backyard, moreover, triggered the development of parallel crisis-management mechanisms in the context of the EU. As NATO doctrine constituted the only internationally accepted reference standard in terms of military doctrine, which was taught in military academies across the Western world, the planning tools it contained migrated into these other organizations. NATO doctrine thus provided a common normative framework. A process of emulation contributed to the adoption of NATO doctrine in a range of countries and international organizations.

In the context of the EU's Common Security and Defence Policy, an elaborate institutional structure was created for conducting civilian as well as military crisis management operations. The military component of this structure was explicitly built in NATO's image. As most EU member-states are also NATO allies, it made sense to ensure maximum compatibility between the different institutional structures. This could in addition to learning and emulation also hint at the competition mechanisms having shaped policy-makers' decisions. Enshrining NATO structures in the EU reduced adaptation costs and generated efficiencies.

While the procedures at the political level of the Brussels institutions were written with the peculiarities of the EU in mind, the lower-level military documents systematically copied from NATO doctrine. The standing operating procedures for EU operation headquarters, most importantly, fall back on the NATO guidelines for operational planning. As a result, the conceptual toolkit described above was directly imported into the EU framework. While this is entirely logical as far as the military structures are concerned, the more intriguing aspects of this diffusion relate to the fact that this military planning mindset was to some extent transposed to the planning of civilian crisis management operations (i.e., missions geared toward police training, security sector reform, rule of law, etc.). It is not uncommon in Brussels to hear civilian planners refer to center of gravity analysis—even if this is a tool originally conceived within a mindset involving traditional warfare.

The transfer of NATO doctrine to the UN framework was more problematic. Given the much more diverse membership structure of the UN—and the fact that NATO is seen by many non-Western nations as *the armed branch of the West*—the direct adoption of NATO doctrine for UN peacekeeping operations was politically impossible. These factors relate to the scope conditions of diffusion. A more diverse set of country contexts and norms can hamper transfer and diffusion. That being said, the multinational nature of UN peacekeeping operations necessitated the adoption of a procedural mechanism allowing for planning operations in a multinational environment. The adoption of the UN Integrated Mission Planning Process and concepts outlining the UN command and control structure, for example, constituted important steps forward in this regard. When comparing these documents with their NATO equivalents, the similarities are obvious even if they are largely left implicit.

This demonstrates that policy transfer and diffusion require a deeper analysis of the process. Merely searching for the adoption of the same policy in different contexts does not necessarily reveal the entire causal mechanism. Sometimes policy diffuses in a more implicit manner. The influence of NATO doctrine, furthermore, becomes much more prominent when actual NATO members participate in UN operations. Whereas European nations by and large left the framework of UN peacekeeping in the aftermath of the debacles in the former Yugoslavia, the 2006 Israel-Hezbollah war set the stage for a much commented upon return of European nations to a UN mission (Mattelaer 2009). De facto, this implied the importation of NATO planning doctrine at the operational level: in the absence of detailed UN doctrinal guidance, French, Italian, Spanish, and other European planners fell back on their common NATO background. Even at the political level, this led to a French push for an alternative type of command chain by inserting a strategic military cell in New York in the absence of strategic-level command.

The above is not meant to suggest that the emulation of NATO planning doctrine in other multinational organizational forums did not feature any type of adaptation. The organizational cultures of both the EU and the UN assimilated but also transformed this doctrinal toolkit. One manifestation of this is the stronger emphasis on what is labeled *integrated planning* in the UN (i.e., integrating different UN policy instruments of which blue helmets are but one) and *civil-military coordination* in the EU. While this trend in turn became fashionable in NATO circles as well—this time under the label of the *comprehensive approach*—it was substantially more difficult to take this further in the absence of instruments other than diplomacy and military force in the NATO toolbox.

In that regard, one major step forward was taken at the Lisbon summit in 2010 when the heads of state and government decided to "form an appropriate but modest civilian crisis management capability to interface more effectively with civilian partners" (NATO Strategic Concept). The more substantial type of adaptation, however, relates to the gradual dilution of these conceptual planning tools in the new operational context that EU and UN missions represented. The notion of the *end-state* got competition from the idea of the *end-date* and decisive points distilled from center of gravity analysis of actors that could no longer be called opposing forces. Such adaptation risks spilling over to the NATO environment as well. Fundamentally, this relates to the question to what extent these planning tools retain their applicability in a changing security environment. In that sense, emulation may also imply the semantic hollowing out of existing terms.

While this section could only sketch the policy diffusion and transfer process as well as some of its scope conditions in the case of operational planning doctrine, it illustrates the complexities of such an analysis as well as its value added of the deeper insights that can be generated for understanding the origins of a country's foreign policy.

Conclusion

Policy diffusion and transfer concepts can provide frameworks and insights to enrich FPA by adding the external effects of other jurisdictions' policies and the interaction among jurisdictions to the set of factors that can explain the design, adoption, and implementation of foreign policy. While in other policy areas diffusion and transfer studies abound, they rarely have found their way into FPA and have not been exploited to their full potential.

The case study of operational planning doctrine has demonstrated that the ideas and concepts informing the design of military interventions—a foreign policy decision of the highest order—have effectively migrated throughout time and space, from one nation state to another, from states to international organizations and back, and from one international organization to others. Ideas with roots in the age of Napoleonic warfare were studied in multiple countries. The learning process that unfolded within the US military community enshrined key concepts in operational planning doctrine. In the NATO framework, these concepts were eventually standardized across the Alliance's membership. A transnational and trans-historical learning process thus culminated in an established set of norms. The experience of military crisis management operations in the 1990s and 2000s, furthermore, provided a window in which other states and international organizations such as the EU and the UN emulated this conceptual framework and, to some extent, the norms it entailed, even if the latter were often diluted or adapted to changing circumstances.

While there is insufficient evidence to make any claims about the extent to which these diffusion processes constituted an instrument of foreign policy—except in the most subliminal sense—the analysis offered here does shed a new light on how states relate to international organizations of which they are a member. Alliance membership has proven to be a productive arena for engaging in collective learning and defining joint norms and standards. In turn, these can disseminate to a much wider audience through emulation. As such, the international political context and available policy options undergo a constant process of recalibration. This opens new avenues for FPA, but due to the intricacies of the causal mechanisms involved, substantial work lies ahead with respect to identifying scope conditions and other constraints on foreign policy diffusion and transfer.

References

AAP-6 (2010) *NATO Glossary of Terms and Definitions*, Brussels: NATO Standardization Agency.

Adler, Emanuel (1992) The Emergence of Cooperation: National Epistemic Communities and the International Evolution of the Idea of Nuclear Arms Control, *International Organization* 46(1), 101–145.

AJP-3 (2002) *Allied Joint Operations*, Brussels: NATO Standardization Agency.

Alecu de Flers, Nicole and Patrick Müller (2012) Dimensions and Mechanisms of the Europeanization of Member State Foreign Policy: State of the Art and New Research Avenues, *Journal of European Integration* 34(1), 19–35.

Biedenkopf, Katja and Claire Dupont (2013) A Toolbox Approach to the EU's External Climate Governance, in Astrid Boening, Jan-Frederik Kremer, and Aukje van Loon (eds.) *Global Power Europe*, Heidelberg: Springer, 181–200.

Biedenkopf, Katja, Sarah Van Eynde, and Hayley Walker (2017) Policy Infusion Through Capacity Building and Project Interaction in the Case of Greenhouse Gas Emissions Trading in China, *Global Environmental Politics* 17(3), 91–114.

Braun, Dietmar and Fabrizio Gilardi (2006) Taking "Galton's Problem" Seriously: Towards a Theory of Policy Diffusion, *Journal of Theoretical Politics* 18(3), 298–322.

Breuning, Marijke (2011) Re-Constructing Development Assistance: Analogies, Ideas, and Norms at the Dawn of the New Millennium, in Vaughn Shannon and Paul Kowert (eds.) *Psychology, Constructivism, and International*

Relations: An Ideational Alliance, Ann Arbor: University of Michigan Press, 119–149.

Breuning, Marijke (2013) Roles and Realities: When and Why Gatekeepers Fail to Change Foreign Policy, *Foreign Policy Analysis* 9, 307–325.

Brown, Lawrence A. (1969) Diffusion of Innovation: A Macroview, *Economic Development and Cultural Change* 17(2), 189–209.

Checkel, Jeffrey T. (2001) Why Comply? Social Learning and European Identity Change, *International Organization* 55(3), 553–588.

Checkel, Jeffrey T. (2005) International Institutions and Socialization in Europe: Introduction and Framework, *International Organization* 59(4), 801–826.

Checkel, Jeffrey T. (2008) Process Tracing, in Audie Klotz and Aseem Prakash (eds.) *Qualitative Methods in International Relations: A Pluralist Guide,* London and New York: Palgrave Macmillan, 114–127.

Clark, Jill (1985) Policy Diffusion and Program Scope: Research Directions, *Publius: The Journal of Federalism* 15(4), 61–70.

Clausewitz, Carl von (1976) *On War,* ed. and trans. M. Howard and P. Paret, Princeton: Princeton University Press.

Coxwell, Charles W. (1995) *On Lines of Operation: A Framework for Campaign Design,* Fort Leavenworth: School of Advanced Military Studies.

Cross, Mai'a K. Davis (2011) *Security Integration in Europe: How Knowledge-Based Networks are Transforming the European Union,* Ann Arbor: University of Michigan Press.

Cross, Mai'a K. Davis (2015a) The European Defence Agency and the Member States: Public and Hidden Transcripts, *European Foreign Affairs Review* 20(3), 83–102.

Cross, Mai'a K. Davis (2015b) The Limits of Epistemic Communities: EU Security Agencies, *Politics & Governance* 3(1), 90–100.

Davies, Sara E. and Jacqui True (2017) Norm Entrepreneurship in Foreign Policy: William Hague and the Prevention of Sexual Violence in Conflict, *Foreign Policy Analysis* 13(3), 701–721.

Denca, Sorin Stefan (2009) Europeanization of Foreign Policy: Empirical Findings From Hungary, Romania and Slovakia, *Journal of Contemporary European Research* 5(3), 389–404.

DiMaggio, Paul J. and Walter W. Powell (1983) The Iron Cage Revisited: Institutional Isomorphism and Collective Rationality in Organizational Fields, *American Sociological Review* 48(2), 147–160.

Dolowitz, David P. (2009) Learning by Observing: Surveying the International Arena, *Policy & Politics* 37(3), 317–334.

Dolowitz, David P. and David Marsh (1996) Who Learns What from Whom: A Review of the Policy Transfer Literature, *Political Studies* 44(2), 343–357.

Dolowitz, David P. and David Marsh (2000) Learning from Abroad: The Role of Policy Transfer in Contemporary Policy-Making, *Governance: An International Journal of Policy and Administration* 13(1), 5–24.

Drezner, Daniel W. (2001) Globalization and Policy Convergence, *International Studies Review* 3(1), 53–78.

Echevarria, Antulio J. (2002) *Clausewitz's Center of Gravity: Changing Our Warfighting Doctrine – Again!* Carlisle: Strategic Studies Institute.

Eikmeier, Dale C. (2004) Centre of Gravity Analysis, *Military Review* July–August, 2–5.

Eikmeier, Dale C. (2010) Redefining the Center of Gravity, *Joint Force Quarterly* 59, 156–158.

Elkins, Zachary and Beth A. Simmons (2005) On Waves, Clusters, and Diffusion: A Conceptual Framework, *The Annals of the American Academy of Political and Social Science* 598(1), 33–51.

Etheredge, Lloyd S. (1985) *Can Governments Lean? American Foreign Policy and Central American Revolutions*, New York: Pergamon Press.

Eyestone, Robert (1977) Confusion, Diffusion, and Innovation, *The American Political Science Review* 71(2), 441–447.

Finnemore, Martha and Kathryn Sikkink (1998) International Norm Dynamics and Political Change, *International Organization* 52(4), 887–917.

Gilardi, Fabrizio (2012) Transnational Diffusion: Norms, Ideas, and Policies, in Walter Carlsnaes, Thomas Risse, and Beth A. Simmons (eds.) *Handbook of International Relations*, London: Sage Publications, 453–477.

Graham, Erin R., Charles R. Shipan, and Craig Volden (2013) The Diffusion of Policy Diffusion Research in Political Science, *British Journal of Political Science* 43(3), 673–701.

Gray, Virginia (1973) Innovation in the States: A Diffusion Study, *American Political Science Review* 67(4), 1174–1185.

Greenhill, Brian and Michael Strausz (2014) Explaining Nonratification of the Genocide Convention: A Nested Analysis, *Foreign Policy Analysis* 10, 371–391.

Haas, Peter M. (1992) Introduction: Epistemic Communities and International Policy Coordination, *International Organization* 46(1), 1–35.

Hägerstrand, Torsten (1967) *Innovation Diffusion as a Spatial Process*, Chicago and London: University of Chicago Press.

Holzinger, Katharina, Helge Jörgens, and Christoph Knill (2007) Transfer, Diffusion und Konvergenz: Konzepte und Kausalmechanismen, *Politische Vierteljahresschrift Sonderheft* 38, 11–35.

Hook, Steven W. (2008) Ideas and Change in U.S. Foreign Aid: Inventing the Millennium Challenge Corporation, *Foreign Policy Analysis* 4, 147–167.

Hudson, Valerie M. (2005) Foreign Policy Analysis: Actor-Specific Theory and the Ground of International Relations, *Foreign Policy Analysis* 1(1), 1–30.

Johnston, Alastair Iain (2001) Treating International Institutions as Social Environments, *International Studies Quarterly* 45(4), 487–515.

Kaarbo, Juliet (2015) A Foreign Policy Analysis Perspective on the Domestic Politics Turn in IR Theory, *International Studies Review* 17, 189–216.

Knill, Christoph and Jale Tosun (2009) Hierarchy, Networks, or Markets: How Does the EU Shape Environmental Policy Adoptions Within and Beyond its Borders?, *Journal of European Public Policy* 16(6), 873–894.

Lavenex, Sandra and Emek M. Uçarer (2004) The External Dimension of Europeanization: The Case of Immigration Policies, *Cooperation and Conflict: Journal of the Nordic International Studies Association* 39(4), 417–443.

Lazer, David (2001) Regulatory Interdependence and International Governance, *Journal of European Public Policy* 8(3), 474–492.

Lazer, David (2006) Global and Domestic Governance: Modes of Interdependence in Regulatory Policymaking, *European Law Journal* 12(4), 455–468.

Levy, Jack S. (1994) Learning and Foreign Policy: Sweeping a Conceptual Minefield, *International Organization* 48(2), 279–312.

Levy, Jack S. (2011) The Initiation and Spread of the First World War: Interdependent Decisions, *Foreign Policy Analysis* 7, 183–188.

March, James G. and Johan P. Olsen (1989) *Rediscovering Institutions: The Organizational Basis of Politics*, New York: The Free Press.

Marsh, David and J. C. Sharman (2009) Policy Diffusion and Policy Transfer, *Policy Studies* 30(3), 269–288.

Mattelaer, Alexander (2009) *Europe Rediscovers Peacekeeping? Political and Military Logics in the 2006 UNIFIL Enhancement*, Brussels: Egmont Institute.

Meseguer, Covadonga (2005) Policy Learning, Policy Diffusion, and the Making of a New Order, *The Annals of the American Academy of Political and Social Science* 598(1), 67–82.

Most, Benjamin A. and Harvey Starr (1980) Diffusion, Reinforcement, Geopolitics, and the Spread of War, *The American Political Science Review* 74(4), 932–946.

Naroll, Raoul (1965) Galton's Problem: The Logic of Cross-Cultural Analysis, *Social Research* 32(4), 428–451.

NATO Strategic Concept (2010) *Active Engagement, Modern Defence*, Brussels.

Polillo, Simone and Mauro F. Guillén (2005) Globalization Pressure and the State: The Worldwide Spread of Central Bank Independence, *The American Journal of Sociology* 110(6), 1764–1802.

Rieker, Pernille (2006) From Common Defence to Comprehensive Security: Towards the Europeanization of French Foreign and Security Policy?, *Security Dialogue* 37(4), 509–528.

Rogers, Everett M. (1995) *Diffusion of Innovations*, New York: The Free Press.

Savage, Robert L. (1985) Diffusion Research Traditions and the Spread of Policy Innovations in a Federal System, *Publius: The Journal of Federalism* 15(4), 1–27.

Schimmelfennig, Frank and Ulrich Sedelmeier (2004) Governance by Conditionality: EU Rule Transfer to the Candidate Countries of Central and Eastern Europe, *Journal of European Public Policy* 11(4), 661–679.

Shipan, Charles R. and Craig Volden (2008) The Mechanisms of Policy Diffusion, *American Journal of Political Science* 52(4), 840–857.

Simmons, Beth A. and Zachary Elkins (2004) The Globalization of Liberalization: Policy Diffusion in the International Political Economy, *American Political Science Review* 98(1), 171–189.

Simmons, Beth A., Frank Dobbin, and Geoffrey Garrett (2006) Introduction: The International Diffusion of Liberalism, *International Organization* 60(4), 781–810.

Simon, Herbert A. (1965) *Administrative Behavior: A Study of Decision-Making Processes in Administrative Organiztions*, New York: The Free Press.

Strange, Joseph L. (1996) *Centers of Gravity and Critical Vulnerabilities: Building on the Clausewitzian Foundation So That We Can All Speak the Same Language*, Quantico: Marine Corps Association.

Strange, Joseph L. and Richard Iron (2004) Center of Gravity: What Clausewitz Really Meant, *Joint Force Quarterly* 53, 20–27.

Terzi, Özlem (2016) *The Influence of the European Union on Turkish Foreign Policy*, London: Routledge.

Tews, Kerstin (2005) The Diffusion of Environmental Policy Innovations: Cornerstones of an Analytical Framework, *European Environment* 15(2), 63–79.

Thies, Cameron G. and Marijke Breuning (2012) Integrating Foreign Policy Analysis and International Relations through Role Theory, *Foreign Policy Analysis* 8, 1–4.

Tonra, Ben (2001) *The Europeanization of National Foreign Policy: Dutch, Danish and Irish Foreign Policy in the European Union*, Aldershot: Ashgate.

Vasquez, John A., Paul F. Diehl, Colin Flint, Jürgen Scheffran, Sang-Hyun Chi, and Toby J. Rider (2011) The ConflictSpace of Cataclysm: The International System and the Spread of War 1914–1917, *Foreign Policy Analysis* 7, 143–168.

Vego, Milan (2007) Clausewitz's Schwerpunkt: Mistranslated from German – Misunderstood in English, *Military Review* January–February, 101–109.

Vogel, David (1997) Trading Up and Governing Across: Transnational Governance and Environmental Protection, *Journal of European Public Policy* 4(4), 556–571.

Walker, Jack L. (1969) The Diffusion of Innovations Among the American States, *American Political Science Review* 63(3), 880–899.

Wong, Reuben (2007) Foreign Policy, in Paolo Graziano and Maarten P. Vink (eds.) *Europeanization: New Research Agendas*, Houndmills: Palgrave Macmillan, 321–334.

Zürn, Michael and Jeffrey T. Checkel (2005) Getting Socialized to Build Bridges: Constructivism and Rationalism, Europe and the Nation-State, *International Organization* 59(4), 1045–1079.

9

Policy learning in public policy studies: toward a dialogue with foreign policy analysis

Sebastian Harnisch

Since the 1970s, policy learning has been examined in Foreign Policy Analysis (FPA), bringing it more in line with public policy studies (PPS) where such changes have been analyzed since the 1940s. It follows that policy learning constitutes no stand-alone approach in Public Policy (PP) but rather figures as a central theoretical template in several approaches. The major difference vis-à-vis FPA learning, however, is that the latter foregrounds fundamental policy changes involving the learning agent's identity or interests rather than the strategies or instruments of policy. This social constructivist focus, which involves ontological, epistemological, and substantial propositions, sets FPA apart from much of the PPS literature on learning.

In this chapter, I take up the quest of this volume and carry it to this diverse field of learning literature. My first claim is that the different learning approaches in PP and FPA can be brought into dialogue with each other. However, in order to do so, they have to be understood as a variety of distinct approaches. My second claim is that while dialogue is possible, these different approaches should not be understood as being part of one coherent learning theory. Learning as such, in PPS and FPA, lacks a theory of action and therefore cannot provide a comprehensive explanation or understanding of policy change. However, I will try to show below how different learning approaches may be integrated into more comprehensive explanatory accounts in PPS and FPA and thereby serve as theoretical mechanisms to explain policy flows between status quo and change.

The next section sets forth a systematic account of the evolution of the PPS learning literature based on the degree of uncertainty and its impact on agency and the sociality of the learning process, i.e., the involvement of a social relationship in the learning process. The following section explores the transferability of PPS approach to FPA. The chapter then discusses several FPA learning accounts of the foreign policy changes under Gorbachev and examines their findings against the background of the extant PPS learning literature. The concluding section discusses three areas of common interest for PP and FPA learning scholarship to structure and deepen their dialogue.

Learning in public policy studies

To start the dialogue between public policy learning and foreign policy learning, I briefly delimit learning from neighboring concepts and identify the central features and research alleys of public policy learning. I argue that some of these features are useful for the study of foreign policy change because national and international politics have become more interwoven and technological change has enabled policy-makers and society alike to learn from a much broader variety of cases when facing critical policy challenges.

Policy learning may be understood as the change of beliefs, or more generally, shared ideas to avoid unwanted or unintended policy outcomes. As an analytical concept, the term does not imply a particular normative order and thus differs from its colloquial application. Learning also differs from similar concepts, such as policy convergence, policy diffusion, and policy transfer (see chapter 8 in this volume), depicting particular forms of policy change in interaction with identifiable others (Trein 2015: 9).

Policy learning is widely understood to describe a cognitive and social capacity, in which competent policy actors (individuals and collectives) are the unit of analysis, each of which is sovereign enough to make or influence an identifiable policy choice (Freeman 2006). It is this condition of sovereign choice that separates learning from other related concepts of policy change, such as socialization, imitation, and coercion, which either render the conscious or the sovereign choice unimportant (Sommerer 2011: 33; Marier 2012: 404).

"Lessons drawing," then, is a related but distinguishable concept. It does apply policy instruments and strategies originating in one policy arena into another. Richard Rose's conceptualization of lesson drawing has been an important source of inspiration for the learning literature (Rose 1991, 1993, 2004). But in Rose's reading, civil servants and policy-makers are considered first and foremost practitioners who make sensible decisions in the face of uncertainty, thereby reducing the motivational aspect of public policy choices to uphold the status quo or respond to situational factors. In a similar vein, the literature on "policy feedback" stresses the rising costs of reversing a policy choice over time because these choices tend to empower beneficiaries, i.e., interest groups, and implementing bureaucracies alike.

In sum, for most public policy scholars, policy learning does not figure as an independent research interest because it has been popularized in the field as part and parcel of other research approaches, among others advocacy coalitions (see chapter 4 in this volume), the study of public administration, especially in the EU, or enquiries of policy change in various policy fields (Grin and Loeber 2007; Marier 2012).

Learning approaches assume that identifiable actors react to uncertainties emanating from current policies by changing policy instruments, strategies, and goals of underlying belief systems. Depending on the "depth" of the uncertainty, scholars have identified "simple" or "complex" learning processes, "thick" or "thin" learning (see figure 9.1). In simple learning processes, an unanticipated mismatch between policies and their outcomes forms the independent variable, triggering thin learning, i.e., the adaptation of instruments and strategies so as to improve the utility of the policy without changing its goals. In complex learning processes, however, unanticipated outcomes of policies lead to a reconsideration of policy goals, which also involves changes in the self-interest of actors. In doing so, the interaction between an actor and his or her environment (agent-structure) leads to changes in the self the agent is interested in preserving and nurturing. As a result, action and interaction transform the causal relationship of simple learning into the co-constitutive relationship between interdependent variables.[1]

Learning approaches thus point us into two directions. On the one hand, learning may involve cognitive change only (without resulting policy change), thereby opening up the field of policy implementation and public administration. On the other hand, learning may involve agency change, thereby giving us an enriched understanding of whether an actor's identity, interest, or preference has (fundamentally) changed, e.g., in terms of autonomy or willingness to delegate authority. As a consequence, the notion of preventing unwanted outcomes is therefore foundational for the learning literature (May 1992).

Policy learning also points us to the question as to how far the actor defines his/her identity, interests, and preferences autonomously or not, i.e., whether there is an additional agent involved who teaches norms, beliefs, ways of doing things, etc. Depending on the pattern of interaction between the learning actor and the teacher, the variant institutionalization of those roles prescribes detectable structures of verified

---

[1] Whether complex learning always involves a partial or total recomposition of an actor's identity may be challenged on theoretical and empirical grounds. Theoretically speaking, complex learning raises the question whether a causal explanation and constitutive reasoning may complement each other or not (see Tannenwald 2005: 33–41).

| Learning constellation: Degree of individual/ organizational/national mismatch between anticipated benefit and effect | Simple learning: Causation ⟹ | Degree of instrumental and strategy change without change of goals (thin learning) |

Interdependent variable   *Dependent variable*

| Learning constellation: Degree of individual/ organizational/national mismatch between anticipated benefit and effect | ⟺ Complex learning: Co-Constitution | Degree of change in instruments, strategy and goals (potentially) leading to change in actor's identity (thick learning) |

Interdependent variable   *Interdependent variable*

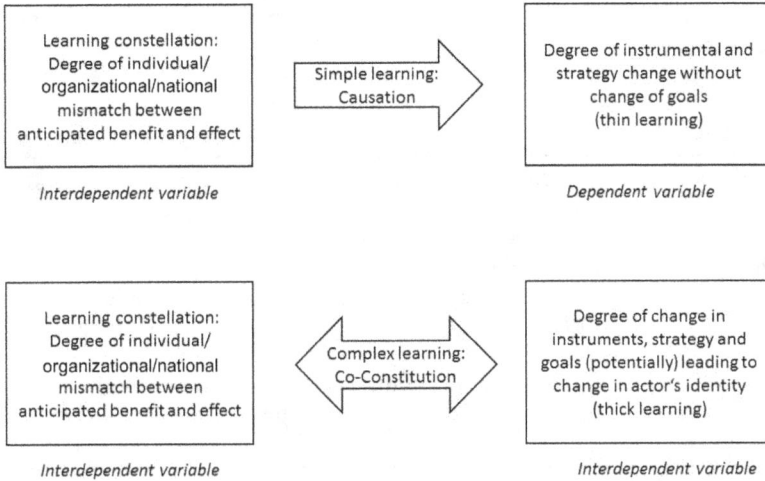

Figure 9.1 Explanatory model of simple (thin) and complex (thick) learning approaches

(and often enforceable) expectations, e.g., trust and authority, which enable learning processes (Jones and McBeth 2010). While learning does happen in non- or less institutionalized settings, such as international relations, the degree of sociality is a very important characteristic of the learning process, when we reflect upon the differences and commonalities of learning transcending national borders.

Indeed, the growing institutionalization of world politics may be one of the most potent trends why FPA should seek the dialogue with PP on learning. As institutions establish self-reinforcement mechanisms, i.e., mechanisms that change opportunities, beliefs, and goals of involved actors in favor of an existing practice, they do establish stable social positions to initiate, facilitate, or sanction learning processes in the respective institutions. It follows that the roles of international institutions (or their organs) as teachers of norms multiply over time. This means that a certain type of learning, involving a low degree of uncertainty (because of the path dependency of institutional outcomes) and a high degree of sociality (because of the strong institutionalized position of the teaching organ vis-à-vis the member-states) becomes ever more important, resulting in the establishment of new concepts, such as socialization.

The variations in uncertainty and sociality of learning processes are summarized in table 9.1. The columns capture the main protagonists and their respective approaches. These depictions of course are highly aggregated and should be further differentiated when used in empirical analysis as some of the concepts do overlap.

Table 9.1 Typology of selected learning approaches in PP: uncertainty and sociality

Sociality uncertainty	Low	High
Low	Dunlop (2009) policy-makers learn from epistemic groups	Dunlop and Radaelli (2016) introduce interactive learning involving EU Commission
High	Argyris and Schön (1978) Double learning Nye (1987) Complex learning: introduces change of goals rather than instruments only	Adler (1992); Haas (1992) introduce epistemic communities, allowing interactive learning processes which may also involve strategic use of epistemes by policy makers (Boswell 2009)

Source: Author's depiction.

The assumption that learning is constituted by uncertainty of actors and their sociality in the learning process is widely shared in the PP literature, but the meaning and consequences of these assumptions are answered in a broad variety of ways. For the so-called "instrumentalists," uncertainty produces a cost/benefit reassessment by actors with given interests and preferences, i.e., political survival (Pierson 1994). "Political learning" then describes an adaptation of existing policies when (external) circumstances change, for example the emergence of major scientific innovations or changes in the power position of interest groups. Instrumentalists usually assume and detect a low level of agency change but various degrees of sociality.

In contrast, ideationalists see uncertainty as a condition arising from the conception of reality, that is, the perception or social construction of one's own identity (and subsequent) interests. Unlike instrumentalists, uncertainty does not impose independently the adaption of instruments and strategies but rather calls for "social learning," i.e., the deliberated change of ideas, paradigms, or identities and subsequent policies. As a consequence, ideationalists do foresee a higher degree of agency change as possible and probable and they do focus on the mechanisms of tracking the sociality of the learning process.

Overall, both of these broad schools have made important contributions to the empirical-analytical literature in a broad variety of policy areas, including tax, social, environmental, health, police, and justice as well as economic and cultural policies (for recent overviews, see Trein 2015; Maggetti and Gilardi 2016). Nevertheless, the apparent difference in conceptualization and learning mechanisms has hampered substantial theoretical progress (see below).

Since the 1950s, there have been significant shifts between the two constitutive components of uncertainty and sociality. During the foundational era of policy learning studies (1950–1980), scholars focused on patterns of innovation emanating from and between members of a social system, most often governments (Freeman 2006: 370–373). For example, in his seminal study on changes in policy-making in Britain and Sweden, Hugh Heclo (1974) argued that politics did not only involve power but also uncertainty: "Policy is a form of collective puzzlement on society's behalf; it entails both deciding and knowing ... Much political interaction has constituted a process of social learning expressed through policy" (Heclo 1974: 306). In Heclo's depiction, civil servants as individuals dominate the learning process. They code, store, interpret, and discuss policy experience as they formulate their response to unforeseen events. Adding some sociality to the process, "policy middlemen" outside the normal run or other organizational actors become crucial for transmitting changes in the societal environment to governments. But these policy middlemen do not have unique cognitive capacities, i.e., persuasiveness. Their influence flows from their sensitivity to changes in the social environment and their access to important institutions (Heclo 1974: 311). Hence, they are "facilitators of change" but not "teachers or entrepreneurs of change." In sum, in Heclo's conceptualization, uncertainty induces limited policy changes, i.e., shifts in instruments and strategies rather than in belief systems. Moreover, the sociality remains low as policy-makers hold on to control the objectives of the learning process vis-à-vis the policy middlemen.

In contrast, Peter Hall's oeuvre (1989, 1993, 2013), which has informed much of the learning literature in the 1990s, shifts the focus into two new directions: first, Hall explicitly sets up a three-stage learning continuum, in which only first and second order learning depict the re-prioritization of policy instruments and the acceptance of new ones, which had been the focus of Heclo's concept. In contrast, third order learning involves a re-prioritization of policy goals, moving beyond the instrumental focus.[2] Integrating insights from natural sciences and the theory of science, Hall's third order changes closely resemble Thomas Kuhn's paradigm shifts (Hall 1993: 280–281). In doing so, he introduces socially constructed ideas and standards to the learning process, implying that social problems (uncertainty) themselves are constituted by a much wider group of discourse participants than policy-makers alone (Hall 1993: 279; Cairney and Weible 2015: 89). Second, and in contrast to Heclo, Hall specifies political, administrative, and contextual factors that need to be present for policy learning to occur: learning has to be able to explain and solve

---

[2] Hall (1993: 293, n. 21) also mentions "fourth order learning" or "deuterolearning" as learning to learn, but does not explore the concept any further.

the unforeseen policy challenges (economic viability); it also has to be "political viable," i.e., satisfying important party interests (political viability); and it has to meet the conditions of independent administrative actors, such as central banks, to meet an "administrative viability" test (Hall 1989: 370–375).

In sum, Hall's approach diverts considerably from Heclo's conceptualization: it involves the constitutive beliefs of learners about their own goals and problems. These beliefs or policy paradigms are socially constituted since the uncertainty component, as the origin of the learning process, becomes socialized. But Hall's ideationalism does not involve a deeper conceptualization of sociality because the learning process is self-directed by the learner, who faces a policy problem, but most often not a physical agent, as Heclo's policy middlemen, or a teacher (Rayner 2015: 72).

In the second (ongoing) era, the consolidation phase of the learning field, the literature has used three conceptual entry points to achieve progress: the composition of agency (advocacy coalition and epistemic communities), specific mechanisms of sociality (bargaining and hierarchy) and variance in institutional roles (autocratic learning).

First, the composition of agency blends the learning literature into the broader framework of public policy approaches. In this realm, Paul Sabatier and his advocacy-coalition framework modify Heclo's earlier approach by introducing coalitions of policy-makers and stakeholders, rather than individuals, as the unit of analysis (see chapter 4 in this volume). Broadly based on neo-institutionalist assumptions, these coalitions respond in (bounded) rational ways to policy challenges in the context of (relatively stable) constitutional, economic, and normative settings, which do impose a certain degree of necessary acceptance for policy change to occur. The coalitions share belief systems that can be depicted as being organized in three tiers: deep core beliefs or ideologies, applying across policy domains and very stable over time; policy cores of domain-specific commitments and non-essential commitments of greater detail. Here, learning does occur in two ways: first, core commitments may change after some external fundamental shock occurred and one or all coalitions face total policy failure. However, this rarely ever happens. Second, learning may also occur between advocacy coalitions, when policy strategies fail to deliver some expected outcomes and policy brokers facilitate new policy consensus. This latter process depicts learning primarily as a cognitive process of finding more efficient or effective strategies after consulting with other members (and policy brokers) of the same coalition. Underlying this concept is not a particular rationality but the historical institutionalist conviction that individuals acquire certain worldviews during a socialization phase, which often become self-reinforcing over time (see chapter 6 in this volume).

In a nutshell, the advocacy coalition framework posits itself between Heclo's and Hall's learning approaches: while aggregating agency on a higher level than Heclo and integrating Hall's notion of ideas as areas of cognitive convergences, it sets itself apart from Hall by reducing the sociality of the learning process. In the advocacy coalition framework (ACF), learning is self-directed by learning agents and occurs more frequently when independent measuring is easy rather than when resonance with the norms held is strong (see chapter 4 in this volume).

The composition of the learning agent takes a slight but important turn in the epistemic community approach. Although epistemic communities are coalitions too, they serve as teachers of expert policy knowledge when uncertainty about the problematic situation and respective policy solutions is low (Haas 1992). By providing such guidance, and in contrast to advocacy coalitions, these expert groups—which develop and hold scientific epistems consensually and "strive to insinuate that aspect of expert knowledge into the public bureaucracies and legislative channels that produce public policy" (Haas and Haas 2016: 239)—intervene in the learner's autonomy of decision about learning objectives as well as the instruments and strategies to reach these objectives (Dunlop 2009). To be sure, epistemic communities rarely hold mandatory institutional positions from which they can simply change PP (Haas and Haas 2016: 240). Also, as Cristina Boswell (2009) has pointed out, these expert groups may be used strategically by decision-makers to either legitimize a policy set before or to set certain standards to which public policies then comply. In this instrumentalist perspective, decision-makers "learn" how to make use of new information for given purposes, regularly their political survival and well-being (see also Fleckenstein 2011). Consequently, the sociality of the learning process cannot be conceived of as a one-way street. Rather, as the diverse use in the public policy learning literature shows, it must be thought of as a social relationship, in which both partners may co-define the role of the other to varying degrees.

In another strand of the learning literature, the relationship between agents is asymmetrical in the sense that one agent has lost (or delegated) his autonomous choice to another agent, so that he/she, the teacher, can control the objectives of the learning process through coercion or incentives. These circumstances do resemble situations under conditionality or during socialization periods where socializees accept obligations of an institution they want to join or co-operate with but who are (negatively or positively) sanctioned to comply with specific standards during the accession period. As these situations imply a substantial amount of coercion, i.e., loss of autonomous choice, and a low level of uncertainty, various scholars do not treat them as "learning processes" anymore (see Dunlop and Radaelli 2013 v. Freeman 2006). Among these latter situations, a particular kind of situation arises when actors have deferred the competence to adjudicate controversial issues to a third party in a highly institutionalized setting. In such a setting the degree of uncertainty over policy outcomes is low and the institutionalization of delegation so high that a third party, for instance a constitutional or supreme court, holds the right to control the re-prioritization of learning objectives (Schmidt 2000). This mix of low uncertainty and high sociality in a deferred learning process may also be considered as outside the remit of a learning process because the delegation of adjudicatory powers over time implies the choice of intertemporal self-binding behavior.

Overall, these latter studies have been primarily brought to bear on the EU. While many other international organizations act as facilitators of "lessons" and "benchmarks" in various policy diffusion and transfer studies (among others Meseguer 2005; Dobbin *et al.* 2007; Gilardi 2010; Füglister 2012; Maggetti and Gilardi 2016), the EU, and especially the European Commission, is unique in seeking to create legitimacy for its own institutional role as an initiator of integration by either directly "teaching" new policy modes to its member and acceding states or indirectly by facilitating policy transfer among them (Eising 2002; Sabel and Zeitlin 2008; Zito 2009; Marier 2009; Zito and Schout 2009; Dunlop and Radaelli 2016).

Methodologically, Maggetti and Gilardi (2016) find in a recent critical survey of the diffusion literature (144 articles over the period from 1990 to 2012) that the respective analyses on learning do not reveal any clear causal or constitutive patterns because the operationalization of learning is too diverse. What can be said, though, is the following: Learning studies in PP tend to focus on the country or federal state level. They tackle mostly economic policies and they do most often employ quantitative methods. When reflecting upon central causal or constitutive as well as context variables, both qualitative and quantitative studies use indicators such as "policy success," "similarity," and "proximity" to explain learning behavior (Maggetti and Gilardi 2016: 99).

A host of "formative events" and "critical junctures," such as the Global Financial Crisis or the Eurozone Crisis and the so-called Arabellion, have recently attracted much attention by learning scholarship (Bamert *et al.* 2015; Fenger and Quaglia 2015; Dunlop and Radaelli 2016). The Arab Spring and the subsequent policy reaction by the regimes in the Middle East and North Africa region have drawn particularly intense interest in this respect (Weyland 2012; Hale 2013; Lynch 2014; Bamert *et al.* 2015). In terms of categorization, there is an emerging consensus in the qualitative and quantitative research community that protesters "learned" from successful events (and their peers) in Tunisia and Egypt in the sense that many protesters, deprived of substantial leadership, used cognitive shortcuts which led them to extrapolate the successful experiences into their own, often very different, local context (Weyland 2012; Lynch 2014: 3–4; Bamert *et al.* 2015). In turn, Heydemann and Leenders (2011) have established the term "authoritarian learning" to describe the adaptation processes of autocratic regimes that, after witnessing the toppling of several incumbents, used a mix of repression and hunkering down to overcome the protests (see also Heydemann and Leenders 2014).

On a theoretical level, these latter studies do focus on single loop or instrumental learning process. In this view, cost–benefit estimates change first and protest behavior ensues later because analogical reasoning (wrongfully) produces hope that autocratic rulers could be toppled by the people. As a consequence, these PP studies again focus on the question of whether learning has been successful in producing anticipated outcomes of instrumental and/or strategic change rather than asking what impact the unintended consequences of protest or repressive behavior may have had for the underlying identities and interests of the parties involved.

In sum, and when compared to the field of foreign policy and international learning (Knopf 2003; Harnisch 2012; Thies 2016), PP studies (primarily) focus on first and second order learning (in Hall's terminology). The sociality level of learning is (often) low to mid-range so that learning agents more often than not face facilitators or producers of standards that improve informational deficits and allow for (Bayesian) updating of policy instruments and strategies, as in the case of the Arabellion.

The promises of dialogue between PP learning and FPA learning

Transferring learning approaches from PP to FPA is a challenging task because FPA has developed autonomously its own set of approaches to explain policy changes. Several additional reasons come to mind to account for the dearth of dialogue between the two sub-disciplines. First, and in contrast to domestic politics, as realism stresses, the scarcity of reliable information induced a deep-seated mistrust between rivaling poles during the Cold War so that foreign policy changes mostly amounted to adaptation, instrumental changes rather than shifts in underlying beliefs and identities (Bar-Simon-Tov 2003). It follows that substantive interest in FPA learning approaches was driven by Cold War concerns, such as rivalry, crisis management, and deterrence (Leng 1983, 2000; Nye 1987; Breslauer and Tetlock 1991; Tetlock 1991; Wallander 1992). The implication for PP learning approaches is not that they do not apply at all, but that they may have to be adapted to the specific context of foreign policy-making, i.e., when the well-being of a nation is at stake and the economic and administrative viability of a solution, as suggested by Hall's learning concept, may play a lesser role than in domestic politics.

Second, international politics and related foreign policies often involve ill-structured problems as liberal theoreticians would argue. Not only do these problems regularly involve several different levels of governments and international actors, thus begging the question who learns: individuals, organizations, governments, or even groups of states (Etheridge 1985; Vertzberger 1986; Khong 1992; Goldstein and Keohane 1993; Stein 1994; Lebovic 1995; Farkas 1998). In one major study, Yuen Khong found that in crisis situations, such as the simmering Vietnam conflict in 1965, US decision-makers rely on analogical reasoning between different historical episodes (Munich decision and Korean War) to overcome decision-making constraints and that their private and public reasoning tends to be highly consistent, the latter finding building the basis for much of discourse analysis (Khong 1992).

In turn, collective action problems also do entail challenges to communicate clearly and consistently over time. As a consequence, liberal rationalists and ideationalists have stressed the importance of "signaling" and "reputation" for learning processes (Mercer 1996; Copeland 1997; Crescenzi 2007; Peterson 2013) because the signals and reputation involved do clarify what type of co-operation partner or rival a country has to face and what kind of policy appears appropriate. Based on similar meta-theoretical underpinnings, it is easy to imagine a fruitful dialogue between the ACF and the signaling literature as both rely on a rationalist core of ideas. Similarly, the Epistemic Community approach assumes that the "reputation" of independent scholarship serves as an entrée to the policy community, thereby overcoming the crucial hurdle of defining a policy problem in such a way that it becomes susceptible to a new solution. It follows that reputation already does play a role in PPS learning approaches but that scholars have not yet grasped the opportunity to evaluate the respective implications of their research for each other.

Moving on to other FPA approaches, a plausible argument can be made that learning could be integrated into Prospect theory. While Prospect theory provides a useful template to describe and explain foreign policy decision-making processes under uncertainty (Kahneman and Tversky 1979; Levy 1992), critics argue that it lacks and adequate understanding of how the central causal mechanism "reference point," the basis for loss and gain calculations, evolves over time (Levy 1997: 98). Learning scholarship could be of help by suggesting causal pathway for shifts of reference points.

It follows then that the challenges of transferring learning approaches between PP and FPA should not be overrated. As stated above, the institutionalization of world politics makes PP approaches more accessible for

FPA because institutions routinize expectations, define policy problems, and stabilize respective behavior through sanctions.

Learning in FPA: change in Soviet foreign policy and the end of the Cold War

Learning theories have been applied to a wide array of foreign policy decisions and international relations subfields, such as conflict studies and environmental policies (Breslauer and Tetlock 1991; Levy 1994; Reiter 1996; Jänicke and Weidner 1997; Farkas 1998; Harnisch 2000, 2012; Leng 2000; Kowert 2002; Knopf 2003; Koremenos 2003; Crescenzi 2007; Sommerer 2011; Thies 2016). But, arguably, there has been no more controversial and well researched issue in the FPA learning literature than the changes in the Soviet Union's foreign policy in the 1980s that led to the demise of the Cold War (Brooks and Wohlforth 2000; English 2002; Petrova 2003; Tannenwald and Wohlforth 2005). Moreover, this case has also been tackled by different learning concepts as well as qualitative and quantitative methods (Deudney and Ikenberry 1991/1992; Checkel 1993; Zubok 1993; Stein 1994; Kratochwil and Koslowski 1995; Brown 1996; Herman 1996), so that a broad variety of theoretical and operational lessons may potentially be drawn for our purpose.

What is more, practical lessons drawn from the end of the Cold War are abound and, indeed, persist until today: in the United States, a majoritarian view holds that the Reagan administration's unrelenting armament made the Soviet Union leadership give up its goal to outcompete the United States. It follows that the United States should face up with potential rivals to prevent them from competing. In contrast, in Europe a majority of policy-makers are inclined to believe that dialogue and cooperation infused Gorbachev's "new thinking" and that this thinking was by far not the only possible reaction to the intensifying arms race under President Reagan (Herrmann 2004).

Following up on the theoretical discussion of the PPS learning approaches above, the following expectations may be derived from Peter Hall's concept and the Epistemic Community approach.[3] The former suggests that policy change occurs only if three conditions are met: it has to be economically, politically, and administratively viable so that policy-makers, facing electoral and bureaucratic pressure, support learning. The latter approach expects that policy communities of experts, who present

---

[3] Both approaches have been explicitly integrated in the FPA learning literature on the changes in the Soviet Union foreign policy and are therefore chosen to show the practicability of transferring theoretical templates or whole approaches between sub-disciplines.

alternative explanations for policy failure and respective policy changes, play a crucial role in learning processes.

The debate

In the debate, scholars have been at issue with the question as to why the Soviet Union abandoned its class-struggle ideology since the mid-1980s, even though the material capabilities to uphold the confrontation with the liberal-democratic and capitalist West were still in place (Tannenwald and Wohlforth 2005: 5). A sophisticated realist explanation holds that the relative material deprivation of the Soviet economy induced adaptive behavior, so that policy-makers around Gorbachev "learned" that they could not compete with the United States for much longer and thus took an "optimal decision" to shed the burdens of Soviet imperialism (Brooks and Wohlforth 2000; Wohlforth 2005: 168). Learning in this case derives from experiencing a deficit in policy implementation (imperial overstretch), resembling a simple and instrumental learning process by which instruments and strategies change, but the underlying ideas, i.e., identities, persist. In a similar vein, Jack Snyder suggests that material forces—the industrial modernization of the Soviet Union—created a constituency of critical intellectuals who supported a peaceful foreign policy and reintegration into the world economy and who were able to effectuate Gorbachev's policy change (Snyder 1995).

Constructivist interpretations of Soviet foreign policy learning disagree on the chain of events and chains of reasoning presented by realists (Checkel 1993; Mendelson 1993; English 2000, 2002; Petrova 2003). In their view, the ideas that led to Perestroika and Glasnost changed prior to the events in the mid-1980s, for instance in the late 1960s as a consequence of the failed Soviet Union intervention in Czechoslovakia, and these ideas, not a desperate economic situation, effectuated the change in the Soviet foreign policy (English 2003: 245). In fact, constructivists argue that only because of these new ideas Gorbachev initiated the reforms, which then resulted (unintentionally) in the dissolution of the Soviet Union (English 2003: 245; Zubok 2003: 208). Moreover, protagonists of the constructivist learning process, such as English (2002, 2003) and Evangelista (2004), reason that the policy change chosen neither reflected a "necessity," since there were substantial differences between the old and new thinking with regard to the reaction to the various policy challenges, nor did the path chosen resemble an "optimal choice" (English 2002: 74; Zubok 2003: 209).

In sum, the two contending learning approaches in the debate differ with regard to the extent of change (first/second order v. third order), but also with regard to the sociality, i.e., adaptation to material forces v. experimental learning and epistemic communities as the sources of change. Most importantly, the constructivist learning argument holds that the dissolution of the Soviet Union was an unintended consequence of the earlier change in Soviet Union foreign policy while the realist explanation argues that both processes were, by and large, separate.

Individual and collective learning: Gorbachev and the "new thinkers"

In one of the first major treatments of learning as a potential explanation for Soviet foreign policy change, Janice Gross Stein (1994) argues that the dramatic changes can be most plausibly explained when conceptualizing Gorbachev "as an uncommitted thinker eager to learn." In her view, Gorbachev held solid views of the necessity to reform the domestic political economy of the Soviet Union, but his knowledge and leanings on foreign and security policy were much less developed. Accounting for change in foreign policy, Stein suggests that Gorbachev's unilateral initiatives, such as the suspension of countermeasures in response to Intermediate-Range Nuclear Forces deployments by NATO and a moratorium on SS-20 deployment, resulted from domestic concerns about the economic effects of expansionist foreign policy goals (Stein 1994: 179). However, as Gorbachev is identified as an "uncommitted thinker," even before taking office, he started to consult and organize a steady stream of meetings and policy papers from a group of liberal policy intellectuals, such as Alexander Yakovlev and Georgi Arbatov, to develop new policies. In addition, and as a result of his unilateral initiatives, Gorbachev met and discussed his policies with foreign officials, most notably Secretary of State George P. Shultz (Stein 1994: 179, see also Brown 2004: 42). In sum, Gorbachev developed a stable internationalist and integrationist foreign policy identity for the Soviet Union over time so that third order changes (at least) on an individual level can be detected.

In terms of categorization of the learning process, Stein (1994) develops a basic nexus between individual and collective learning by introducing policy scientists as an epistemic community and helping to develop new policies for a Soviet leadership that struggled with overextension abroad and domestic contestation of its retrenchment policies at home. The nexus is not fully articulated (yet) but it provides two interesting insights: first, while being one of many options to deal with the external overextension of the Soviet Union, Gorbachev's early retrenchment initiatives appear to have been instrumental in the sense that he wanted to reduce the absolute economic decline of the Soviet society (Stein 1994: 158). Second, the logic of Gorbachev's learning process obviously changed over time, as he developed his policies in response to the advice from the liberal epistemic community and foreign interlocutors. Hence, both the degree of learning (from first/second learning to third order learning) as well as the degree of sociality shifted towards complexity.

The findings by Stein are seconded by various studies on Gorbachev as a decision-maker (Zubok 2003; Brown 2004) and the role of domestic and transnational epistemic communities (Checkel 1993, 1997; Evangelista 1995, 1999; Herman 1996; English 2003). What is more, in these later analyses, epistemic communities do not only figure as teachers or "containers of policy ideas" to be picked up by policy-makers facing uncertainty. Rather, these policy communities also represent larger societal constituencies that are in favor of a policy change (Evangelista 1995; English 2003), connecting the foreign policy learning scholarship directly to the Epistemic Community literature in PP.

Formative events and Soviet foreign policy learning under Gorbachev

One of the crucial questions of the realist-constructivist debate is concerned with the question if, when and in what direction material forces drive ideas that inform a new policy. In this regard, Robert English (2000) traces the social democratic and internationalist policy ideas of Gorbachev back to their intellectual origins in the Khrushchev era and to policy and university circles in the 1970s and early 1980s. Based on Peter Hall's concept of "punctuated learning" (Hall 1993: 277), English develops the concept of "cognitive punch," which may be understood as "a crisis or event that accelerates reevaluation and change from one set of collective understandings or 'paradigms' to another" (English 2000: 244, fn. 26).

English argues that the nuclear catastrophe in Chernobyl (April 1986) dealt the most significant "cognitive punch" to Gorbachev and the new thinkers. Domestically, the reactor meltdown and the subsequent cover up and inadequate rescue measures laid bare the backwardness and corruption of the Soviet command economy. And yet, the disaster also provided reformists with crucial arguments to drastically reform the system and to hold those responsible that tried to block reforms. Externally, the fallout from Chernobyl set in motion a critical rethinking of the Soviet Union's relationship with the rest of the world: on the one hand, the nuclear catastrophe made crystal clear that any use of nuclear weapons in wartime would bring the end of the world as it was known. As a direct consequence, Gorbachev started to portray the world as facing a common threat of nuclear annihilation (English 2000: 217). On the other hand, his subsequent policy initiatives, most notably the Reykjavík Summit and the proposal of drastic nuclear arms reductions, were met with substantial domestic contestation by hardliners who tried to undercut reforms. Again, as a result of those reactions, Gorbachev and his closest confidents came to believe that Western claims about the Soviet Union's untrustworthiness were genuine and had to be taken seriously (English 2000: 215–222).

Policy learning and the case of Gorbachev's new thinking

The case of dramatic changes in Soviet Union foreign policy may be called an archetypical case study for policy learning because several different approaches have been brought to bear upon it. Thus, the case may offer a few more generalizable suggestions about the way and content of the learning process. First, it appears that the origins of the "new thinking" go back to the reform era under Khrushchev in the mid-1950s. It follows that the new thinking was shaped by the social reality in the Soviet Union since the mid-1950s—the mismatch between the communist teachings and subsequent practices—rather than relative material losses vis-à-vis the United States in the 1980s. Hence, in this case foreign policy learning originated from domestic historical malperformance rather than from current international competition. In this line of reasoning, historical experience, as learning scholars starting with Heclo have taught us, also played an important role in this case.

Second, it appears that phases of instrumental learning alternated with phases of third order learning. Early in his tenure of office, Gorbachev used the adverse (budgetary) effect of expansionist foreign policy goals instrumentally as reasons to argue for Soviet retrenchment. Yet later, especially after 1986, he openly identified himself with a circumscribed liberal-international foreign policy identity that prescribed a co-operative and integrationist agenda. In such a line of reasoning, it becomes possible that instrumentalist and ideationalist accounts of learning may complement each other in a two-stage process of identity formation and subsequent interest-based policy-making (and vice versa) rather than compete with each other (see below). It follows that PPS scholars focusing on first and second order learning, and their FPA colleagues, focusing on third order changes, may examine jointly when and how both processes interact functionally or sequentially.

Third, as Jacques Levésque (1997) makes clear in his analysis of the dissolution process of the Soviet Union, Gorbachev's new policy agenda was designed to overcome the East–West conflict and secure a new leadership role for the Soviet Union in its aftermath. However, the ideational forces set in motion (unintentionally) by him did trigger (if not cause) the loss of the East European allies and also led to the subsequent demise of the Soviet Union (Levésque 1997). In this line of reasoning, learning may not always produce success or improvement but can effectuate failure in the sense of triggering unintended consequences.

Finally, Stein's and English's learning studies stress that learning processes are in (constant) motion, either through processes of persuasion and contestation (as in and among most epistemic communities) or through historical experience and interaction (as in the case of Chernobyl). Hence, depending on the institutional setting of deliberating policies, the separation and reintegration of the interaction of learners with material factors and social actors may lead to distinct patterns of learning for specific regime types. In the case of the Soviet Union, as an autocratic regime, the extant literature has it that autocrats do not learn easily but when they do, they may shift policies much faster and more comprehensively than democracies.

Conclusion

Learning processes are definitely worth studying. They provide unique opportunities to observe how learners and teachers, or "teaching circumstances," interact in times of high uncertainty and momentous decisions. And yet, it is not enough to proliferate learning as a conceptual term across PP (or for that matter FPA) approaches without specifying the underlying theoretical assumptions. For the analysis of learning to help resolving ongoing theoretical, methodological, or policy debates, learning scholars must generate systematic expectations (hypothesis) when, how, and for what purpose learning is expected to affect policy behavior and (social) structural outcomes.

The purpose of this chapter has been to set forth a systemic account of learning approaches in PP as they relate to empirical FPA learning analysis. I began by describing the evolution of the PP learning literature as a historical shift from first and second order learning to third order learning and from high to low uncertainty under increasingly institutionalized relationships. I then discussed the veracity of two PP learning concepts (Peter Hall's and the epistemic community approach) and different FPA learning approaches to the explanation of Gorbachev's new thinking in the Soviet foreign policy.

The discussion of the Soviet case illuminated several contested features of the extant learning literature: first, for Gorbachev and the new thinkers, uncertainty in the mid-1980s emanated from the absolute mismatch between the communist teaching and subsequent practices and miserable outcomes rather than from relative material losses vis-à-vis the United States. Thus, historical experience and misguided path-dependencies of the Soviet system trumped current comparisons with the peer competitor as the source of learning. The implication for a dialogue between PP and FPA scholars is clear: since the origin of your subject of study may lie elsewhere, it may be worth talking to those colleagues that examine this elsewhere.

Second, crisis moments, such as the Chernobyl catastrophe, shorten time frames. They do interrupt the historicity of policy evaluations by substantially threatening power positions, institutions, and respective pay-off structures and/or norms and values. As a consequence, they infuse a sense in "learners" that order, i.e., stability of expectations, can only be restored through swift action. In doing so, these moments, or critical junctures, are the most probable situations where the degree, speed, and sociality of learning changes. It follows that PP and FPA scholars should focus on some of these events to gauge the multidimensionality of policy learning also to get a better of the interaction between first, second, and third order learning.

Third, as Stein (1994), English (2000) and Petrova (2003) stress in their respective discussions of the new thinkers as an epistemic community, this group was much less institutionalized and it was (at least partially) established by Gorbachev himself so that the group neither functioned in the role of an "institutionalized teacher" nor as mere "repositories of policy ideas." Rather, as described vividly by English (2000), the interaction between these groups and individuals themselves as well as between them and Gorbachev shaped the new thinking. It follows that epistemic communities are also shaped by policy-makers' openness and initiative toward expert advice, a nexus that could be explored in close co-operation with FPA studies on leadership styles or advisory processes. In this reading, they hardly constitute "independent variables" but should be conceptualized as "role players" who depend on the attribution of their specific role set by others. Fourth, dialogue between PP and FPA is important but as the discussion of PPS learning literature suggests, the dialogue should not stop there. As international institutions multiply and create more self-reinforcing mechanisms, the social position of these institutions (and some designated organs) as teachers of policies and norms multiply too so that the social character of learning changes and concepts, such as socialization, occur more often. To improve our understanding on how, when, and why states delegate competences and authorities to institutions in order to be taught, PP and FPA scholars need to broaden their discussion to include institutionalism.

Overall, these three features, the historicity and cross-fertilization of experience, the temporal pattern of specific learning episodes, and the variant patterns of sociality, including international institutions, should stimulate a healthy dialogue to better grasp policy change across the PPS and FPA spectrum. However, these features do not point at a coherent set of hypotheses about causal or constitutive mechanisms as stepping stones for a comprehensive theory of policy learning. Rather, they may be thought of as modules to be combined in their respective theoretical application, i.e., historical institutionalism, to find better and more inclusive explanations for the interaction between agents and structures across time and policy areas.

References

Adler, Emanuel (1992) The Emergence of Cooperation: National Epistemic Communities and the International Evolution of the Idea of Arms Control, *International Organization* 46(1), 101–145.

Argyris, Chris and Donald Schön (1978) *Organizational Learning: A Theory of Action Perspective*, Reading: Addison Wesley.

Bamert, Justus, Fabrizio Gilardi, and Fabio Wasserfallen (2015) Learning and the Diffusion of Regime Contention in the Arab Spring, *Research and Politics* 2(3), 1–9.

Bar-Simon-Tov, Yaacov (2003) Adaptation and Learning in Conflict Management, Reduction, and Resolution, *International Journal of Peace Studies* 8(1), 19–37.

Boswell, Christina (2009) *The Political Uses of Expert Knowledge: Immigration Policy and Social Research*, Cambridge: Cambridge University Press.

Breslauer, George and Philip E. Tetlock (eds.) (1991) *Learning in U.S. and Soviet Foreign Policy*, Boulder: Westview Press.

Brooks, Stephen and William Wohlforth (2000) Power, Globalization, and the End of the Cold War: Reevaluating a Landmark Case for Ideas, *International Security* 25(3), 5–53.

Brown, Arcie (1996) *The Gorbachev Factor*, Oxford: Oxford University Press.

Brown, Arcie (2004) Gorbachev and the End of the Cold War, in Richard K. Herrmann and Richard Ned Lebow (eds.) *Ending the Cold War: Interpretations, Causation, and the Study of International Relations*, New York: Palgrave Macmillan, 31–58.

Cairney, Paul and Christopher M. Weible (2015) Comparing and Contrasting Peter Hall's Paradigms and Ideas with the Advocacy Coalition Framework, in John Hogan and Michael Howlett (eds.) *Policy Paradigms in Theory and Practice: Discourses, Ideas and Anomalies in Public Policy Dynamics*, Basingstoke: Palgrave Macmillan, 83–100.

Checkel, Jeffrey T. (1993) Ideas, Institutions and the Gorbachev Foreign Policy Revolution, *World Politics* 45(2), 271–300.

Checkel, Jeffrey T. (1997) *Ideas and International Political Change: Soviet/Russian Behavior and the End of the Cold War*, New Haven: Yale University Press.

Copeland, Dale C. (1997) Do Reputations Matter?, *Security Studies* 7(1), 33–71.

Crescenzi, Mark (2007) Reputation and Interstate Conflict, *American Journal of Political Science* 51(2), 382–396.

Deudney, Daniel and G. John Ikenberry (1991/1992) The International Sources of Soviet Change, *International Security* 16(3), 74–118.

Dobbin, Frank, Beth Simmons, and Geoffrey Garrett (2007) The Global Diffusion of Public Policies: Social Construction, Coercion, Competition or Learning?, *Annual Review of Sociology* 33, 449–472.

Dunlop, Claire A. (2009) Policy Transfer as Learning: Capturing Variation in what Policy-Makers Learn from Epistemic Communities, *Policy Studies* 30(3), 291–313.

Dunlop, Claire A. and Claudio M. Radaelli (2013) Systematizing Policy Learning: From Monolith to Dimensions, *Political Studies* 61(3), 599–619.

Dunlop, Claire A. and Claudio M. Radaelli (2016) Policy Learning in the Eurozone Crisis: Modes, Power and Functionality, *Policy Sciences* 49(2), 1–18.

Eising, Rainer (2002) Policy Learning in Embedded Negotiation: Explaining EU Electricity Liberalization, *International Organization* 56(1), 47–84.

English, Rainer (2003) The Road(s) Not Taken: Causality and Contingency in Analysis of the Cold War's End, in William Wohlforth (ed.) *Cold War Endgame: Oral History, Analysis, Debates*, University Park: Pennsylvania State University Press, 243–272.

English, Robert (2000) *Russia and the Idea of the West: Gorbachev, Intellectuals, and the End of the Cold War*, New York: Columbia University Press.

English, Robert (2002) Power, Ideas, and New Evidence on the Cold War's End: A Reply to Brooks and Wohlforth, *International Security* 26(4), 70–92.

Etheridge, Lloyd S. (1985) *Can Governments Learn?* New York: Pergamon.

Evangelista, Matthew (1995) The Paradox of State Strength: Transnational Relations, Domestic Structures, and Security Policy in Russia and the Soviet Union, *International Organization* 49(1), 1–38.

Evangelista, Matthew (1999) *Unarmed Forces: The Transnational Movement to End the Cold War*, Ithaca, NY: Cornell University Press.

Evangelista, Matthew (2004) Turning Points in Arms Control, in Richard K. Herrmann and Richard N. Lebow (eds.) *Ending the Cold War: Interpretations, Causation, and the Study of International Relations*, New York: Palgrave Macmillan, 83–106.

Farkas, Andrew (1998) *State Learning and International Change*, Ann Arbor: University of Michigan Press.

Fenger, Menno and Lucia Quaglia (2015) The Global Financial Crisis in Comparative Perspective: Have Policy Makers "Learnt Their Lessons"? *Journal of Comparative Policy Analysis: Research and Practice* 18(5), 502–517.

Fleckenstein, Timo (2011) *Institutions, Ideas and Learning in Welfare State Change: Labor Market Reforms in Germany*, Basingstoke: Palgrave Macmillan.

Freeman, Richard (2006) Learning in Public Policy, in Robert E. Goodin, Michael Moran, and Martin Rein (eds.) *Oxford Handbook of Public Policy*, Oxford: Oxford University Press, 367–387.

Füglister, Katharina (2012) Where Does Learning Take Place? The Role of Intergovernmental Cooperation in Policy Diffusion, *European Journal of Political Research* 51(3), 316–349.

Gilardi, Fabrizio (2010) Who Learns from What in Policy Diffusion Processes?, *American Journal of Political Science* 54(3), 650–666.

Goldstein, Judith and Robert O. Keohane (eds.) (1993) *Ideas and Foreign Policy: Beliefs, Institutions, and Political Change*, Ithaca, NY: Cornell University Press.

Grin, John and Anne Loeber (2007) Theories of Policy Learning: Agency, Structure, and Change, in Frank Fischer, Gerald J. Miller, and Mara S. Sidney (eds.) *Handbook of Public Policy Analysis: Theory, Politics and Methods*, Boca Raton: CRC Press, 201–222.

Haas, Peter M. (1992) Introduction: Epistemic Communities and International Policy Coordination, *International Organization* 46(1), 1–36.

Haas, Peter M. and Ernst B. Haas (2016) Learning to Learn: Improving International Governance, in Peter M. Haas (ed.) *Epistemic Communities, Constructivism, and International Environmental Politics*, New York: Routledge, 234–260.

Hale, Henry E. (2013) Regime Change Cascades: What We Have Learned from the 1848 Revolutions to the 2011 Arab Uprisings, *Annual Review of Political Science* 16(1), 331–353.

Hall, Peter A. (1989) Conclusion: The Politics of Keynesian Ideas, in Peter A. Hall (ed.) *The Political Power of Economic Ideas: Keynesianism Across Nations*, Princeton: Princeton University Press, 361–391.

Hall, Peter A. (1993) Policy Paradigms, Social Learning, and the State, *Comparative Politics* 25(3), 275–296.

Hall, Peter A. (2013) Brother, Can You Paradigm, *Governance* 26(2), 189–192.

Harnisch, Sebastian (2000) *Außenpolitisches Lernen. Die US-Außenpolitik auf der koreanischen Halbinsel*, Opladen: Leske und Budrich.

Harnisch, Sebastian (2012) Conceptualizing in the Minefield: Role Theory and Foreign Policy Learning, *Foreign Policy Analysis* 8(1), 47–71.

Heclo, Hugh (1974) *Modern Social Politics in Britain and Sweden*, New Haven: Yale University Press.

Herman, Robert G. (1996) Identity, Norms and National Security: The Soviet Foreign Policy Revolution and the End of the Cold War, in Peter Katzenstein (ed.) *The Culture of National Security*, New York: Columbia University Press, 271–316.

Herrmann, Richard K. (2004) Learning from the End of the Cold War, in Richard K. Herrmann and Richard N. Lebow (eds.) *Ending the Cold War: Interpretations, Causation, and the Study of International Relations*, New York: Palgrave Macmillan, 219–238.

Heydemann, Steven and Reinoud Leenders (2011) Authoritarian Learning and Authoritarian Resilience: Regime Responses to the "Arab Awakening," *Globalizations* 8(5), 647–653.

Heydemann, Steven and Reinoud Leenders (2014) Authoritarian Learning and Diffusion in the Arab Counter Revolution, in Marc Lynch (ed.) *The Arab Uprisings Explained: New Contentious Politics in the Middle East*, New York: Columbia University Press, 75–92.

Jänicke, Martin and Helmut Weidner (1997) Summary Global Environmental Policy Learning, in Martin Jänicke and Helmut Weidner (eds.) *National Environmental Policies: A Comparative Study of Capacity-Building*, Heidelberg: Springer, 299–313.

Jones, Michael D. and Mark K. McBeth (2010) A Narrative Policy Framework: Clear Enough to Be Wrong?, *Policy Studies Journal* 38(2), 329–353.

Kahneman, Daniel and Amos Tversky (1979) Prospect Theory: An Analysis of Decision under Risk, *Econometrica* 47(2), 263–292.

Khong, Yuen F. (1992) *Analogies at War: Korea, Munich, Dien Bien Phu, and the Vietnam Decisions of 1965*, Princeton: Princeton University Press.

Knopf, Jeffrey W. (2003) The Importance of International Learning, *Review of International Studies* 29(2), 185–207.

Koremenos, Barbara (2003) Loosening the Ties that Bind: A Learning Model of Agreement Flexibility, *International Organization* 55(2), 289–325.

Kowert, Paul A. (2002) *Groupthink or Deadlock: When Do Leaders Learn from their Advisors?*, New York: State University of New York Press.

Kratochwil, Friedrich V. and Rey Koslowski (1995) Understanding Change in International Politics: The Soviet Union's Demise and the International

System, in Richard N. Lebow and Thomas Risse-Kappen (eds.) *International Relations Theory and the End of the Cold War*, New York: Columbia University Press, 109–126.

Lebovic, James H. (1995) How Organizations Learn: US Government Estimates of Foreign Military Spending, *American Journal of Political Science* 39(4), 835–863.

Leng, Russell J. (1983) When Will They Ever Learn? Coercive Bargaining in Recurrent Crises, *Journal of Conflict Resolution* 27(3), 379–419.

Leng, Russell J. (2000) *Bargaining and Learning in Recurring Crisis: The Soviet-American, Egyptian-Israeli, and Indo-Pakistani Rivalries*, Ann Arbor: University of Michigan Press.

Lévesque, Jacques (1997) *The Enigma of 1989: The USSR and the Liberation of Eastern Europe*, Berkeley: University of California Press.

Levy, Jack S. (1992) An Introduction to Prospect Theory, *Political Psychology* 13(2), 171–186.

Levy, Jack S. (1994) Learning and Foreign Policy: Sweeping a Conceptual Minefield, *International Organization* 48(2), 279–312.

Levy, Jack S. (1997) Prospect Theory, Rational Choice, and International Relations, *International Studies Quarterly* 41(1), 87–112.

Lynch, Marc (ed.) (2014) *The Arab Uprisings Explained: New Contentious Politics in the Middle East*, New York: Columbia University Press.

Maggetti, Martino and Fabrizio Gilardi (2016) Problems (and Solutions) in the Measurement of Policy Diffusion Mechanisms, *Journal of Public Policy* 36(1), 87–107.

Marier, Patrik (2009) The Power of Institutionalized Learning: The Uses and Practices of Commissions to Generate Policy Change, *Journal of European Public Policy* 16(8), 1204–1223.

Marier, Patrik (2012) Policy Feedback and Learning, in Eduardo Araral, Scott Fritzen, Michael Howlett, M. Ramesh, and Xun Wu (eds.) *Routledge Handbook of Public Policy*, London: Routledge, 401–414.

May, Peter J. (1992) Policy Learning and Failure, *Journal of Public Policy* 12(4), 331–354.

Mendelson, Sarah E. (1993) Internal Battles and External Wars: Politics, Learning, and the Soviet Withdrawal from Afghanistan, *World Politics* 45(3), 327–360.

Mercer, Jonathan (1996) *Reputation and International Politics*, Ithaca, NY: Cornell University Press.

Meseguer, Covadonga (2005) Policy Learning, Policy Diffusion, and the Making of a New Order, *Annals of the American Academy of Political and Social Science* 598(1), 67–82.

Nye, Joseph S. (1987) Nuclear Learning and U.S.-Soviet Security Regimes, *International Organization* 41(3), 371–402.

Peterson, Timothy M. (2013) Sending a Message: The Reputation Effect of US Sanction Threat Behavior, *International Studies Quarterly* 57(4), 672–682.

Petrova, Margarita H. (2003) The End of the Cold War: A Battle or Bridging Ground Between Rationalist and Ideational Approaches in International Relations? *European Journal of International Relations* 9(1), 115–163.

Pierson, Paul (1994) *Dismantling the Welfare State: Reagan, Thatcher, and the Politics of Retrenchment in Britain and the United States*, Cambridge: Cambridge University Press.

Rayner, Jeremy (2015) Is There a Fourth Institutionalism? Ideas, Institutions and the Explanation of Policy Change, in John Hogan and Michael Howlett (eds.) *Policy Paradigms in Theory and Practice: Discourses, Ideas and Anomalies in Public Policy Dynamics*, Basingstoke: Palgrave Macmillan, 61–80.

Reiter, Dan (1996) *Crucible of Beliefs: Learning, Alliances, and World Wars*, Ithaca, NY: Cornell University Press.

Rose, Richard (1991) What Is Lesson-Drawing? *Journal of Public Policy* 11(1), 3–30.

Rose, Richard (1993) *Lesson-Drawing in Public Policy: A Guide to Learning Across Time and Space*, Chatham: Chatham House Publishers.

Rose, Richard (2004) *Learning from Comparative Public Policy: A Practical Guide*, London and New York: Routledge.

Sabel, Charles F. and Jonathan Zeitlin (2008) Learning from Difference: The New Architecture of Experimentalist Governance in the European Union, *European Law Journal* 14(3), 271–327.

Schmidt, Susanne K. (2000) Only an Agenda Setter? The European Commission's Power over the Council of Ministers, *European Union Politics* 1(1), 37–61.

Snyder, Jack (1995) Myths, Modernization, and the Post-Gorbachev World, in Richard N. Lebow and Thomas Risse-Kappen (eds.) *International Relations Theory and the End of the Cold War*, New York: Columbia University Press, 109–126.

Sommerer, Thomas (2011) *Können Staaten voneinander lernen? Eine vergleichende Analyse der Umweltpolitiken von 24 Staaten*, Wiesbaden: VS Verlag.

Stein, Janice G. (1994) Political Learning by Doing: Gorbachev as Uncommitted Thinker and Motivated Learner, *International Organization* 48(2): 155–183.

Tannenwald, Nina (2005) Ideas and Explanation: Advancing the Research Agenda, *Journal of Cold War Studies* 7(2): 13–42.

Tannenwald, Nina and William C. Wohlforth (2005) Introduction: The Role of Ideas and the End of the Cold War, *Journal of Cold War Studies* 7(2), 3–12.

Tetlock, Philip E. (1991) In Search of an Elusive Concept, in George Breslauer and Philip E. Tetlock (eds.) *Learning in U.S. and Soviet Foreign Policy*, Boulder: Westview Press, 20–61.

Thies, Cameron (2016) Political Learning and Socialization, in Patrick James (ed.) *Oxford Bibliographies in International Relations*, Oxford: Oxford University Press. DOI: 10.1093/obo/9780199743292-0142.

Trein, Philipp (2015) Literature Report: A Review of Policy Learning in Five Strands of Political Science Research, INSPIRES Working Paper, available at www.researchgate.net/publication/296196015_Literature_Report_A_Review_of_Policy_Learning_in_Five_Strands_of_Political_Science_Research (last accessed May 5, 2017).

Vertzberger, Yaacov Y.I. (1986) Foreign Policy Decisionmakers as Practical-Intuitive Historians: Applied History and its Shortcomings, *International Studies Quarterly* 30(2), 223–247.

Wallander, Celeste A. (1992) Opportunity, Incrementalism, and Learning in the Extension and Retraction of Soviet Global Commitments, *Security Studies* 1(3), 514–542.

Weyland, Kurt (2012) The Arab Spring: Why the Surprising Similarities with the Revolutionary Wave of 1848?, *Perspectives on Politics* 10(4), 917–934.

Wohlforth, William C. (2005) The End of the Cold War as a Hard Case for Ideas, *Journal of Cold War Studies* 7(2), 165–173.

Zito, Anthony R. (2009) European Agencies as Agents of Governance and EU Learning, *Journal of European Public Policy* 16(8), 1224–1243.

Zito, Anthony R. and Adriaan Schout (2009) Learning Theory Reconsidered: EU Integration Theories and Learning, *Journal of European Public Policy* 16(8), 1103–1123.

Zubok, Vladislav (1993) The Collapse of the Soviet Union: Leadership, Elites, and Legitimacy, in Geir Lundestad (ed.) *The Fall of the Great Powers*, Oslo: Scandinavian University Press, 157–174.

Zubok, Vladislav (2003) Gorbachev and the End of the Cold War: Different Perspectives on the Historical Personality, in William C. Wohlforth (ed.) *Cold War Endgame: Oral History, Analysis, Debates*, University Park: Pennsylvania State University Press, 207–242.

10

Conclusion: the promise and pitfalls of studying foreign policy as public policy[1]

Juliet Kaarbo

One of the most intellectually stimulating roundtables at a professional political science conference that I have been to was about connecting the study of public policy with the study of foreign policy. It was inspiring because it was a meeting of minds and the participants, as representatives from both areas of research, discovered common grounds as well as new ways of thinking. The two subfields shared similar conceptual ideas, methods, and challenges, although they communicated in different languages. In other ways, there were clear differences in their approaches and the exciting part was the spontaneous conversation over how the subfields could learn from one another.

That roundtable took place in the 1990s and I know of no sustained attempt to bridge Foreign Policy Analysis (FPA) with Public Policy (PP).[2] For all the reasons mentioned in the introduction (see chapters 1 and 6 in this volume; also Hudson 2005; Lenter 2006; Smith *et al.* 2016), the disconnect between foreign policy scholarship and public policy scholarship remains. This volume addresses this separation with the application of several public policy approaches to foreign policies. In each chapter, the contributors to the volume summarize the evolution and state-of-the-art of public policy approaches, grapple conceptually with the questions of transferability from public policy to the foreign policy arena,

---

[1] This chapter was previously presented at the workshop "Foreign Policy Analysis and Public Policy: Towards Theoretical Dialogue and Integration," 4th European Workshops in International Studies, European International Studies Association, Cardiff, June 7–10, 2017. I thank the workshop participants and the editors of this volume for very helpful comments.

[2] Efforts by Lentner (2006) and Charillon (2018) are more recent attempts to call for a dialogue between public policy and foreign policy scholars.

and empirically experiment with applying public policy approaches to foreign policy.

This is an extremely important exercise. The subfields of FPA and PP have been disconnected for historical and sociological-institutional, not intellectual, reasons. That they share the same explanandum—policy, only modified by a qualifier (foreign or public)—is reason enough to have a dialogue. Both subfields stand much to gain from this engagement. While the benefits to FPA are the focus of this chapter, the contributors to this volume (e.g., chapters 2, 4, and 5) also note the advantages of this connection for the study of public policy.

The benefits to approaching foreign policy through a public policy lens are not, in my opinion, only appropriate to contemporary politics. While it may be the case that post-Cold War globalization, interdependence, and regional integration dynamics have opened up the foreign policy-making process, made foreign policy more salient to more actors, and have blurred the distinction between foreign and domestic policy (e.g., Lentner 2006; see also chapters 1, 7, and 8 in this volume), this may only be a matter of degree. As some of the chapters in this volume demonstrate, foreign policy debates in previous times (e.g., chapter 4 on the 1947 US decision to support the partition of Palestine; chapter 9 on Gorbachev's foreign policy; and chapter 8's NATO military planning doctrines) and around "traditional" security policies (e.g., chapter 2 on Turkish–Greek relations and the Oslo Accords; chapter 6 on US sanctions on Russia; chapter 5 on German troop deployment; and chapter 7 on nuclear proliferation policies) are also amenable to public policy approaches. The applicability of public policy approaches to foreign policy across time and policy domains is an important empirical question, a point to which I return later in this chapter.

This chapter draws key lessons from this collective exercise. I discuss several benefits to the use of public policy approaches in FPA. I also assess some of the difficulties and challenges in doing so. To conclude this chapter, and this book, I offer avenues for future research, including further work on the application of public policy models to foreign policy, on a mirror-image exercise of applying foreign policy approaches to public policy, and on a mutually benefiting integration of the two subfields. This chapter builds directly on the insights of the previous contributions but avoids summarizing the volume's contents. I offer instead a more holistic assessment of this important endeavor.

Reaping rewards? Promises and benefits of studying foreign policy as public policy

The use of public policy approaches in FPA holds many promises. The benefits are not simply the particular advantages that each specific approach provides (as articulated in the individual chapters). More generally, the rewards to reap from a FPA–public policy dialogue are connected to some of the enduring criticisms of FPA. In this way public policy approaches offer a promising intervention into FPA, prompting and pushing FPA to address some of its own shortcomings. I argue that the primary benefits are: (1) theoretical innovation; (2) methodological innovation; (3) a widening of scope; (4) novel internal–external connections; and (5) reflections on the very nature of foreign policy.

Public policy approaches offer FPA opportunities for *theoretical innovation*. This is important because the toolbox of FPA middle-range theories is rather stale. With some exceptions, the table of contents of FPA textbooks and FPA course syllabi that are organized theoretically have not changed much in the past several decades. The standard "sources" or "factors"—such as public opinion, political opposition, bureaucratic institutions, elite beliefs and information processing, leader personality, and small group decision-making—for explaining foreign policy have remained fairly constant. To be sure, there have been theoretical innovations within these FPA traditions, but FPA as a whole has not evolved very much since the 1980s.

An infusion of public policy approaches could change this. The approaches used in this volume bring new theoretical concepts (such as critical junctures, punctuated equilibrium, path dependency, and policy entrepreneurs, and relational power) and novel ways of thinking about policy-making. The chapters demonstrate the individual empirical payoffs from each of these theoretical angles, but the point here is that, collectively, FPA can benefit from a conceptual makeover. An additional advantage of new public policy concepts in FPA is that many of these frameworks—such as the veto player approach and new institutionalism—provide very rich and systematic vocabularies and previous theoretical work on the conceptual front. These frameworks thus offer FPA not just new ideas, but sophisticated theoretical toolkits.

Another way FPA can benefit theoretically from public policy scholarship relates to more general theoretical traditions. It is clear from the chapters in this volume that many public policy approaches include rational choice and constructivist-normative versions. This is certainly the case with policy transfer and diffusion, new institutionalism, network, and multiple streams approaches. Including divergent meta-theoretical orientations, such as rational choice and constructivism, under a single umbrella can be problematic, given some epistemological differences that may be irreconcilable. But there are advantages to this as well (Sil and Katzenstein 2010). FPA has not engaged as much with these larger debates. FPA instead has spent time situating itself vis-à-vis realism and constructivism in IR theory (Hudson 2005; Houghton 2007; Kaarbo 2015) but has not seriously grappled with the complementarity of rational and normative perspectives. By using public policy approaches that have already mapped this terrain, FPA can learn and benefit from PP in this way.

Two more theoretical and conceptual benefits are worth mentioning here. Many public policy frameworks integrate multiple levels. While FPA has some of its own multilevel approaches (such as Brecher 1972; Putnam 1988; Hermann 1990; Hermann 2001), most FPA research remains at one level, source, or factor, with little integration across its islands of middle-range theories (Smith 1986; Vertzberger 2002). Utilizing public policy approaches (such as the multiple streams approach, new institutionalism, and advocacy coalition framework) offers FPA some much-needed coherence. Finally, some of the public policy approaches presented in this volume (such as punctuated equilibrium theory, new institutionalism, and the veto player approach) have conceptualized cross-national differences. This is not new for FPA and indeed some of its origins lie in its comparative foreign policy tradition (Hudson 2005), but much of FPA is still single-country focused. Using ideas from PP about differences in policy making across states not only gives FPA new ideas about how to theorize variation in foreign policy-making across states, but can also steer FPA back to its more comparative roots, with all the benefits that come with comparative research (Rosenau 1968; King *et al.* 1994; Peters 1998; Kaarbo 2003; George and Bennett 2004; Hudson 2005).

Public policy approaches also offer FPA opportunities for *methodological innovation*. FPA is and always has been a multi-methodological endeavor, perhaps more so than most other subfields in the study of politics and international relations (Schafer 2003). FPA includes, for example, experiments, content and discourse analysis, comparative case studies, quantitative analysis, and counter-factual analysis. Similar to its theories, this set of methods has remained fairly constant over decades of research. New analytical techniques and new data are extremely important to the continued development of any area of study. Public policy approaches with methodologies not typically used in FPA thus provide opportunities for novel empirical research. Three approaches from this volume stand out in this respect: (1) the advocacy coalition framework's method of assessing distances between policymakers' beliefs and changes in distances over time; (2) punctuated equilibrium theory's techniques for modeling change and stability; and (3) the network approach's computer analyses for representing complex social networks. While there has been some use of these methodologies in FPA, they are not part of the standard toolkit and thus give FPA new methodological "blood."

A public policy approach to foreign policy can also *widen the scope* of FPA by bringing attention to some issue areas and actors that public policy research naturally includes, that may be relevant to foreign policy, but that FPA has traditionally neglected. For reasons mentioned throughout this volume, public policy approaches might most easily transfer to intermestic issues, issues that are both foreign and domestic policy. Issues such as immigration, environmental policy, criminal law, tax policy, and subsidization are policy areas are already included in public policy research. Although these issues have a clear international and foreign policy dimension, they are rarely included in FPA's scope. If using public policy approaches brings FPA's attention to these areas, this will address the enduring critique of FPA as too narrowly preoccupied with "high" security policies (see, for example, White 1999; Vertzberger 2002; Baumann and Stengel 2014).

As the introduction to this volume notes, public policy approaches to foreign policy also promise to widen the scope of the political actors examined in FPA. As several of the chapters in this volume demonstrate, although foreign policy is often assumed to be very centralized and restricted to top decision-makers, the circle of actors who have policy inputs (and not just in the form of public opinion) and are involved in the implementation of foreign policy may be larger. Approaches, such as the advocacy coalition framework, network analysis, and new institutionalism give FPA conceptual tools to include a broader range of actors and more informal policy-making arenas.

Drawing on public policy scholarship, FPA can also explore *novel connections between internal and external* processes. It is a bit ironic that FPA would reap this reward from public policy approaches, given that public policy has historically been more about domestic politics and FPA should naturally be externally-oriented. Yet many public policy scholars have recognized the arbitrary or at least porous boundaries between internal and external factors and include external actors, policy networks and sources of learning that are international or transnational. Public policy work on the European Union has arguably developed the most in problematizing state boundaries, given the nature of the EU (see chapter 8, this volume). Research on the EU as a foreign policy actor is perhaps the most promising bridge between FPA and public policy approaches as EU foreign policy work has employed public policy frameworks (such as network analysis, principal-agent models, policy diffusion, and socialization) more than has FPA. The lack of engagement between EU foreign policy research and FPA, noted by Brian White in 1999 and still largely true today is as strange as the disconnect between FPA and PP. A three-pronged connection—FPA, EU studies, and PP—thus holds considerable promise.

Finally, FPA can reap rewards from public policy approaches through the necessary *reflection on very nature of foreign policy*, and whether, and how, it is *sui generis*, distinct, or at least different from domestic policy.

This benefit was mentioned in this volume's introduction although it goes hand-in-hand with the potential challenge of transferring public policy approaches to foreign policy. In each chapter, the contributors to this volume note the differences as potential obstacles to applying their framework to the foreign policy area. Whatever the challenge, there is still value in the exercise of unpacking what are often assumed to be differences between foreign and domestic policy. If nothing else, this volume clarifies and problematizes the domestic–foreign policy distinction. These include differences in the environment, policy-making process, and nature of the policies. Figure 10.1 outlines and categorizes some of the distinct characteristics of foreign policy, as compared to public policy, discussed in the previous chapters. Identifying these possible differences through a comparison between foreign and domestic policy is beneficial to FPA, as this exercise forces assumptions to be more explicit. It also cries out for empirical study, a point I return to later in this chapter. Are, for example, foreign policy decisions made in the context of more mistrust, ambiguity, and focusing events, as compared to public policy decisions? Are public policy issues more structured, clear, salient, and contested? Is policy-making in foreign policy more centralized, informal, and secretive than public policy-making? As the chapters in this volume make clear, there are good reasons to advance these differences, but also good reasons to challenge them. If the differences are small, or simply a matter of degree, then the disconnect between FPA and public policy approaches is hardly justifiable.

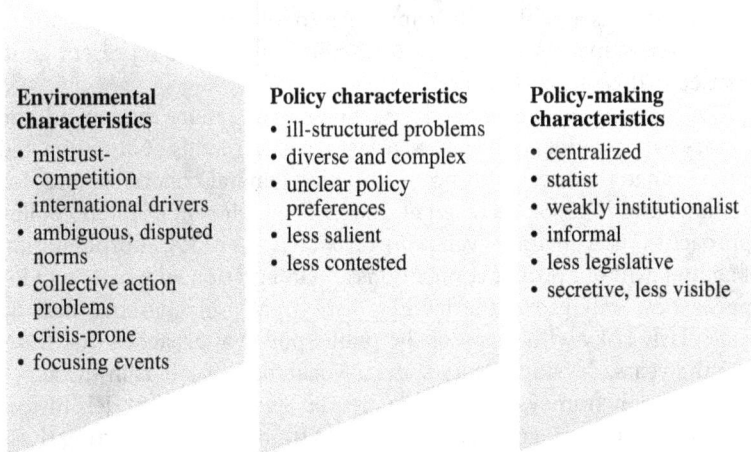

Environmental characteristics

- mistrust-competition
- international drivers
- ambiguous, disputed norms
- collective action problems
- crisis-prone
- focusing events

Policy characteristics

- ill-structured problems
- diverse and complex
- unclear policy preferences
- less salient
- less contested

Policy-making characteristics

- centralized
- statist
- weakly institutionalist
- informal
- less legislative
- secretive, less visible

Figure 10.1 Assumed characteristics of foreign policy as compared to public policy

Precarious pitfalls? Potential drawbacks of studying foreign policy as public policy

As the contributions to this volume note, the use of public policy approaches to explain and understand foreign policy is not without challenges and potential drawbacks. Each of the previous chapters explored those disadvantages with respect to the particular framework they were using. But there could be more general pitfalls for FPA as a subfield, including: (1) the inappropriateness of public policy frameworks to the foreign policy arena; (2) the introduction of more incoherence into the field; and (3) the dangers of inheriting the problems of public policy studies.

If domestic policy and foreign policy are so different, as has often been assumed (particularly in the study of international relations), then *public policy approaches may be inappropriate to the study of foreign policy*. The editors, in this volume's introduction, recognized this fundamental challenge to this project, raised the potential difficulties of transferability, and asked each chapter to reflect on this. As argued above, I see this as more of a benefit than a challenge. Beyond the value of critical reflection on the nature of foreign policy, however, the chapters themselves argue, and demonstrate, that these difficulties are not insurmountable. Even if there are differences between the two policy-making arenas, most contributors saw this as a matter of degree. In addition, if prior public policy research was oriented toward the nature of domestic policy, this was not seen as inherent to the approach. The assumed differences should be part of the research agenda going forward and the issue of transferability should be something addressed by each piece of scholarship that applies a public policy approach to foreign policy. Applications should not be made blindly; the chapters in this volume represent good practice in this respect.

FPA has long been criticized for being nothing more than an ad hoc laundry list of sources and factors, a vast sea with islands of disconnected middle range theories, with no overarching general coherence (see, for example, Smith 1986; Vertzberger 2002). The inclusion of public policy approaches risks creating even *more incoherence for FPA*. A proliferation of factors, without proper connections and integration with existing FPA approaches, only grows the laundry list. Greater incoherence may be particularly risky with many of the public policy approaches that have, over the years, developed very specific vocabulary (such as in the advocacy coalition framework, the punctuated equilibrium model, historical institutionalism, and multiple streams framework). Importing these approaches may mean the expansion of more jargon, with some similar terms meaning different things and different terms just reproducing other terms for the same phenomena. Public policy research uses the veto player framework, for example, in a similar way as foreign policy analysts talk about decision units (Hermann 2001; see also chapter 5 in this volume) and selectorates and audience costs (e.g., Bueno de Mesquita *et al.* 2003). Punctuated equilibrium may be just a different term for foreign policy change.[3] And work in public policy on advocacy coalitions has a specific, yet inclusive, definition of coalitions. Most research in FPA on coalitions, on the other hand, has a different definition, sticking closely to government coalitions as defined in comparative politics scholarship (Oppermann *et al.* 2017). In addition, the specialized vocabularies of some public policy frameworks raise difficulties for FPA scholars, not trained in these approaches, to apply terms consistently.

Finally, and relatedly, borrowing the good may also mean *borrowing the bad*. No public policy approach is perfect and FPA needs to be careful to not repeat mistakes or import problems. A few contributors (such as Harnisch on learning, Oppermann and Brummer on the veto player approach, Schieder on new institutionalism, Ansell and Torfing on networks, and Biedenkopf and Mattelaer on policy diffusion and transfer) note that these approaches are in some ways hampered by internal differences and disagreements and are underdeveloped with regard to underlying theoretical assumptions and causal mechanisms. Another "bad" trait of public policy approaches is that, despite the internal–external connections in some of the frameworks, public policy scholarship rarely engages with work in international relations. If FPA wholly embraces the public policy route, it might further distance itself from the field of international relations, cementing its minority status as "footnotes to grand theories of international relations" (Smith 1986: 13; see also Houghton 2007; Kaarbo 2015).

Forging futures: a research agenda for connecting FPA with public policy

On balance, the advantages of using public policy approaches in FPA outweigh the risks. So what is the way forward? In this section, I discuss three categories of research pathways in which to build on the foundation laid by this volume: (1) future applications of public policy frameworks to foreign policy; (2) FPA applications to public policy; and (3) an integration of public policy and foreign policy approaches.

There are several possible ways to forward this volume's main goal of *using public policy scholarship to understand and explain foreign policy*. One obvious strategy would be to build on previous scholarship that has already done so, including the previous chapters. All of the contributors to

[3] I am grateful to Klaus Brummer for this point.

this volume identified the (albeit rare) previous work that had used their public policy approach, or something akin to it, to analyze foreign policy. Each chapter then expanded these earlier efforts in their own application. It makes sense, therefore, to continue with this research trajectory, developing more added value within each public policy perspective.

Another strategy to direct future efforts is to integrate public policy approaches by focusing on some of the concepts common across many of them. There are two concepts that stand out from the chapters in this volume: change and learning. A focus on policy change (or its absence, its stability) is common across many public policy approaches, including multiple streams, advocacy coalition, veto player, new institutionalism, and punctuated equilibrium theory. The combined insights on policy change from public policy scholarship could be connected with existing FPA work on foreign policy change (see, for example, Goldmann 1982; Hermann 1990; Gustavsson 1999; Welch 2005; Kuperman 2006) to move forward with public policy approaches to foreign policy in a more targeted way. Learning is another concept that comes into play in many public policy frameworks, including policy learning, policy transfer and diffusion, historical institutionalism, and veto player approaches. Future applications of public policy approaches to foreign policy could focus around learning, also connecting it to existing FPA scholarship on learning (see, for example, Etheridge 1985; Breslauer and Tetlock 1991; Levy 1994; Stein 1994; Harnisch 2012). While learning in public policy is treated more institutionally, learning in foreign policy is often at the individual-psychological level, thus providing complementarity.[4] This integration around common concepts may help future work avoid the pitfall, discussed earlier, of proliferating different approaches and contributing to FPA's incoherence.

Another way to integrate public policy perspectives is to combine two or more perspectives for their application to foreign policy. Many of the chapters noted the already existing connections across these approaches. These include alliances between multiple streams, punctuated equilibrium, advocacy coalition, and policy learning approaches and between network and policy transfer and diffusion approaches. Public policy perspectives that already include complementary constructivist or rationalist streams of public policy scholarship could be another way of combining more than one approach. This combination might best realize the promise mentioned above regarding FPA's need to engage with general epistemological debates. Finally, one might want to combine the perspectives covered in this volume into a single, integrated "public policy approach" to foreign policy, taking the best from all, and creating a single framework that is bespoke to FPA needs. Again, for the sake of

[4] I am grateful to Kai Oppermann for this suggestion.

more coherence, a combined public policy approach to foreign policy, along one of the lines suggested here, may be a fruitful strategy.

Finally, future research applying public policy approaches to foreign policy approaches could problematize and empirically investigate some of the related assumptions and claims that were evident in this volume. One assumption, discussed in this chapter's introduction, is that public policy approaches have become more relevant to foreign policy over time. A second assumption is that public policy approaches can best explain "new" areas of foreign policy, such as immigration and climate change policy. Finally, there is the argument that foreign policy is different from public policy along a variety of characteristics (see figure 10.1 and related discussion above). These assumptions could be explored through appropriate research designs to assess these expected differences and whether they have diminished in contemporary politics, as compared with previous eras, and across issue areas. As I noted before, many of this volume's chapters already demonstrate the ability of public policy models to explain older, more traditional foreign policy. This suggests the promise of and need to extend this type of analysis across time and policy space.

A second major pathway for future research would be to pursue the mirror image of this volume by *applying FPA frameworks to the study of public policy*. There are several solid candidates for such an exercise, including approaches focusing on role theory, national identity, public opinion, parliaments, bureaucratic politics, small group dynamics, elite beliefs and decision-making, and leader personality. Of course, many of the insights offered by these FPA approaches overlap with ideas already in public policy scholarship, but because of the historical disconnect between FPA and the field of PP, their differences may be enlightening and catalyze new research directions.

Political psychological research in FPA may be a particularly beneficial approach to bring to PP. Many of the chapters in this volume noted the importance of policy-makers' beliefs and bounded rationality (e.g., chapter 2 with the multiple streams approach; chapter 4 on the advocacy coalition framework; chapter 3 with punctuated equilibrium theory; chapter 8 on policy diffusion and transfer). This psychological element of public policy scholarship is consistent with psychologically oriented research in FPA. Psychological approaches in FPA have a long legacy and political psychology is one of the main areas of contemporary FPA scholarship (see, for example, DeRivera 1968; Holsti 1976; Singer and Hudson 1992; Ripley 1993; Rosati 2000; Levy 2003; Hudson 2005; Houghton 2007; Shannon and Kowert 2012; Kaarbo 2015). Compared to public policy approaches, FPA research on the psychology of decision-making and leader characteristics is much broader, more directly interdisciplinary (drawing on psychology research and, in some cases, using methods more traditional in psychology), more theoretically advanced, and has produced a larger and longer record of empirical findings. This rich area of research in FPA, I would argue, is FPA's comparative advantage and has great promise for application in the study of public policy. Harnisch (this volume) offers a specific example along this point when he notes that FPA research on leadership styles could provide the policy learning approach with ideas about when policy-makers are open to epistemic communities. Oppermann and Brummer (see chapter 5) make a similar point on leaders' orientations toward veto players. Biedenkopf and Mattelaer (see chapter 8) note that the actor-centered approach of FPA fits well with the importance of agents in policy transfer research. Ansell and Torfing (see chapter 7) concede that network approaches overlook micro-processes. It is at this level that psychological research from FPA could most directly contribute.

A third pathway of future research is to discard the idea of applying a framework from one subfield to another and work toward a mutually benefiting *integration of public policy and foreign policy perspectives*. One strategy for this would be to pair a public policy approach with a foreign policy approach. Possible pairs were noted in some of the chapters in this volume. Oppermann and Brummer, for example, propose that the veto player approach links up nicely with FPA work on bureaucratic politics and decision units. These pairings could be complementary (combining the best of the two approaches) or competing (assessing which framework best explain the foreign policy).

Another, more radical, way forward to integrate the two subfields is by altogether abandoning the distinction between foreign policy and public policy. All approaches, from FPA and public policy scholarship, would be used to explain all policy, whether domestic or foreign. This is a logical extension of this volume's contributors' arguments that foreign policy is not *sui generis* and that different explanatory frameworks transfer quite easily across what is arguably an arbitrary boundary across policy areas. Others have made this argument with regard to internal and external politics (see, for example, Carlsnaes 1992; Caporaso 1997; Hill 2013), and Goldmann (1989) offered several specific models for combining international and domestic politics, with one model being simply that politics (internal and external) explains policies (foreign and domestic).

Abandoning the distinction between public and foreign policy wholeheartedly may be extreme, and it may have negative, unintended consequences. Sub-disciplinary boundaries organize research and provide identity and a sense of community to researchers working within them, which in turn can foster progress in scholarship. Yet, as this volume demonstrates, cross-community dialogue can be beneficial. The added value of a public policy approach to foreign policy is multi-dimensional and clear: it prompts researchers to try out novel theoretical, conceptual, and methodological tools with improved explanatory power, it encourages FPA to venture into new empirical domains, and it forces critical reflection on the nature of foreign policy. Let us hope that future research sustains this conversation between foreign policy and public policy.

References

Baumann, Rainer and Frank A. Stengel (2014) Foreign Policy Analysis, Globalisation and Non-State Actors: State-Centric after All? *Journal of International Relations and Development* 17, 489–521.

Brecher, Michael (1972) *The Foreign Policy System of Israel: Setting, Images, Process*, New Haven: Yale University Press.

Breslauer, George and Philip E. Tetlock (eds.) (1991) *Learning in U.S. and Soviet Foreign Policy*, Boulder: Westview Press.

Bueno de Mesquita, Bruce, Alastair Smith, Randolph M. Siverson, and James D. Morrow (2003) *The Logic of Political Survival*, Cambridge, MA: MIT Press.

Caporaso, James A. (1997) Across the Great Divide: Integrating Comparative and International Politics, *International Studies Quarterly* 41(4), 563–592.

Carlsnaes, Walter (1992) The Agency-Structure Problem in Foreign Policy Analysis, *International Studies Quarterly* 36(3), 245–270.

Charillon, Frédéric (2018) Public Policy and Foreign Policy Analysis, in *Oxford Research Encyclopedia on Foreign Policy Analysis*, Oxford: Oxford University Press, 483–496.

DeRivera, Joseph H. (1968) *The Psychological Dimension of Foreign Policy*, Columbus: Charles E. Merrill Publishing Company,

Etheridge, Lloyd S. (1985) *Can Governments Learn?*, New York: Pergamon.

George, Alexander L. and Andrew Bennett (2004) *Case Studies and Theory Development in the Social Sciences*, Cambridge, MA: MIT Press.

Goldmann, Kjell (1982) Change and Stability in Foreign Policy: Détente as a Problem of Stabilization, *World Politics* 34(2), 230–266.

Goldmann, Kjell (1989) The Line in Water: International and Domestic Politics, *Cooperation and Conflict* 24, 103–116.

Gustavsson, Jakob (1999) How Should We Study Foreign Policy Change? *Cooperation and Conflict* 34(1), 73–95.

Harnisch, Sebastian (2012) Conceptualizing in the Minefield: Role Theory and Foreign Policy Learning, *Foreign Policy Analysis* 8(1), 47–71.

Hermann, Charles F. (1990) Changing Course: When Governments Choose to Redirect Foreign Policy, *International Studies Quarterly* 34, 3–21.

Hermann, Margaret G. (2001) How Decision Units Shape Foreign Policy: A Theoretical Framework, *International Studies Review* 3(2), 47–81.

Hill, Christopher (2013) *The National Interest in Question: Foreign Policy in Multicultural Societies*, Oxford: Oxford University Press.

Holsti, Ole (1976) Foreign Policy Formation Viewed Cognitively, in Robert Axelrod (ed.) *Structure of Decision*, Princeton: Princeton University Press, 18–54.

Houghton, David P. (2007) Reinvigorating the Study of Foreign Policy Decision Making: Toward a Constructivist Approach, *Foreign Policy Analysis* 3(1), 24–45.

Hudson, Valerie (2005) Foreign Policy Analysis: Actor-Specific Theory and the Ground of International Relations, *Foreign Policy Analysis* 1(1), 1–30.

Kaarbo, Juliet (2003) Foreign Policy Analysis in the Twenty-First Century: Back to Comparison, Forward to Identity and Ideas, *International Studies Review* 5(2), 156–202.

Kaarbo, Juliet (2015) A Foreign Policy Analysis Perspective on the Domestic Politics Turn in IR Theory, *International Studies Review* 17(2), 189–216.

King, Gary, Robert O. Keohane, and Sidney Verba (1994) *Designing Social Inquiry: Scientific Inference in Qualitative Research*, Princeton: Princeton University Press.

Kuperman, Ranan D. (2006) A Dynamic Framework for Analyzing Foreign Policy Decision Making, *International Studies Review* 8(3), 537–544.

Lentner, Howard H. (2006) Public Policy and Foreign Policy: Divergences, Intersections, Exchange, *Review of Policy Research* 23(1), 169–181.

Levy, Jack S. (1994) Learning and Foreign Policy: Sweeping a Conceptual Minefield, *International Organization* 48(2), 279–312.

Levy, Jack S. (2003) Political Psychology and Foreign Policy, in David Sears, Leonie Huddy, and Robert Jervis (eds.) *Oxford Handbook of Political Psychology*, New York: Oxford University Press, 253–284.

Oppermann, Kai, Juliet Kaarbo, and Klaus Brummer (2017) Introduction: Coalition Politics and Foreign Policy, *European Political Science* 16(4), 457–462.

Peters, B. Guy (1998) *Comparative Politics: Theory and Methods*, Basingstoke: Macmillan.

Putnam, Robert D. (1988) Diplomacy and Domestic Politics: The Logic of Two-Level Games, *International Organization* 42, 427–460.

Ripley, Brian (1993) Psychology, Foreign Policy, and International Relations Theory, *Political Psychology* 14, 403–416.

Rosati, Jerel A. (2000) The Power of Human Cognition in the Study of World Politics, *International Studies Review* 2, 45–75.

Rosenau, James (1968) Comparative Foreign Policy: Fad, Fantasy, or Field, *International Studies Quarterly* 12, 296–329.

Schafer, Mark (2003) Science, Empiricism, and Tolerance in the Study of Foreign Policymaking, *International Studies Review* 5(2), 171–202.

Shannon, Vaughn P. and Paul A. Kowert (2012) *Psychology and Constructivism in International Relations*, Ann Arbor: University of Michigan Press.

Sil, Rudra and Peter Katzenstein (2010) *Beyond Paradigms: Analytic Eclecticism in the Study of World Politics*, New York: Palgrave.

Singer, Eric and Valerie Hudson (eds.) (1992) *Political Psychology and Foreign Policy*, Boulder: Westview Press.

Smith, Steve (1986) Theories of Foreign Policy: An Historical Overview, *Review of International Studies* 12, 13–29.

Smith, Steve, Amelia Hadfield, and Tim Dunne (eds.) (2016) *Foreign Policy: Theories, Actors, Cases*, 3rd edition, Oxford: Oxford University Press.

Stein, Janice G. (1994) Political Learning by Doing: Gorbachev as Uncommitted Thinker and Motivated Learner, *International Organization* 48(2), 155–183.

Vertzberger, Yaacov (2002) Foreign Policy Analysis: Steady Progress and a Half-Empty Glass, in Michael Brecher and Frank P. Harvey (eds.) *Millennial Reflections on International Studies*, Ann Arbor: University of Michigan Press, 479–501.

Welch, David A. (2005) *Painful Choices: A Theory of Foreign Policy Change*, Princeton: Princeton University Press.

White, Brian (1999) The European Challenge to Foreign Policy Analysis, *European Journal of International Relations* 5, 37–66.

Index

EU authorised representative for GPSR:
Easy Access System Europe, Mustamäe tee 50,
10621 Tallinn, Estonia
gpsr.requests@easproject.com